Staging Consciousness

THEATER: Theory/Text/Performance

Enoch Brater, Series Editor

Staging Consciousness

Theater and the Materialization of Mind

William W. Demastes

Ann Arbor

THE UNIVERSITY OF MICHIGAN PRESS

2005   2004   2003   2002   4   3   2   1

A CIP catalog record for this book is available from the British Library.

Library of Congress Cataloging-in-Publication Data

Demastes, William W.
    Staging consciousness : theater and the materialization of mind /
William W. Demastes.
        p.   cm. — (Theater—theory/text/performance)
    Includes bibliographical references and index.
    ISBN 0-472-11202-3 (cloth : alk. paper)
    1. English drama—History and criticism—Theory, etc.   2.
Consciousness in literature.   3. American drama—History and
criticism—Theory, etc.   4. Theater—Production and direction.   5.
Drama—Psychological aspects.   6. Mind and body in literature.   I.
Title.   II. Series.
PR635.C69   D46 2002
822.009'384—dc21   2001003754

For Jean and Erin

Contents

Acknowledgments

In many ways this book is a celebration of ten years of teaching at Louisiana State University. During that decade dedicated students pushed me to find better and more relevant explanations of what was going on in works by such varied artists as Oscar Wilde and Antonin Artaud, Samuel Beckett and Peter Shaffer. What I have discovered in fits and starts is that the notion of consciousness pervades all theater in ways I feel has yet to be articulated. I thank my students for whatever success this book may find.

I am also very much in debt to two anonymous readers. Through several drafts they offered encouraging and incredibly insightful advice. I really can't thank them enough, though, if they reveal themselves, I will try. In the same vein I must thank LeAnn Fields at the University of Michigan Press. She stuck with me as I found what I wanted to say even when it wasn't entirely clear that I would get to that point. Thanks, LeAnn. And Mike Vanden Heuvel, devil in my ear, hovers over my shoulder throughout this work.

It's always a treat to say, finally, that none of this would have been possible without the support and encouragement of my family, Jean and Erin. To them this book is dedicated.

Chapter 1

Toward a Materialization of Consciousness in Theater and the Sciences

"There is a special providence in the fall of a sparrow," concedes Hamlet in the late stages of Shakespeare's masterpiece, a famous image the point of which is repeated moments later in the play when Hamlet observes, "There's a divinity that shapes our ends." This rather humbled Hamlet toward play's end—falling into destiny's lap—is a far cry from the self-confident, ego-centered, proto-modern man who in act 1 declares of the world, "O cursèd spite / That ever I was born to set it right."

In these few choice lines from *Hamlet* Shakespeare proleptically outlines both the problem modern society has created for itself and the way to fish ourselves out of the mess we've gotten ourselves into. Post-Cartesian (post-Galilean, post-Newtonian) Western culture has arrogantly assumed command of setting the world right, dissecting it for its secrets and reconstituting it as we see fit. What Hamlet learns—too late to save himself but in time to save Elsinore—is that he is very much part of that world and has been called upon to serve it rather than to manipulate it. Belatedly realizing that he is integrally part of that creation he is trying so hard to fix, Hamlet learns that, rather than fixing the world as might some cosmic mechanic with special expertise, he must accept his part in the great ebb and flow of nature that will ultimately fix itself, albeit with a little help from humanity.

Giving in to "the Force"—recalling Hamlet's much-reduced twentieth-century incarnation, Luke Skywalker—is precisely Shakespeare's seventeenth-century advice to Hamlet and to *Hamlet*'s audience. But how can twentieth-century audiences do that, encrusted today as we are by the scientistic spirit of Hamlet's Wittenberg? Can we today only "feel the Force" playfully depicted in our entertainments, or is there a serious charge built into that latter-day command that we can actually activate?

Modern science from the Renaissance to the present day has persistently preached to us the virtues of viewing the world from some objectivist, Olympian height and controlling the world/environment beneath us, that world placed before our feet to manipulate as we please. We have consistently striven to dominate *our* world to *our* own ends rather than to accept our place within that world and to immerse ourselves in its enfolding, creative energies. Science has preached to us that the world is a "dumb" mechanism ruled by empty coincidence and susceptible to our ever-increasing capacities to control it. And we have increasingly accepted the attendant insistence that any ascription of meaning or purpose to this universe is little more than wishful fiction making. After all, as the earlier cocksure Hamlet remarks (the act 2 Hamlet who still believes in his powers), "nothing is either good or bad but thinking makes it so."

So today we watch *Hamlet* and are touched by the transformation of its central character as he moves from being a tormented though distant analyst—striving to find a way to set the world right—to a fully engaged participant who learns to play his part in the bigger picture. But there's always a sneaking suspicion among modern audiences that the fall of a sparrow Hamlet envisions simply means that the sparrow's life has come to an end. Providence, fate, and destiny really have no place in our ontologies. We are simply what *we* make of ourselves. Believing anything more is foolishness or mere superstition. Sure, some of us might see certain omens or signs that might tell of a larger design of which we are to be part, but we quickly engage our rational faculties and discount any such silly notions. We might shudder slightly at the ill omen of a cracked mirror, but we quickly recover to signal that our concern is over the inconvenience of replacing the piece. We may experience momentary concern when a black cat crosses our path, but the shadow soon passes. Some of us are even heartened by the sight of a rainbow, but few of us really sees signs of any covenant in this commonplace act of refraction. Science has taught us to know better than to expect signals from some "undiscovered country, from whose bourn / No traveler returns." In fact, science has pretty much convinced us—sometimes seemingly against our better instincts—that this "undiscovered country" does not even exist and that sighting such denizens of that domain is merely proof of one's madness.

Toward the end Hamlet learns not to unquestioningly valorize what he has learned at school in Wittenberg: he has learned to accept that Wittenberg does not offer all there is to know of existence, that there truly are "more things in heaven and earth . . . , / Than are dreamt of" by rational minds. But then Hamlet was not mired in a culture so thoroughly inundated by the spirit of science as for centuries ours has been. He was there at the beginning of this revolution and so was better able to turn away from the tantalizing opening tunes of a dissecting scientific certainty, retraining his ear to hear the harmonizing music of the spheres, instead. Perhaps living at the apparent end of this period of tyrannical empirical certainty, we, too, may soon be able to follow Hamlet and retune ourselves to a long-forgotten integral natural harmony and to become participants in rather than mere auditors/observers/manipulators of this world.

The Risen Spirit of Scientism

There is little doubt that modern Western culture has handed the manufacture of truth over to the sciences. The scientific claims to objectivity have mesmerized our culture, leading to a general acceptance of scientific premises and conclusions. Traditional physics and its attendant scientifically supported mechanistic reductionism—breaking down nature-as-machine and engaging in piecemeal study—have long ago supplanted any humanities-initiated metaphysics and the artistically inspired imagination that have sounded a resistant note to such a process. A mechanistic worldview has replaced vitalism and mystery, and reductionism has triumphed over organicism. There is little doubt, too, that the contemporary arts to a great degree have conceded the dominance of the sciences, often merely imitating scientific enterprises by generally withdrawing to slice-of-life dissections or escaping to solipsistic, elitist enterprises of personal discovery having little to do with larger, more integrally organic issues. The arts even frequently adopt coldly analytical scientific procedures in the bargain.

It is not entirely clear, however, that the scientific juggernaut should be considered the culmination of human endeavor, the many triumphs of that process notwithstanding. Rationalist science has admittedly produced innumerable beneficial technological breakthroughs and has "explained" countless once-mystifying natural events. But it has also led to global ecological crises of untold proportions. In many ways, however, these ecological troubles which are so frequently (and recently) attributed to this scientific juggernaut are the least troubling legacies of scientific progress when one considers the attendant spiritual devastation it has unleashed. The mechanistic conclusions of the reduc-

tionist scientific process leave little more for humanity to conclude than
that the universe is an inert, amoral, causally created mass of discrete
entities tumbling toward their respective final positions in a universe
void of purpose or any real direction other than that of attaining an
inevitable universal heat death.

Many scientists, of course, see no problem with this "worldview"
and simply pursue knowledge without any hunger for moral stabilizers
or any longing for greater purpose than to piece together the puzzle of
existence placed before us and to manipulate that knowledge for still
greater human control and material advancement. Life is the culmination of temporary organizing conditions, uniting otherwise inert matter
that will shortly once again become inert. Positivism (reality is only that
which is physically measurable) and reductionism (to understand reality
one must understand its elemental components) rule the day. Take what
we see, break it down, see how it works, and reconstruct it for our own
purposes. Science has proposed, as Joseph Wood Krutch has observed,
"a declaration of faith in the senses . . . and in the visible world as
opposed to the unseen."[1] The "unseen," at very least, is simply not
important or, at most, does not exist.

This amoral, mechanistic perspective is, of course, a relatively new
perspective in the long history of human thought, though it perhaps feels
to us like it has been a universal constant or that it is the natural culmination of the evolution of human thought. After all, we at least *appear*
currently to be in control of our own collective destiny: science has
solved many of life's former riddles/mysteries, and technology can
manipulate that newfound knowledge to fit the needs (even the whims)
of its human masters.

From our (post)modern vantage point the argument goes that the
vitalist perspective that the mechanistic worldview replaced has no basis
in empirical evidence and so should be discarded because it really offers
no concrete hope for a better (material) future. The vitalist position
rather quixotically posits that some higher order (often called God) has
imposed a purpose onto the cosmic fabric and that the universe is in the
process of fulfilling what it has been set up to do. There is, of course, no
solid evidence to support this vitalism, according to traditional science or
the culture slipstreaming behind science's advance. In fact, this "top-
down" perspective is undermined by the many "bottom-up" triumphs
of the reductionist scientific approach. Clearly, contemporary science
and technology have discredited vitalist illusions. In moments of intellectual weakness we may choose to long for such a progressive world of

meaning/purpose/design, but we ultimately need to accept the facts of positivist empirical study. So goes the argument.

Interestingly enough, however, the monolith of traditional mechanistic science is beginning to reveal cracks. Quantum mechanics, chaos theory, and the growing pursuit of complexity (wherein the whole is more than the sum of its parts) within the more traditional sciences are examples of such moves to adjust the paradigm from the mechanistic to a more organic vision that in many instances at least tentatively supports some of the conclusions posited by the vitalists. These cracks don't entirely discredit the mechanistic vision, but they do suggest that we revisit the vitalist perspective, perhaps update it, and then consider at least the possibility of an unseen hand (though the anthropomorphism of traditional religions is not strictly necessary) controlling cosmic events. In fact, without needing necessarily to invoke a vitalist higher being, reductive science itself is beginning to question the dumb blindness of the universe it has envisioned.

While scientifically inspired technology has produced untold triumphs, it has also produced unexpected by-product dangers. And in many cases more and better technology is not the answer to the problems created by technology in the first place. Rather, there is a begrudgingly growing sense of respect for natural patterns of order that can't be controlled or dominated by our superior technology. For example, Laurie Garret, in *The Coming Plague*,[2] has proposed that the relatively recent and alarming increase in incurable diseases is the complex result of our technological "triumphs" placing the world out of balance, creating unnaturally ripe conditions conducive to rapidly developing strains of disease, and making humanity—and the globe—susceptible to numerous plaguelike onslaughts. The unanticipated developments she documents, and many more like them, lead inevitably to the question: what are these unanticipated and uncontrollable forces that we are throwing out of balance? (Are these akin to the forces of providence Hamlet learns to live with?)

In the process of trying to answer these questions, mechanistic views of the world are being challenged at various levels by a sense that we need to enter (or reenter) the realm once allocated to artists, religious figures, and other non- or anti-empirical dreamers and visionaries. But this time we must enter with a full sense of the kinds of evidence our culture relies on to validate those visions. Rather than invoking a sense of mystery from on high and insisting on faith or "visions" to sustain us, this new (re)turn must accept the reality of the empirical world, working from the bottom up (material to spiritual) rather than from the top down.

Seemingly following a trajectory parallel to this agenda, some scientists are beginning to think like dreamers and artists, in the process rocking the boat of mechanistic reductionism. Their reevaluations in many cases actually echo positions and perspectives advanced by their humanist colleagues. In fact, Western culture may be on the verge of a reengagement of the arts and sciences that it has abandoned at least since scientistic ascendancy in the Renaissance. It is perhaps possible that these first halting scientific steps toward reevaluation may lead to a reunion of the arts and sciences.

In an earlier study entitled *Theatre of Chaos: Beyond Absurdism, into Orderly Disorder,* I suggested parallels between ideas presented in the theater (primarily contemporary British and American theater) and the revolutionary twentieth-century sciences of quantum mechanics and chaos theory.[3] Noting crucial points of convergence, the study observed that the theater, quantum physics, and chaos theory have conjoined to challenge the linear and causal foundations of traditional reductionist science as well as our cultural worldview, which is built upon those foundations. Quantum physics has worked at the subatomic level of existence to undermine the scientifically supported concept of the world as linearly causal. Likewise, chaos theory has made similar challenges at the level of the visible, "real" world. With the help of such breakthroughs a 1914 statement by Henri Poincaré (considered the father of chaotics) resonates more fully than ever: "Modern man has used cause-and-effect as ancient men used the gods to give order to the Universe. This is not because it was the truest system, but because it was the most convenient."[4] What these new sciences present is a revolutionary belief in systems of complex behavior irreducible to the former reductionist, strictly linear cause-and-effect doctrines. There's more going on out there than we've previously been willing to see or even to look for. It may not be a convenient proposition, but it appears to be more true.

Events flow in unexpected, nonlinear ways. But randomness is not what is located in this flow; rather, what has been posited is an existence that is richly varied, grounded in myriad patterns of interrelating forces whose actual interplay can never precisely be anticipated. In that rich soup of creative existence on the edge of chaos (between the domains of strict order and unfathomable randomness) is a varied pattern of life rather than the one-to-one interactions of automata previously assumed to be the model for life.

In theater terms chaos theory is a creative, interactive fusion of naturalism/determinism and absurdism/randomness, the two dramatic extremes that have held sway in the twentieth century. Because the naturalist's insistence on the determinism of existence fails to acknowledge the rich variety of the universe, an absurdist vision of the world as random seemed a viable latter-day counter-option to assume. But it now appears that the absurdist position was too extreme: existence is not random, as the absurdists oppositionally concluded, only more complexly ordered than previously imagined by the naturalists. The world can best be explained by a philosophy that falls somewhere between naturalism and absurdism. To use a scientific description, existence is controlled by the unpredictability of nonlinear determinism.

The arts and sciences both are reintroducing themselves to a sort of neostructuralist notion that life is richly patterned. The result is that we are seeing more and more viable patterned alternatives to an entrenched linear reductionism. Significantly, however, these revolutionary insights have yet to be pursued to their full, potentially even more revolutionary, conclusions. Can we accept that the diversity and richness explicated in these new visions are merely more complex forms of an empirically verifiable, still meaningless mechanism? Or is there an emergent quality that transcends positivistic comprehension and asks that we look to uncover some "mindful hand" at work? Sighting patterns is clearly an advance beyond our former isolating and reductionist tendencies, but thus far we have fallen short of pursuing the sources/causes of these structures. What (or who) is responsible for them?

While science can perhaps be faulted for failing fully to consider the option of some mindful hand at work, it is a bit surprising to be able to make the same charge against the arts. Consider that this lingering positivist urge to avoid the big question can be seen to exist within the theater community as well. While a critical shift toward pattern sighting has indeed occurred in the theater, the theater likewise has stopped short of seeking the source of these newly sighted patterns. Recent shifts in theater challenge our obsession with reductionism by challenging, for example, the traditional obsession with the psychology of character, predicated as it is on a system of thought that strives to comprehend discrete units of life through systematic, linearly causal reduction. As Elinor Fuchs has reported in *The Death of Character*,[5] this still-lingering urge to understand individual motive is being replaced by an increasing regard for more pervasive systems of *pattern* revealed through an experience of performance as a single organic unity. Evaluating the alternative theater scene in New York City, Fuchs observes of character that "much of its signifying power has been taken over by abstract pattern" (44).

This growing shift away from psychology and character clearly allies itself with (and perhaps even anticipated) the scientific re-visionings cited earlier. But what is missing in Fuchs's analysis, and what is missing in much of the experimental theater she discusses, are answers to the questions regarding from whence these patterns. It's the same problem we see occurring in the sciences. Is there a way to move beyond merely *describing* what is seen and trying to *explain* what is being described? For example, are these patterns simply reflections of our own self-willed postmodern metatheatrical obsession with the nature of theatricality in our culture, merely a reflection of how everything we do in one way or another is metaphorically "theatrical"? Or can this new idea of theater, like the idea of chaos theory, be a way to engage these emergent fundamental patterns and get them to get us closer, in some way, to the emergent essence of life itself? Is the game of performance merely a postmodern, theoretical pastime, or is there really something of existential substance to this enterprise of theater artifice?

Simply put, the questions we have reached involve the matter of consciousness itself, what it is and how it works. We seem to be at the point where we need to pursue the possibility of "mindfulness" intermingling with physical existence. Consciousness has, in fact, begun to be confronted by the sciences, expanding beyond the positivist perspective to suggest that some nonpositivist element of "universal" consciousness might ultimately play a part in the evolving new worldview. Somehow there appears to be a feedback loop between thinking and nonthinking matter that shapes our ends, an apt contemporary and material alternative to Hamlet's "divinity." Some notion of consciousness seems crucial in our full pursuit of knowing how the universe operates, for, if the universe is more than dumb mechanism, then something akin to universal consciousness might very well exist. And if, as the trend in the sciences now suggests, we can find a way to see consciousness as an integral part of material reality, then we move closer to an integrated vision of order materially self-generating a sense of control and purpose. What is occurring today is a process in the sciences that suggests consciousness is the evolutionary result of nature itself. The materialist Darwinian machine may actually have produced the thing we call consciousness, from the bottom up (the dumbly physical to the mental).

This is a revolutionary shift in thinking about life and consciousness, and the consequences are far-reaching, though one could suggest that this connection is actually what Shakespeare revealed to us four hundred years ago when he created Hamlet. We have risen from and are therefore connected to our world in ways we have not yet fully come to accept. But, though we may not yet accept this line of thinking, I suggest that the point has been placed before our eyes even before Hamlet walked out of the dark ages and onto the stage of modernity, at least as early as when Thespis stepped out of the chorus self-consciously to stand alone. Although we often choose to forget, the theater has been pursuing these material connections since its inception, giving rise to the very point that consciousness—and life, too—is materially grounded rather than mysteriously dropped into the world from above.

We do need to recall, of course, that theater history and criticism are loaded with responses by observers acknowledging being swept away by the enigmatic, mystical magic of the theater and being mesmerized by the mysteries of talent. It's as if the breath of a muse is somehow the prerequisite for good theater. What such invocations imply is that theater emerges in vitally inexplicable ways, unfathomable by standards of analysis and therefore impossible to recuperate with any real regularity. But giving in to urges to concede a magic in the theater is for many an unsatisfactory option. If, in fact, we look closely at the heart of theater, we can see it doing something quite different. The life that grows from the theater can better be seen—in the same manner as the sciences are seeing things—as the result of material realities drawn together in ways that create a "life in the theater" not altogether different from a rising sense of consciousness. Theater is a concrete reality that sparks an "essence" through a process we often call "magic." But it isn't magic at all, at least not in the traditional sense. Rather, a sort of spiritual *something more* has resulted from the emergent combining of numerous material *somethings less*. What we need to be able to do is explain how that concrete reality produces essence or spirit and what exactly that magical process is. Do that, and a new awareness, even a new consciousness, will be the result.

A Scientifically Emergent "Holy" Theater?

Several recent studies in the philosophy of science have incorporated theatrical metaphors in an effort to explain recent scientific advances. Among them is Robert P. Creases's *The Play of Nature*. In his discussion of the interrelationship between scientific inquiry and theatrical performance—in the process arguing against the linear, objective, and reductionist paradigm of traditional scientific thinking—Crease categorizes four types of performance and four parallel types of scientific experimentation: "(1) a *failed* performance; (2) the mechanical *repetition* of a performance; (3) a *standardized* performance; and (4) an *artistic* performance."[6] The first two categories are of little real interest—neither adding to nor inspiring new awareness or knowledge—except for the unfortunate fact that they are often nevertheless called art or science. The third Crease considers a "transformation of science into technology" (110), drawing from what he describes as a transformation of formerly artistic performance into canon/repertoire repetition.

Crease's fourth category "is an action at the limit of the already controlled and understood; it is risk." This edge-of-chaos activity is the crucial category, where true creativity occurs. Crease continues:

> The artistry of experimentation involves bringing a phenomenon into material presence in a way which requires more than passive forms of preparation, yet in a way so that one nevertheless has confidence that one recognizes the phenomenon for what it is. Artistic objects "impose" themselves—they announce their presence as being completely or incompletely realized—but this imposition is not independent of the judgement and actions of the artist. (110)

Out of nothing, seemingly, arises creatively inspired presence. We have here a case of science involved in an "artistic" engagement with the material that belies former scientific assertions of objective distance and study of inert, inactive matter. And it is an engagement that is invested in the complexities of inspiration and creativity, but it is inspiration grounded in concrete reality.

Crease's primary task is to enlighten his audience to the processes of groundbreaking science; in addition, however, his analogy between science and art crystallizes the nature of transcendent, adaptive complexity inherent in the theater itself. Artistry operates at the edge of the known world, beyond "terra firma" but this side of oblivion. As chaos theory would have it, artistry lies firmly in the realm where life itself arises and thrives. Agreeing with Crease, Gordon Armstrong argues in "Theatre as Complex Adaptive System" that we see significance in the interactive *process* as much as in the product arrived at:

> When spectators see a production of *Twelfth Night* at Stratford-upon-Avon, and hear Eamon William as the Fool uttering the words, "I am a man for all waters," and the hair on the back of the neck tingles, and spec-

tators say to themselves, "Yes, Of course!" nothing has happened: a "nothing" has happened.[7]

But, of course, an emergent "very much out of very little" has also happened, revealing a good deal of rising and adaptive complexity, which for the moment takes us to several critics whose work in many ways anticipates and parallels the work of the new scientists.

In 1968 Peter Brook announced the unfortunate triumph on the stage of what he called the "Deadly Theatre."[8] Deadly Theatre is typically the theater we identify as mere entertainment, a generally commercial theater that has given up on its former duties of advancing new thought or experience within its culture. But, according to Brook, the popular theater is not the only source of the Deadly: "The Deadly Theatre finds its deadly way into grand opera and tragedy, into the plays of Molière and the plays of Brecht. Of course nowhere does the Deadly Theatre install itself so securely, so comfortably and so slyly as in the works of William Shakespeare" (10). Text itself, the raw material of the theater, is obviously not necessarily the reason for Deadly Theatre, though in many cases it does contribute. Rather, it is the *habit* of performance and engagement that produces Deadly Theatre. Empty formalism, discovering a method or style seemingly appropriate to the text and robotically going through the necessary motions, is what is at fault. The formula of linearly predicated repetitive practices is at fault.

But, if all forms of theater (even serious theater engaging the classics) can potentially sink to the level of the Deadly, so can all forms of theater (even commercial theater) transcend the Deadly. In order to do so, however, it must capture the complex, nonlinear spontaneity and vitality of performance, engage the audience through that spontaneity, and fuel itself from the feedback of that engagement. Brook speaks of an interactive organicism that escapes even the most sophisticated analyses of ultimately reductionist semioticians and semiologists. What we have in his living theater is an interactive complexity that transcends a linearly mechanistic, reductionist production and a reductionist critic's analysis. In 1992 Brook explained himself "quasi-scientifically" as follows: "Let's take an explosion as an example. If mixed according to very precise specifications, a certain number of elements will explode, whereas the same elements, combined in a different way, won't do anything at all."[9] Brook is speaking essentially of a theater of chaotic complexity wherein the whole is more than a mere sum of its parts, wherein self-organization and interactive adaptability are observable but are nonlinearly or even spontaneously derived. As noted earlier, Elinor Fuchs makes a similar point when she observes the need for—and in experimental theater a turn toward—"a systems-awareness that moves sharply away from the ethos of competitive individualism toward a vision of the whole, however defined in any given setting" (107).

In the case of interpreting both Brook and Fuchs, we can come dangerously close to an intangible mysticism on the stage. In fact, Fuchs leads us in that direction when she observes that "modern drama never shed its mystery impulse" begun in the late nineteenth century (37). But she also notes that this urge stems from a symbolist impulse that—Fuchs quotes Jean Moréas in 1886—"seeks to clothe the Idea in tangible form" (29). In other words, though Brook and Fuchs assault the reductive materialism of much current theater and suggest a needed reemphasis of "mystery," it is not the case that mystery need be *intangibly* or *immaterially* mysterious. Mystery itself may find material incarnations; in fact, mystery may be materially explicable, and this explicability needs neither to return to premodern models nor to be entirely demystified by modern processes. Our (post)modern sensibility need not disenchant as it explains the world. We can, however, redefine *mystery* as we pursue it through these enchanting, though explicable, avenues.

It is apparent for both Brook and Fuchs that the theater must be more than an abstracted "touchy-feely" embrace, merely an intuitional presentation that simply announces, as many tabloid critics often pronounce, "magic has occurred this night." The new theater can be analyzable because there is more than inexplicable mystery or magic at work, but the parts emergently fall together in patterns more complex or chaotic than linearly causal predicates dictate, and formulas will never capture its essence. On these points Crease would clearly agree. There is more to Holy Theatre (and to the dynamism of life itself) than reductive analysis of component units can comprehend. Some self-organizing principle—an order rising out of disorder—is at work that escapes "formula" and that never precisely duplicates itself regardless of controls we may try to place upon it. For most of us an exclusively vitalist's/mystic's conclusion that life, or Holy Theatre, is emergent mystery is unacceptable, given that a humanity immersed in postlapsarian scientism wants more than medieval or premodern reverence for that which is just beyond its current, immediate, empirical grasp. In this regard we all follow in the footsteps of Hamlet.

To a large degree both traditional mechanism/scientism and traditional vitalism/mysticism need to work together to answer these questions. If mechanism has been given a new analytic shot in the arm via the antireductionist though still materialist machinations of the new sciences, so, too, can we begin to see that the visions of the vitalist have new, evolving, postmodern equivalents. But, instead of the vitalist's charge to look from the top down, the magic invoked can now be seen to be firmly grounded in explicable bottom-up material reality.

The Push-Pull of Mechanism and Vitalism

Much of this problem is grounded in our collective visions of reality, determining whether or not there is something beyond the reality our senses perceive. We generally—though, as will be seen, not totally—accept the point that there is more to reality than inert matter bouncing around in a frenzy of deterministic interaction (like a break in a pool game), that there is something in existence that is pulsingly "alive," more than inert, and whose activities are more than that which the traditional mechanistic or linear and deterministic models identify.

Speaking of the theater, Bert O. States observes, "The convincing idea that there is no art but that art which nature makes is inconceivable in a world where nature and human consciousness lie in two different realms."[10] States's "convincing" perspective on art needs the realms of nature and consciousness to (re)connect. Here States is speaking specifically of the shortcomings of traditional realism or naturalism, which "like the science that inspired it, . . .was essentially an art of pinning things down" in isolation (61), void of considering the "big interactive picture," consciousness issues certainly included. To illuminate the limits of the movement, States cites a passage by Zola: "Instead of abstract man I would make a natural man, put him in his proper surroundings, and analyze all the physical and social causes which make him what he is."[11] For this movement, it seems, anything beyond the inertly material must remain officially outside the realm of direct consideration. States particularly notes that the effect of the reductive, positivist urge in the realist/naturalist form is most pointedly evident in the realist setting itself:

> Like all realistic locales, the living room is invariably a conditioning environment and all things that pass in it do so by virtue of the limitations it implies. . . . Thematically, they are the limitations of the inhabitants' own history of birth, choice, and class made visible in what we might call a moment of space. (66)

What is measurable is what is real, and nothing presumably can transcend the limitations observed: the parts necessarily add up to the whole,
and the whole is a vastly reduced reality of virtually inert objects acting
upon a generally inert life form. Here art echoes the conclusions of traditional science.

What has, of course, been overlooked or denied is that of consciousness possibly overriding, or stepping outside of, such a positivistic
grasp of existence. Somehow, States argues, we need to (re)unite consciousness with nature, especially if nature is to be the inspiration of art.
But David H. Hesla notes the following in his study of Samuel Beckett,
pinpointing the dilemma inherent in the philosopher-artist's task:

> When a philosopher tries to move from a discussion of the nature of
> knowledge to the nature that is known, he sometimes encounters great
> difficulties, and needs to call upon some mediating principle or mechanism
> (as Descartes did) or upon some larger concept which can contain and
> integrate the perceiver and perceived (as did Malebranche and Berkeley) in
> their notions of the relation of ideas to God's vision or mind.[12]

For philosophers and artists—as well as for scientists—integrating the
two worlds is a dicey task at best.

Here is where the other side of modern theater takes over. In the
same manner that Fuchs speaks of the symbolist strain, for States it is the
related form of expressionism that enters the picture:

> To abbreviate a complex metamorphosis: once realism had perfected the
> fusion of psychology and scenery—finding, as it were, the mind's con-
> struction in the environment—the next step was immanent. The clearest
> moment of conventional transformation . . . is expressionism, which [Ray-
> mond] Williams says, is realism turned inside out. Once you have trapped
> your protagonist in one of these *real* rooms, leaving him (or her) in the
> posture of Munch's creature in *The Cry,* you take away the room—which
> is no longer *real* enough—and reconstruct it as the visible extension of his
> ravaged state of mind. (83–84)

At the convergently overlapping edges of both traditional realism and
conventional expressionism, we see a complexly complementary, parallel activity at work. Realism moves from the bottom up, traveling
through the material world and (in the better examples of the form) ultimately penetrating the world of consciousness, while expressionism

moves from the top down, sojourning through consciousness and affecting the "reality" of the material world beneath it.

The Cultural Matrix

A key point here is that, if current theater is basically a Deadly Theatre, it is not necessarily the case that the theater is entirely dead, and it is far from certain that the theater cannot be resuscitated or, if necessary, even resurrected to play a central role in the life of our culture, at least as a catalyst to trigger redirected research in other disciplines, at most as integral in creating our collective postmodern cultural "consciousness" of identity and place. Unfortunately, the twentieth-century theater legacy has been, as Robert Brustein has suggested,[13] a fundamentally negativist "theatre of revolt" against held beliefs rather than for new ones. The theater, and most of the arts of the twentieth century, has done little more than tear down the old bastions of truth and faith, failing to replace what it has rightly demolished with anything of constructive contemporary relevance.[14] Largely a modernist phenomenon, the legacy of revolt now seems in critical need of being updated through constructive postmodern regeneration stemming from a reengagement with culture in an effort to confront the problems that revolt so devastatingly exposed in recent decades.

Condemning a culture that lost its way is essential, but perhaps even more essential today, and far more difficult, is the need to find regenerative options that can be made acceptable to the postmodern mind. We need to dispense with "diaper dramas," that whining, adolescent, last-gasp theater of revolt, as well as the more sophisticated deconstructions of a culture off track. And we need to dispense with the isolationist escapism—founded upon its own reductivist visions—found in much contemporary performance art. Likewise, we need to abandon euphoric messages asserting salvation through simple acts of will. "Happy thoughts" overriding Hegel's notorious "unhappy conscious" and feel-good entertainments merely sugar-coat the ugly, troubling reality that we are fundamentally spiritually lost amid our material "progress."

This proposed theater of emergent regeneration, however, is not magical in any simple conventional sense of the word. Brook again makes an appropriate observation when he says of his Holy Theatre, "it could be called The Theatre of the Invisible-Made-Visible: the notion that the stage is a place where the invisible can appear has a deep hold on our thoughts" (42). The invisible-made-visible clearly echoes the trick of the magician, but the theater's event is no more trick than a Christian's act of communion (at least for the believer). In the theater the invisible *is* made visible; the immaterial *is* made material in a genuine and not just metaphorical sense. Moving beyond the metaphorical is precisely the goal of those we could call today's "new alchemists," the new scientists and artists who are seeking the same "magical" connections in the world at large. Theater, it seems, has already paved the way.

Brook asserts, "We are all aware that most of life escapes our senses: a most powerful explanation of the various arts is that they talk of patterns which we can only begin to recognize when they manifest themselves as rhythms or shapes" (42). States echoes Brook when, speaking of Artaud and Grotowski, he observes the need for a theater embracing "the pleasure of magic, trance, and participation . . . reaching us below the threshold of critical thought" (112–13). Fuchs does likewise by quoting Maeterlinck, who in 1896 sought a theater that would show "the mysterious chant of the Infinite, the ominous silence of the soul and of God, the murmur of Eternity on the horizon, the destiny or fatality that we are conscious of within us, though by what tokens none can tell" (38). Today we are materially closer than ever to understanding the magic and grasping the "tokens" unavailable to our predecessors. Behind, beneath, under, and throughout it all, we move closer and closer to an understanding that a materially manifested consciousness is the cornerstone of existence as we know it.

Chapter 2

The Science of Consciousness

Amid the vast webwork of patterns revealed through the new sciences, a sense creeps in that there must be a meaning or even purpose behind the orders revealed. Surely dumb mechanistic luck and blindly random selection cannot be the cause of such intricacy. In his work *At Home in the Universe* Stuart Kauffmann summarizes a growing sense among scientific theorists that creation could not have begun through random, dumb luck. Rather, he argues that to the generally accepted scientific tenets of natural selection and historical accident must be added the universal reality of patterns and rhythms leading to the third ingredient of self-organization. Kauffmann suggests that this third ingredient is a material reality that made life virtually inevitable. And it is also the thing that made consciousness, by way of an evolutionary path, also virtually inevitable. As Kauffmann repeats throughout his work, rather than holding onto the uncomfortable feeling that humanity is an unexpected accident of dumb and blind natural selection, "we may be at home in the universe in ways we have hardly begun to understand."[1]

Given the idea that self-organization is a universal constant waiting to create emergent complexity out of simple ingredients (what is known as complexity theory, a near cousin of chaos theory), it seems that we are coming closer to confirming our suspicions that, if there is a built-in sense of inevitable ends or purpose, then we are also coming to a sense that there is something at least akin to a consciousness that directs the universe. Religious thought has, of course, already sided in favor of such a thought, but science is beginning to lean that way as well, though in rather unexpected ways. The scientific result is similar to the religious response in that a true sense of enchantment ensues but this time in a way relevant to our postmodern urges to *know* that which we hold in awe.

Modern theater has done likewise, occasionally invoking a religious (top-down) approach to such questions but more often working from the bottom up and invoking a sense that the spiritual inheres in the material, that spirit or consciousness rises out of the world in which we live. The result is a challenge to the Cartesian separation of mind and body. In "Theatre as Complex Adaptive System" Gordon Armstrong identifies this element of theater as pervasive on the stage throughout time though rarely explicated by critics or articulated by reviewers: "Theatre is a complex adaptive system of biological intentionality, composed of infinitely probable componential strata of human evolution, neuro-anatomical change, and cultural imperatives."[2] Theater confirms our material place in the universe through its activation of physical means of (re)presentation, despite a still often pervasive critical sense that theater presents the enchanted mystery of life through rather mysterious means. Theater and science in essence combine to reveal the materialistic sources of our existence, from the inert to the conscious. In the process they are sighting the means by which these two halves of our existence interact.

The Quagmire of Dualism: The Ghost in the Machine

To gain a sense of our culture's turn toward scientific reductionism, one must turn to Shakespeare's near contemporary, René Descartes (1590–1650). To this day we are victims of what Antonio Damasio has called "Descartes' error," the celebrated separation "of mind, the 'thinking thing' (*res cogitans*), from the nonthinking body, that which has extension and mechanical parts (*res extensa*)."[3] The legacy of that persistent "error" has been, as Erich Harth has observed, the creation of intellectual "chasms [that] separate the individual from the rest of the cosmos, life from the inanimate, humans from animals, man from machine, image from reality."[4] At the heart is our conception of consciousness, specifically its fundamental separateness from the rest of creation.

Descartes's *cogito ergo sum* argument has clearly contributed to the belief that humanity is something more than merely a cog in the universal machinery. It posits that we are above that machinery, potentially masters of it, as the early, cocksure Hamlet would argue. Thought ("I think") is what validates and verifies human existence ("therefore, I am") in ways that the same argument fails to verify the existence of anything else: rocks *presumably* exist, but they don't think, so do they *really* exist? And, if such material entities do exist, how is it that we know they exist? Thought and humans who possess it are apparently different "stuff" from the rest of the material world because it and we extend beyond a certain physical tangibility that the rest of the world has. Thought in humans effectively separates us from that world, even though we are manifest, via body, in that world (though, of course, even the existence of body is suspect, given Cartesian skepticism). Furthermore, thought grants us the potential to choose actions, apparently to operate beyond the causal or mechanical and to become agents within our own universe, determining value, evaluating behavior, and choosing activities. As such, humanity appears separate from the rest of nature while still, arguably at least, being part of it. Descartes further sees a higher consciousness in operation when he propounds the existence of God, likewise an agent within as well as beyond the universe. Finally, however, for Descartes consciousness splits creation into that which naturally functions solely by habit and that which mentally moves beyond habit.

Contemporary philosophy and science see this dualism as invoking a fundamental debate between the separate existences of brain and mind, the organ that can be dissected and the "thing" that appears to have no material reality but that interacts and even directs material reality despite its apparent immateriality. As Daniel C. Dennett observes, "The idea that a *self* (or a person, or, for that matter, a soul) is distinct from a brain or a body is deeply rooted in our ways of speaking, and hence in our ways of thinking."[5] But how is it that we can remain wedded to this material-immaterial root of inconsistency? Cartesian dualism essentially argues the existence of two worlds and two unique sets of rules governing each. The result is that either we must acknowledge the incompleteness of our positivist, materialist leanings and accept a world at times overruled by the "magic" of consciousness, or we need to find a materialist alternative that unites these two *seemingly* separate worlds. Ignoring the reality of consciousness, choosing to see it as not really there, seems an unacceptable option, though some have suggested it, and many more rather surreptitiously practice it. And denying the world outside of consciousness seems equally unacceptable, though it, too, has been suggested (by mystics and religious thinkers for example).

The central problem of dualism can perhaps best be seen from a scientist's point of view. A dualist necessarily argues that immaterial consciousness affects material reality and overrules the mechanistic laws of nature, but this consciousness is not itself subject to those laws. This immaterial consciousness can disrupt computational, mechanistic behavior and, through free will, can dictate events and outcomes (to lesser or greater degrees, depending on one's epistemological philosophy). Here is the fundamental flaw in Cartesian dualism from the scientist's perspective. The physicist's cornerstone notion of the "conservation of energy" cannot accept the fact that an endless source of energy—the "soul" or consciousness—can infuse itself into the material world. Where does that interactionist energy come from, and how can it be boundless? In other words, if consciousness actually engages the material world, why can't it be positivistically quantified (measured)? Ultimately, what is it that allows for this contact between the material and immaterial? Descartes suggested that such interaction literally occurred *materially* in the brain's pineal gland, but hard science has effectively refuted this suggestion. In a similar turn nineteenth-century mystics submitted "ectoplasm" as the transitional ooze between the two realms, but that suggestion ultimately supported little more than an industry of flimflam mediums.

Generally, when our culture has even attempted to bridge this chasm, it has envisioned some extra-material substance uniting mind and brain, immaterial and material. These types of resolutions are centered around what Gilbert Ryle in 1949 identified as Descartes's "dogma of the Ghost in the Machine,"[6] inserting an operational creature—a homunculus—within the brain that/who operates between the realms of the material and immaterial to direct our behavior. But the problem is that, if we accept such a "ghost" (be it ectoplasm, a homunculus in the pineal gland, or something else), we have actually only deferred the real problem by placing the question of interaction in a smaller package. Is there a ghost driving the ghost in the ghost, etc.? And what exactly is the glue that operates within this immaterially material ectoplasm? Somewhere in the unavoidable gap must lie a substance that bridges the two worlds. While some thinkers have attempted to defend the Ghost in the Machine,[7] the attendant inconsistency has led others first to discredit the concept and then to support alternative, materialist options. As Dennett observes:

> How can mind stuff *both* elude all physical measurement and control the body? A ghost in the machine is of no help in our theories unless it is a ghost that can move things around—like a noisy poltergeist who can tip over a lamp or slam a door—but anything that can move a physical thing is itself a physical thing (although perhaps a strange and heretofore unstudied kind of physical thing). (35)

The apparently obvious option—other than to ignore the problem altogether—is to find a materialist alternative to this immateriality in our efforts to comprehend consciousness.

This search for an alternative has proven immensely difficult; even those professionally engaged in cognitive field research often tend to acknowledge an incipient dualism, studying peripheral elements of the mind/brain and leaving unstudied some unfound, unknown "central processing unit" that apparently pulls everything together. But what we see with such research is a fundamental, reductionist failure of our current scientific process, in which fragmented, isolated studies reveal to us the parts but never the whole, because somehow the parts never add up to the whole. This failure of reductionism, however, should not be seen as a failure of materialism. It is, according to some contemporary materialists (Dennett included), quite simply a failure of *reductionism,* requiring a more embracing acknowledgment of the complexities of the subject/object at hand. For these thinkers it has become apparent that Cartesian dualism is itself a reductionist conclusion, ultimately as unsavory as those conclusions coming from blindered thinkers who simply deny any sort of consciousness in favor of pure behaviorist mechanism. In both cases the position is founded upon the assumption that mechanism is all that humanity can "know" and that mind/consciousness remains in the realm of mystery, *if,* that is, we even accept its existence.

One argument posited is that consciousness is merely an illusion, that it really does not exist. After all, behavior can and in many instances does occur clearly without conscious engagement of any sort. But this argument that consciousness is fundamentally inessential belies, at the very least, common sense and has caused numerous theorists, among them Owen Flanagan, to feel compelled to argue the apparently obvious: "Consciousness *is* essentially involved in being intelligent and purposeful in the ways in which we are."[8]

Postmodern society cannot long last, much less strive, under such oppressive inconsistency. Sticking our heads in the sand and ignoring consciousness in our efforts to create ontological and epistemological order cannot succeed. As Dennett notes, however, "finding suitable replacements for the traditional dualistic images will require some rather startling adjustments to our habitual ways of thinking" (37).

David J. Chalmers, in *The Conscious Mind,*[9] outlines the arguments for and against various materialist claims by positing the following premises:

1. Conscious experience exists.
2. Conscious experience is not logically supervenient on [connected to] the physical.

3. If there are phenomena that are not logically supervenient on the physical facts, then materialism is false [because it is incomplete].
4. The physical domain is causally closed.

(161)

Chalmers observes that scientists and philosophers have worked with these premises and typically posit theories by rejecting one or more of these commonsense premises. Denying premise 1 leads to eliminativism, namely, that notions of consciousness are delusional and that, for example, behaviorism is the best explanation of human activity. Denying premise 2—arguing that consciousness is physical and therefore causal—leads to one form or another of material reductivism, namely, that discrete physical functions in, say, the neural system add up to consciousness. Denying premise 3 leads to nonreductive materialism, namely, that consciousness is physical but that it does not strictly adhere to physical laws as other physical objects do. Denying premise 4 leads to an interactionist dualism. This view differs from Cartesian dualism in that it argues some degree of physical and conscious causal interplay, in the process acknowledging a much looser or open causal world.

Chalmers's own view accepts all four premises and leads to another form of non-Cartesian dualism, "naturalistic dualism," which he rather mysteriously describes as having consciousness supervening "naturally on the physical without supervening logically or 'metaphysically'" (162).

These premises and responses are worth noting because they are the cornerstones of the whole materialist dilemma stemming from our efforts to avoid the sloppy ontology resulting from acknowledging the Cartesian conclusion that there are discrete physical and mental realities. I throw in Chalmers's own theory as evidence that explaining how this thought/leaning will work involves answers that, as Dennett confirms, are in no way easy, simple, or straightforward. Such difficulties notwithstanding, however, the pursuit of a cohesive theory that incorporates consciousness into the material world persists.

Given that accepting a traditional mechanist's view of human behavior (resulting in a denial of human consciousness) is as unacceptable as the Cartesian dualist's view, something new and more comprehensive is necessary, though very problematic to our current ways of thinking. A new view needs to include more of a total embrace of the actual dynamics and interplay between human consciousness and the actions it triggers, more than a robotic or zombie-like diagram of human behavior. As Dennett notes and Chalmers implies, we need to move beyond commonsense projections, move beyond our traditional habits of thought in regard to consciousness and agency. We must remain unwilling to accept a *"Don't-have-a-clue materialism"* (Chalmers's own italicized phrase [162]) as our alternative to Cartesian dualism.

Dramatic Parallels

Typically, the naturalist movement in theater seems to work within the scientific eliminativist's realm in that in its purest sense it rejects premise 1. In a reversal of Husserlian phenomenology—wherein Husserl "bracketed" out the external world in order to study consciousness—the theatrical naturalists essentially bracketed out consciousness in their pursuit of understanding our physical "place" in the external world. Consciousness was not considered nonexistent; it simply was not of central import to the naturalists. It is simply not something to concern ourselves with as we pursue the Newtonian assumptions of a tight, physically causal existence. A conventional naturalist merely asserts a belief in premises 3 and 4 (with 3 forcing a rejection of premises 1 and 2). The naturalist believes, simply, that the world is causally closed and fundamentally material.

Some variations, we will see, occur within the naturalist camp, which fruitfully complicates the issue by acknowledging some manifestation of consciousness. But the typical naturalist process of bracketing out consciousness (in favor of genetics and environment) rather reductively eliminates the lively and necessary complications inherent in Cartesian dualism. To one degree or another all of the materialist options Chalmers outlines—from strict behaviorism to naturalistic dualism—can be located within the naturalist's canon. (It should be observed here that the two uses of *naturalism* are in no relevant sense related.)

At the other extreme the typical impressionist/expressionist playwright seems predisposed simply to accepting premises 1 and 2. They argue that separate conscious and physical worlds exist. In extreme versions a sense of spiritual monism may arise wherein physical existence is deleted from the ontological picture altogether, but this is rare indeed. More frequently than either of these two cases, however, the impressionist/expressionist—like some naturalists—slips into some level of interactionist dualism, if for no other reason (though I will later suggest that this is an important point) than for the fact that theater is a physical/material medium.

Taking a complex example and speaking of Chekhov, Bert O.

States suggests that we "can see his plays as a demonstration of how far the descriptive [behaviorist?] function of realism could be carried, how close art could come to the rhythm of 'life as it is.' "[10] But Chekhov, the causalist/naturalist behaviorist,

> cannot be circumscribed in the terms of realism and naturalism. We can also see a lyrical, or impressionistic, or Maeterlinckian side of Chekhov. . . . It is not that there are two discrete sides of Chekhov, for the impressionism is, in one sense, only a refinement of the naturalism. (80)

In the hands of the century's stronger—more complex—playwrights, the theater muscles out a vision of reality that pulls together the two apparently discrete realms of mind and matter. We may at first glance see in a realist work such as Ibsen's *Ghosts* merely a play of behaviorist action, while at the other extreme, as States suggests, we may see a string of "impressionistic plays from Maeterlinck to Beckett where the characters seem to be enacting a drama of pure consciousness." But the exclusivity of one or the other type becomes less clear when one considers, as States has, that, on the one hand, these dramas of pure consciousness materially operate "under a naturalistic shell of language" and that, on the other hand, we see emanations of consciousness bubble up in the materially naturalistic *Ghosts* (81). So, from both sides of the mind-body and expressionist-naturalist chasm, these playwrights are tossing out grappling hooks and striving to pull the two realms together. If these earlier efforts are less obvious because they come from a time and theater in which these terms—*naturalism* and *expressionism*—forced certain conceptual prejudices upon their audiences, one can look at less encumbered contemporary works by Shepard, Pinter, and Weiss, among many others, to see this cross-pollination and hybridization perhaps more obviously, if not any more fruitfully, at work. Stanton B. Garner Jr., in *Bodied Spaces: Phenomenology and Performance in Contemporary Drama*,[11] makes just this point by observing that among these playwrights a phenomenologically predicated nexus operates between the material/real and immaterial/expressionist worlds.

In the more effective, memorable, and powerful theater of the last hundred years, we are seeing consciousness staged but not as some discrete, autonomous entity; rather, we are seeing full efforts at bridging the very mind-body chasm that the new scientists have been attempting. Finally, if this account seems reasonable, then perhaps the agendas of

Ibsen's "behaviorist" *Ghosts* is not so far distant from, say, Strindberg's spiritualist *The Ghost Sonata* as may appear at first glance.

What is needed here is a critical agenda that accepts the responsibility of highlighting this interactionist process and that sees this interaction as being first and foremost a process physically and materially undertaken. Both Bert O. States and Stanton B. Garner Jr. take on the task by studying the theater from a phenomenological perspective. Both clearly and convincingly argue for increased understanding via concentrating on the physicality of the theater. The theater itself is the thing to attend to, unmediated and unmediating. Garner utilizes the work of Maurice Merleau-Ponty, whose writings, Garner notes, "center on corporeality and the 'embodiedness' of consciousness" (25). Succinctly put in his *Phenomenology of Perception*, Merleau-Ponty's philosophical task was to "restore to things their concrete physiognomy, to organisms their individual ways of dealing with the world, and to subjectivity its inherence in history."[12] Mind, self, consciousness, are all inextricably bound to the material world. To know one realm is to know the other.

When theater works unpolluted by idiosyncratic agendas (when it is Holy?), it likewise necessarily sees consciousness not as an evanescent "something" but as a physical and material reality, something to be reckoned with not as an abstraction but as an extension and physical embodiment to be materially reckoned with. Challenging reductive semiotics, States takes a similar tack by observing, "To speak of the signifier is already to begin gossiping about a signified, to be thrown back into an elsewhere of assignable meaning" (24). We should recognize here that the thing States identifies as signifier—rather than signified—is the thing to pursue. The charge given by both critics, Garner and States, is to work with the physicality of the theater in order to understand this something other that appears to be beyond the physical. This something extra known as consciousness is not something other; rather, it inheres within the physical.

Gordon Armstrong argues a similar point when he observes theater's inextricable bond with the physical/material in the specific form of the biological: "Theatre's entire repertoire is induced and articulated 'fight,' 'flight,' 'sexual encounter,' and 'hunger,' There are no other options." And up from these primitive urges develop the more complex urges and manifestations, including consciousness. While States and Garner approach Armstrong's proposed agenda of moving up the level of complex behavioral adaptivity to consciousness itself, their reliance on

phenomenological philosophy needs the added push of scientific theo-
rizing from positions not fully in place when they produced their works.
We need, in essence, to move beyond even the phenomenological
agenda. Nevertheless, States and Garner point to directions we need to
take, for, as Armstrong asserts, "Our [current and past] theatrical description of character, stage events, historic events, and methodologies are
secondary—and academic" (284).

Turning away from incipient dualism is a goal that reintroduces us
to one of the central strengths the stage offers its culture; its very physicality is a reflection of existence, offered up to us in ways no other
medium can.

Revisiting the "Cartesian Theater" and The
Materialist Alternatives

Traditional consciousness theory, in its attempt to unite the material
world and immaterial mind, generally follows a commonsense perspective picked up and expanded upon by Descartes himself, wherein some
mental entity—in Descartes's case, a homunculus—operates in the brain
as a central operating system. This is often described as the "Cartesian
Theater" of consciousness. Daniel C. Dennett describes the Cartesian
Theater theory of consciousness as "a metaphorical picture of how conscious experience must sit in the brain" (107). Somewhere in the brain
exists a central operating system that a homuncular control center of consciousness operates in order to compile a coherent picture, which gets
"observed" by the "I." Descartes's homunculus, the "little human" or
"ghost in the machine," receives material data from the brain on a sort of
screen projected for that homuncular "mind's eye" to review. This theatrical description has dominated our perspective for centuries if for no
other reason than that it seems to conform to our commonsense vision of
how things work: we have an inner eye observing phenomena, and a
"something" (soul? the self?) attached to that eye reacts to what it sees.

As Dennett puts it, in order to be conscious of something, "traffic
from the senses had to arrive at this station [Descartes's pineal gland, the
home of the homunculus], where it thereupon caused a special—indeed,
magical—transaction to occur between the person's material brain and
immaterial mind" (105). If Descartes is right, and many fundamentally
still believe he is, then there is no need to search further for the seed of
religion: consciousness proves God. But we should add that just because
the model seems accurate doesn't mean it is accurate. Recall that the

Ptolemaic system of a flat Earth likewise arose from our commonsense perception of the universe. In other words, common sense often belies the facts.

According to the Cartesian Theater, the homunculus is consciousness, literally the mind's eye, a thing that is actually an immaterial nothing. But, of course, this homunculus idea solves nothing since it is merely a smaller-scale version of the dilemma: is there a homunculus in the homunculus? So, even if there is a homunculus sitting in a command tower observing the world and directing our behavior, the Cartesian Theater still begs a necessary chasm between matter and nonmatter, between things and thought, between brain and mind.

Dennett makes a further logical assault on the notion of a Cartesian Theater. If this Cartesian processor is materially and integrally part of the brain, why does the homuncular processor need a "screen" or "stage" to view what the brain is doing? Dennett suggests that, as with a computer system, a monitor for the brain is only necessary if it requires input from some external operator. If input is necessary, then the processor is merely a mindless (consciousless) machine—part of the material brain, in fact— and consciousness is that outside other still needing explanation, leading to yet another endless regression. Who/what is viewing the monitor and manipulating the machine? We're back to dualism again, now articulated in a more complicated manner.

Common sense seems, finally, to be of little help in any effort to escape dualism. But, given our mind's-eye prejudice, any new materialist option that rejects this inclining is in turn common-sensibly difficult to grasp. Dennett admits that it is counterintuitive to reject the Cartesian Theater idea. It so obviously *appears* that we perceive a unified picture, that our senses compile data, and that a "something" brings it all together in some place in our brain for "us" to see in our mind's eye.

Grappling with this intuitive logjam, Dennett agrees that a materialist view would be much more palatable/defensible if a clear and commonsensible alternative could be devised, one that is as equally intuitively alluring as the Cartesian Theater. But he cannot, ostensibly because, as with Copernicanism, the truth is often not commonsensible. Much like the difficult-to-swallow shift from Ptolemaic geocentricism to Copernican heliocentrism, Dennett argues that an equally counterintuitive concept of consciousness needs fully to be grasped by Western culture, for, while Dennett's perception of truth works counter to intuitive sensibilities, it apparently is not at all counter to the evidence. The sun may *appear* to rise and set daily, but we now know that it's the earth's rotation that creates this illusion. Similarly, we *seem* to have a mind's-eye homuncular view of the world, but perhaps we should learn to think of consciousness otherwise. The materialist asks us to accept a fundamentally counterintuitive paradigm shift, not just in the name of esoteric abstract truth but in the very name of human evolutionary development and survival.

This notion of human survival hinges on an understanding of the brain/mind as an evolutionary necessity for the human species, the thing that has so successfully promoted our survival in a competitive natural world. And the consequences of our new understanding may help us to steer clear of a path that has not only wasted human energies in its misdirected pursuits of errant truth but that may also help redirect us to maximize our uses of continually diminishing and even overextended human and natural resources.

Taking this attack on the Cartesian Theater of consciousness to the theater proper, one can again see parallels. While we traditionally view theater as a discretely observer-observed phenomenon, recent developments in the theater speak to a rejection of the putative homunculus theory, wherein the director/homunculus manipulates events before it, or (from another perspective) wherein the audience/homunculus merely observes materialized events placed before it. To draw from experimental theater one can recall numerous efforts directly involving collaborative and decentralized involvement of multiple members in the decision-making process and of venues converting audiences from passive to active participants. But the theater need not be conceived as necessitating an avant-garde format to reflect the anti-Cartesian perspective. We need not, strictly speaking, eliminate the director or break the observer/observed barrier in order to visualize the anti-Cartesian theater at work. For example, it is frequently evident in many traditionally mounted productions that the putative director is often not in full control of the events onstage, that something much more than planned frequently rises out of a production. And audiences need not be invited onstage to be actively engaged in the theater's goings-on. The audience/mind can be activated by the stage/reality at numerous levels, revealing an actively interactive nexus between the two apparent realities. The nexus is being suggested when Elinor Fuchs sees the "theater as a crucial mediating term between the heterogenous fullness of life [the physical world] and the clarifying abstractions of theory [mind]."[13] Here is where we see what has generally been called the "magic of the theater" arcing between the material world/stage and immaterial mind/audience.

We see this sort of interplay with the *Murder of Gonzago,* through which Hamlet "catches" the conscience of Claudius:

> I have heard that guilty creatures sitting at a play
> Have by the very cunning of the scene
> Been struck so to the soul that presently
> They have proclaimed their malefactions.
>
> —(2.2.574–78)

Though using a different terminology, Shakespeare's point is similar to that of a materialist's position: consciousness/audience actively interacts with the physical/stage and with "telling" results. Indeed, the inability of Brecht himself to reduce his plays to the objectively sighted events his theories propound—in which we are to watch his plays with rational distance rather than "get caught up" in the events—speaks of the complex but fundamental spectator-stage (and director-production) interconnectedness that belies the naive, discrete dualism of a Cartesian Theater. When at its best one does not merely observe a production, and a director is rarely in full control of any but the most trivial stagings. Something more always occurs when theater "works." The centrality of a homunculus implicit in the Cartesian model—even when applied to a literal theater—simply doesn't hold.

Explaining how this decentralizing nexus operates is by no means a simple task, but science again assists in the pursuit.

Materialist Models of Consciousness: The Astonishing Hypothesis

"Theory models" are outlines of scientific theories either as of yet lacking in certain substantiating detail or vulnerable to attack of their details though not necessarily of their overall formulation. For example, the Copernican conception of the sun as the center of the solar system can be considered a theory model supplanting the Ptolemaic geocentric model, a theory model that the Copernican model discredits. The Copernican heliocentric model of circular orbits was refined by Kepler's theory of elliptical orbits, which was later refined by Newton's theory of gravitational attraction, which again was further refined by Einstein's theories of relativity. The error in detail notwithstanding, Copernicus' theory model has not been discredited as the Ptolemaic system had but has since been revised and upgraded to an acceptable and verifiable theory, thanks to the developments that followed Copernicus. The model triggered further speculation and research, and the further research revealed the essential validity of Copernicus' theory model.

In the world of theater one can see how theory models have also been set up, challenged, and refined. From metaphysical models such as, say, the *Oresteian Trilogy* of Aeschylus to the more naturalist models of the twentieth century, theater has likewise evolved, challenged, and refined visions of our essential ontology without necessarily defeating or invalidating its predecessors. As with the theory models in the sciences, these theatrical models (we should forever remember the common roots of the words *theater* and *theory*) lack the certainty of law but offer directions in which we may fruitfully continue to focus our attention.

In the science of mind there are numerous models of materialist consciousness. The following is a discussion of several particularly fruitful and/or intriguing theory models. As *models* clearly conceding a good deal of incompleteness, these theories suggest, Copernican-like, avenues of approach and engagement that should pave the way for solid empirical development that could lead to unraveling one of the final great mysteries of creation with a sophistication acceptable to a postmodernist mind.

Francis Crick, who with James D. Watson collaborated to discover the molecular structure of DNA, is very much a traditional scientist who has seemingly taken on a very nontraditional task in *The Astonishing Hypothesis*,[14] as suggested in his book's subtitle, *The Scientific Search for the Soul*. Tantalizing as the subtitle may be, however, Crick concedes having fallen very short of his goal, though he suggests that the work he outlines in the book is a first step to the soul's scientific discovery. The book is a summary of recent developments that lead him to conclude that " 'you,' your joys and your sorrows, your memories and your ambitions, your sense of personal identity and free will, are in fact no more than the behavior of nerve cells and their associated molecules" (3). Crick is here basically denying Chalmers's premise 2 by arguing that consciousness is causally relevant and therefore an actual physical reality.

Working from a clearly linear and scientifically reductive posture, Crick summarizes the vast complexity of the human neural network, suggesting that consciousness is a relative matter that arises from a complex of rising orders whose sources are decentralized along the vast network of synaptic operators. Consciousness in essence occurs at different levels for different functions along a complex line of mechanical exchanges, denying the existence of both a Cartesian homunculus and a stage on which information is accumulated for homuncular viewing and response. Crick focuses on visual consciousness to make his point, observing that no central operator is at work; instead, throughout the entire receptor operation a variety of types of awareness arises. While we typically perceive consciousness to be a singular, coherent, whole event, Crick suggests that scientific evidence should direct us to other conclusions, namely, that our mind convinces us of a holism that, in fact, never literally occurs except as a sophisticated fabrication of the mind. Countless events occur within the neural network from which an "emergent" whole is accumulated. He explains:

> Much of the behavior of the brain is "emergent"—that is, behavior does not exist in its separate parts, such as the individual neurons. An individual neuron is in fact rather dumb. It is the intricate interaction of many of them together that can do such marvelous things. (11)

Numerous other thinkers agree with this perspective, including William R. Uttal, who concludes that "mind from an operational point of view, does seem to be inherently holistic and not divisable into parts."[15] Oftentimes, those espousing a rising complexity suggest that this element of "emergence" has magical overtones, namely, that something inexplicable (attributable to God?) occurs wherein the parts add up to something *more* than the whole. (Flanagan calls these thinkers the "new mysterians" [312].) Such thinkers echo a conclusion forwarded by John C. Eccles, who is "constrained to attribute the uniqueness of the Self or Soul to a supernatural spiritual creation."[16] Crick, however, derides this notion, observing, "while the whole may not be the simple sum of the separate parts, its behavior can, at least in principle, be *understood* from the nature and behavior of its parts *plus* the knowledge of how all these parts interact" (11).

The idea of the self, simply put, is an evolutionary development rising from a harmonizing of the parts into a holistic fiction. Studying the parts is a first, traditional step; beyond this step the parts' complexity may require nonlinear evaluation. Not surprisingly, Crick the traditionalist actually never draws near a discussion of soul; he barely approaches the idea of consciousness beyond the level of visual awareness, an event that is admittedly one level or degree of consciousness but that does not itself enfold our full concept of consciousness.

Most animals develop a sense of awareness that triggers some "flight-fight-feed-mate" response that is central to survival. But this level of consciousness is quite basic, ignoring higher forms of consciousness. For example, identifying movement is a sort of conscious awareness basic to animal survival; movement locates an object that must be judged food or predator or mate. Distinguishing forms and colors is a higher form that may lead to better guarantees of survival; it's a skill that can refine our primitive reactions to the outside environment. Distinguishing faces is much more complex, however, than either previous type of awareness, and responding to the distinctions is even more complex. Science has yet to move up the ladder to explain/comprehend this complex process, a fact that prevents science from confidently asserting anything of significance about even more complex levels of consciousness.

What Crick centrally attempts to show is that our first halting scientific steps toward understanding the "wiring" of the brain have moved us forward in our understanding of some limited levels of consciousness. His charge is made to scientists to begin looking at the big picture of consciousness itself in their pursuits of the smaller points that many scientists in numerous disciplines are currently pursuing.

Crick does postulate several tentative materialist answers to the consciousness question, based on scientific information. He suggests that "there may be several forms of visual awareness and, by extension, even more forms of consciousness in general" (246). And he argues that current research suggests that "it may well be that there is a hierarchy of processing units, in the sense that some of them may exert some sort of global control over the others" (250). This Processing Postulate has significant empirical support, though it as yet has not been fully validated.

As regards the Cartesian Theater, however, Crick himself seems uncertain of how to deal with this fundamental dualism, confessing, "I myself find it difficult at times to avoid the idea of a homunculus" and even later suggesting a decentralized, multiple-homunculus thesis (258). While he is willing to agree that there likely is not a centralized Cartesian Theater, he says "it is possible that there are distributed Cartesian theaters" (283). Crick clearly subscribes to the concept of decentralization, but he equally clearly has missed the point that the very idea of Cartesian Theaters, decentralized or not, begs an untenable dualism: who/what is watching within these decentralized units? Crick the self-described materialist, and others like him, shows himself actually to be a *quasi*-dualist; at least Eccles is bold enough to concede the problem.

Evolutionary Complexity

As valuable as Crick himself has been to constructing a New System of the World via his DNA discovery, and perhaps via his considerations of consciousness, he nonetheless clearly displays the limitations of the isolated, traditional scientific approach. A primary shortcoming arises in his discussion of emergence. He never fully postulates how emergence—parts adding up to be more than the whole—will be explained via reductionist scientific technique. Crick's view of emergence falls short of the-whole-being-more-than-the-sum-of-its-parts sort of complex emergence that seems necessary.

Daniel C. Dennett, on the other hand, moves more ambitiously to another level, using traditional hard sciences but moving beyond reductionism and toward complexity (patterns of nonlinear self-organization) in the process. From an evolutionary perspective Dennett argues that one must see consciousness as a process, not a thing. As Crick, too, observes, consciousness began as a simple survival technique of awareness of movement, and to a greater or lesser degree it developed in all animal life. Eventually, more complex forms of contact and "communication" (interaction) with the outside world increasingly improved chances of species proliferation. In a major evolutionary move the human brain began a feedback loop wherein it additionally began communicating with itself much as it had at first "communicated" only with the outside world. Patterns of recall streamlined a process wherein each case of externally triggered awareness no longer demanded renewed evaluation but promoted automatic (or near automatic) responses to recollections of like conditions. Further along the line, internal feedback of recollected events promoted a process of choice selection: was this present event more like past event A or past event B? Evidence and recall moved beyond reflex and to the level of decision making: based on selective past experience, should one fight or flee (or eat or mate)? Awareness moved to another plane of consciousness, that of reflection and introspection.

The mechanisms of external and internal awareness are essentially interactive, namely, the mind/brain manipulates data (either current or recalled) in a maximally useful fashion, absorbing parallel (multiple, nonlinear, and simultaneous) external and internal input and fashioning serial (linear) sequencing, which leads to singular decisions on what subsequent behavior is to be activated. The flood of data is at various points edited (say, within the eye, along the optic nerve, and then into and throughout the brain), and that which is considered significant is linearly highlighted. If, however, certain data becomes experientially insignificant, the data becomes stored for potential future conscious recall and use or eventual elimination resulting from disuse. If the overall process is successful, a species thrives. This whole evolutionary process, apparently, is one that developed from simple linear/serial responses (awareness of movement led to flight) to nonlinear/parallel input (multiple signal input) that led to distinctive, though still simplistically programmed, responses (fight or flight), to the flooding of parallel input that was processed, channeled, and serially developed for fully conscious, introspectively evaluated decision making.

Furthermore, one can see, as Dennett does, that this evolution is something other than a series of distinct stages; rather, each process carried into the next evolutionary phase to one degree or another, creating an evolved brain—in the human especially—that today does all of these activities at various stages within the brain and frequently along neural paths outside the actual brain, from simple reflex responses to complex computational responses and even to the fluster (nonlinear invasion) of complex emotions such as love and hate. The result is a mix of awareness processes, each level in one way or another contributing to human experience and each level bleeding into the processes of the other. As Dennett observes, "Today we talk about our conscious decisions and unconscious habits, about the conscious experiences we enjoy (in contrast to, say, automatic cash machines, which have no experiences)—but we are no longer quite sure we know what we mean when we say these things" (23). Every level of our "total" experience occurs in different regions of the brain and neural network. And nowhere do all these processed data accumulate for a single bringing together—there is no literal, centralized theater of display, our commonsense conceptions notwithstanding. In fact, this illusion of centralization, claims Dennett, is one more significant evolutionary process in the material brain that permits us the essential survivalist illusion of an integrated self, amid evidence that such a formulation is anything but a phenomenological fact.

That a single picture *seems* to be a mental reality is what Dennett calls a heterophenomenological truth, one produced by our brains/minds into a fictionalized world made coherent, just as simpler masses of input (like sight) are likewise made coherent by the complex linear machinations of the brain/mind. This evolutionary bringing together of data is, of course, important; otherwise, we may have multiple responses to any given flash of data, one response signaled by high-lighted data that another response urge may have ignored. This fiction-ally created sense of a centralized selfhood is a crucial yet self-delusional necessity, arguing for integrated personal coherence by organizing events of the past and creating a personal sense of teleology that gives us a reason to continue the struggle for survival. This observation fits per-fectly into Armstrong's vision of the theater as an important and essen-tial extension or reflection of our species' collective evolution: "Theatre, with its freedom to interpret discontinuous fictive events according to arbitrary patterns, is the most unique expression of our species' adapta-tion to the visible and fictive worlds" (278).

To draw upon a powerful allusion from O'Neill's *The Iceman Cometh,* pipe dreams *are* finally crucial to our very existence as individu-als and a species. Our individual and collective fictive capacities are not luxuries to be frivolously indulged in but evolutionary necessities to be engaged for survival itself. Without a functional (as opposed to a literal) coming together of our edited data, we might literally self-destruct by simultaneously choosing to fight and flee, turning into hopelessly schiz-ophrenic specimens of our current selves. It is increasingly clear in the sciences that the accumulation of complex data that makes for deliberate activity resides in no central locale in the brain, whether we choose to see that centrality as a homunculus or not.

Awareness and more elevated forms of consciousness, according to Dennett, are the evolutionary results (still ongoing, in fact) of our increased interaction with nature, nature being either immediately per-ceived or (for more complex species of animals) recollected data. There appears to be absolutely no need to invoke some discretely informed top-down mystery of consciousness into the process. It is not a thing breathed into us at some pre- or postnatal stage of our individual devel-opment, at some point before or after which we can say we were uncon-scious and then conscious. Rather, it is an evolving process among species and within individuals that has no real beginning and no real end (unless, of course, we choose arbitrarily to define consciousness only as that which occurs at some higher echelon of decision making or action).

This perspective is important because it provides us with the mate-rial *fact* that we are not different or distinct from our environment—except by a fabricated survivalist twist in brain/mind/human evolution that provides us with the illusion of discrete reality requiring protection from the hostile world of otherness. But, even then, the fabricating potential of consciousness is merely the sophisticated result of yet another natural level designed to increase its possessor's natural fitness in the game of survivability. Nature has provided us from the bottom up with consciousness; we need not invoke the "breath of god" as the source of consciousness. Self-delusion notwithstanding, we are not *other* than nature; we are the latest advance in nature, a point that should make us more fully aware of our essential stake in the world around us, of which we are integral parts rather than distinct entities.

Even Crick, the more traditional and reductive of the two thinkers, agrees with much of Dennett's observations, further noting that many who hold firmly to a traditional religious impulse "believe that to understand Nature is to diminish her, since it removes the mystery and thus the natural awe that we feel when we are confronted with things that impress us but about which we know very little." Considering our recent understanding of the complexity and age of the universe, Crick argues, "This new knowledge has not diminished our sense of awe but increased it immeasurably. . . . To say that our behavior is based on a vast, interacting assembly of neurons should not diminish our view of ourselves but enlarge it tremendously" (260).

Multiple Drafts Materialism

In place of the Cartesian Theater, Dennett suggests what he calls the Multiple Drafts model of consciousness, suggesting that consciousness is a dynamic, continual process of instances of awareness along a continual "stream of consciousness" that never reaches a destination but, rather, feeds back into itself, adjusting itself and achieving "awareness" at countless points along its neural progress. So, consciousness is less a uniquely defined level of information processing than it is a continual process along a spectrum ranging from programmed response to fully aware and creative interplay. Simple awareness, for example, is a form of consciousness that, given the choice of subject or data, occurs any number of places and often simultaneously along the neural stream. A stabilizing mechanism, much like the stabilizing mechanisms of the eye (the eye jumps to many points of focus each second, but the brain nonetheless levels matters off to a stable sense of panoramic vision), creates an illusion of distinct, unified, and stable consciousness amid a mass of actually fragmented input. The argument here is that the mind never fully lies in a leveled state of concrete awareness but flows forward from one instant to the next, with various gaps in information filled in or covered up by countless brain-function editing processes.

If this model is accurate, we can see both the triumph and the short-coming of the mind. The "mind" takes a pandemonium of parallelly received data and an equally pandemonious list of possible reactions, and, through a force of serial, linear manipulation, considers the options and selects the best response for the moment. Without this process of eliminating various data as "noise," human reaction would, of course, be impossible, for, faced with an infinity of input and possible responses, we would be frozen, Prufrock-like, into petrified inaction. The serializing operators reduce our menu of options, which allows for controllable human activity within a reasonable time frame and with minimal panic or confusion.

But the process of eliminating what we habitually label *noise* also restricts human ability for truly original change. New and truly beneficial frames of thought may be floating within the noise field, only ignored by serialized human habit. The seriality of that which we traditionally label *mind* restricts the opportunities provided by the input accumulated by that which we traditionally call the *brain*.

Finding the optimum balance (for any given event) between fully engaging our serial minds (maximizing our rationalist mechanism) and allowing our parallel-functioning brains to operate unhindered (embracing the pandemonium of input and possibilities of output) seems to be the best chance for continuing humanity upon its potentially new reorientation. We see here the mind, at its best, operating at what could be called the edge of chaos.

Chapter 3

Modernist Dramas of Consciousness

Drama in the early twentieth century struggled through much of the same problems regarding consciousness that we see evident in the current scientific struggles previously outlined. As suggested earlier, one way of seeing how Cartesian dualism was confronted in the theater is by looking at the two camps identified as naturalist/realist and expressionist/impressionist. Interestingly, many of the same conclusions seen among the scientific/philosophical camps can be seen intuitively formulated within and between these two dramatic camps, with a crucial observation that what evolves is a dissolution of the logical "law of excluded middle." The result of this crucial breakdown is that some either/or assertion of a dilemma—accept either *A* or *B*—dissolves into an increasingly cross-pollinating fusion of both/and. In other words, though we frequently see drama as falling into either the realist or expressionist camp, often it is more accurately the case that one camp sprawls into the other camp and that the terms only apply to rather uninteresting examples of the extremes of one camp or the other. We have here a case of true creativity operating between what could be seen as two limited extremes of dramaturgical practices but bursting with engaging creativity at the numerous points of intersection.

In his three-volume study of modern dramatic genres entitled *Modern Drama in Theory and Practice,*[1] J. L. Styan frequently acknowledges his discomfort with the legacy of dramatic categories handed down to theater practitioners, noting a consistent muddying of the issue when we see, for example, that "expressionism began as a form of windy neo-romanticism and grew to be a hard-headed, dialectical kind of realism" (3:1). To take the most famous example of a naturalist-turned-expressionist, Styan concedes in his volume on realism and naturalism that Strindberg

> developed new techniques in writing a production which took him further away from the realism of the naturalistic movement. Indeed, Strind-

berg himself recognized the change to expressionism in his own work, and declared, "To me falls the task of bridging the gap between naturalism and supra-naturalism by proclaiming that the latter is only a development of the former." (1:44)

The Strindberg quote actually acknowledges more than Styan recognizes in that Strindberg's expressionism was not a *change* from one form to another but, rather, a development that maintained much of the former form as it *expanded* the breadth of the form's scope, to what Strindberg himself would call "soul-complex."

Styan's point regarding Strindberg may not be surprising given the varied canon Strindberg produced. Yet it rather surprisingly echoes Bert O. States's observation regarding Chekhov, one of the central icons of modern realism, when States observes that Chekhov centrally creates a drama that captures (using Chekhov's own description) the rhythm of "life as it is." States concludes, "It is not that there are two discrete sides of Chekhov, for the impressionism is, in one sense, only a refinement of the naturalism."[2]

These fruitful complications notwithstanding, the tendency remains to see modern drama in terms of strict categories. It is so solidly entrenched in our current critical mind-set that it prompted Marc Robinson, in *The Other American Drama,* to observe:

> If one believed the loudest historians, all good American drama in the first half of this century was essentially plot-based, built on the trusty model passed down by the melodramatists, in which a successful play begins with an exposition, leads inexorably to a conflict among characters (or between characters and their fates), and drives on to a climax and denouement. Stories are told. Crises ensue and resolve. Characters change. We identify.[3]

Just prior to this passage Robinson makes a particularly crucial point: "The one canonized writer who seemed most original, Tennessee Williams, was often discussed only as a naturalist . . .—his ground breaking ideas of character and his poet's sense of language and image are not nearly as interesting to these critics as were his bittersweet narratives" (1–2). In many ways great disservice has been done to modern drama by the categorical manner in which we observe what is going on in the text and on the stage, recalling Gordon Armstrong's charge that "conventional research simply cannot explain the internal complexity and self-regulating mechanisms of living organisms."[4] The stage—and the world—is too complex, finally, to be restrained by comfortable and comforting either/or propositions. We need to remember, for example, that, when we recall even Arthur Miller's *Death of a Salesman* as a highlight of realist drama, it truly is "Certain Private Conversations" (as the subtitle insists), almost of the expressionistic variety, having (as the stage directions note) "an air of the dream cling[ing] to the place, a dream rising out of reality."[5] Returning to Tennessee Williams, we are reminded by Eric Bentley in his 1955 review of *Cat on a Hot Tin Roof* that "the general scheme [of *Cat*] is that not only of *Streetcar* but also of *Salesman:* an exterior that is also an interior—but, more important, a view of *man's* exterior that is also a view of his interior, the habitat of his body and the country of his memories and dreams."[6]

The point is that the theater rarely effectively discounts the world of consciousness in its efforts to deal with the materiality of existence. *Either* consciousness *or* materiality is not really a choice. Inevitably, theater uses a both/and proposition of confronting consciousness integrally through materialism rather than discretely through mystical or spiritual channels. As is usually the case, Shakespeare puts it well in the prologue to *Henry V*. First he asks, "O for a Muse of fire, that would ascend / The brightest heaven of invention," then materially longs for "A kingdom for a stage, princes to act / And monarchs to behold the swelling scene!" He next comes down to the pragmatic point of asking his audience, "Suppose within the girdle of these walls / Are now confined two mighty monarchies, / Whose high-uprearèd and abutting fronts / The perilous narrow ocean parts asunder." Then, crucially, he pleads that the audience "Piece out our imperfections with your thoughts" (1.pro.1–23). Despite teasingly appearing first to long for a top-down muse to activate the play, Shakespeare actually asks that we engage our imaginations with the material, splicing the imagined into the physical. We are asked literally to materialize a world via mechanisms of consciousness, working to transform the mundane boards of the stage before us into the reality already materially surrounding us. Indeed, the "magic" of the stage is created in a conventionally speaking unlikely manner, out of the stuff of daily existence. This is the process of theater, of whose rough rude stuff integrally includes the mind.

So, even invocations of mystery are invariably materially grounded when activated in the theater, if for no other reason than that the theater is by definition a material medium. But, while it *may* appear that such materializations exist only as a matter of craft—being, of course, crucial to any attempt physically to fill a stage—the stagecraft accurately affects our thoughts to think of the material process of consciousness to the point that, if this process is at first merely a necessity of craft, ultimately it reveals itself to be, intrinsically, a matter of how we and the world integrally operate. We work from the material to the seemingly immaterial, and theater, reflecting this epistemological process, insists that we exercise that bottom-up approach and create an ontological fusion in the process.

Unlike poetry, the novel, music, and perhaps even painting and sculpture (though these latter may differ more by degree than by type), the very physicality of the stage succeeds at a level that forces us to think *materially* about everything before us, even the apparently immaterial. Theater even supersedes the medium that is often assumed to replace the theater, for cinema lacks that first degree of materiality inescapably, bodily inherent in the theater. We have in theater real bodies and living breath, not merely shadows of the real. In the theater, of all art forms, we see at work the processes of materialization that embrace the notion of consciousness suggested by the new materialists. The story of theater is quite literally the story of consciousness drawn out of material existence.

Modern Dramatic Grapplings with Consciousness

Even a "Trivial Comedy for Serious People," Wilde's *The Importance of Being Earnest,* contributes to our notion of consciousness in ways every bit as consequential as, say, a work by O'Neill. Wilde's masterpiece actually helps us to identify precisely what we should look for in the theater. It even helps us see that a play by Shaw or Ibsen is far more than "merely" an assault on social myopia. As *all* theater reveals, the material world bleeds up to consciousness and is in turn a first step in understanding how humanity interacts with its physical environment, perhaps especially in Wilde's case, when the process remains uncluttered by discursively revealed social commentary.

Recall that Dennett and others see the brain as loading up on random data accumulated by the senses and sorted through by the serial processes of mind in order to develop a singular, focused consciousness *of something.* The material, however, which may not be immediately serially retrieved, has nevertheless found its way into our neural systems. If we take the point that consciousness is a state of flow rather than the end-product of attentiveness we usually ascribe it as being, then even these scraps and bits not currently responded to have become parts of our conscious process, available to be utilized at a later, perhaps more appropriate, time. Given sufficient amounts of similar input, it is possible that the process of serial selectivity will be forced into a modifying posture and may be compelled to consider data previously subdued by the later process of serialized conscious awareness. This perpetual give-and-take between brain data and mental selection is an edge-of-chaos source of vitality, change, and creativity. And it is something we see in full operation in the theater.

So, while elements such as theme and "author's message" may find quicker access to our serially conscious faculties—having been trained as we have to seek out such "higher-order," already serialized elements—other operations are at work of which we are not fully aware but which themselves are potentially in the process of altering the very processes of "data digestion." Not every mental event, as we all are aware, is necessarily a fully aware, serially ordered event; it is more than possible, however, that such nonserial events within the consciousness stream affect our future conscious processes, increasing the flexibility of mentality and consciousness outlined by the new materialists. As Flanagan notes:

> Brain areas respond in parallel to various aspects of some stimulus and pass the information they compute back and forth to other regions involved in perception and cognition. . . . Perceiving is not the result of a set of serial computations that eventually reach the "perception center." It is the result of coordination among the system of functionally distributed processors vertically and horizontally communicating back and forth.[7]

Furthermore, Flanagan observes, "The key to our magnificent abilities as 'anticipation machines' involved fixing gross architecture while leaving the development of the connections at the level of microstructure undedicated and adaptable" (323). We are, in essence, grossly hardwired but adaptably softwired at the level of thoughtful connectivity.

Laurene Faussett observes that the foundation of this microstructure is the neuron, which requires a sort of exercising of the muscles to grow: "Each neuron is connected to other neurons by means of directed communication links, each with an associated weight. The weights represent information being used by the net to solve problems."[8] Our conscious states do not control these weighting events but, rather, are controlled by them. And in the process our consciousness is altered by these shifting weights. Our soft-wiring is controlled by a pre-aware, preserialized influx of information whose mental life span is determined by its "weight," which is determined by its problem-solving utility. The consequence of this point is that we "learn" at at least two levels. At the "higher" states of consciousness—at the levels of serialized processing—we rather didactically learn information that we can store in our already-wired systems. But at a more fundamental level—we sometimes see this as being the paradigm level—it is possible to rewire our connections, literally to see anew what was previously unavailable but is now given new attention as a result of reweighting what was previously disregarded by our serial mental processes.

We traditionally valorize what is done at the higher level of mental activity while either deploring, refusing to recognize, or struggling to resist changes at the "lower levels." Yet, to take a simple example, *knowing* in our minds that extreme heat is painful to the touch is ultimately less beneficial than being wired simply to reflex away from painful heat the moment we come in contact with it. This latter procedure engages conscious awareness literally as an afterthought: "That was hot." And we are more "fit" to survive such experiences as a result, reflex preceding fully conscious thought. This is a point that calls into question the often unquestioned assumption that the level of serial attentiveness we generally exclusively call "consciousness" is the triumphal endpoint on a long line of rising mentality. That higher consciousness should not invariably be considered quite so superior a quality as we often suppose.

So, having the fitness to react prior to fully aware consciousness as well as having the adaptability to rewire ourselves along the paths toward higher consciousness are of immeasurable value to our species' survival and advancement. Here, then, is where Wilde comes in. We have in *The Importance of Being Earnest* a work that virtually defeats any attempt at "serious" analysis; it is not of the order of, say, *A Doll's House* or *Arms and the Man,* in which ideas in the play correlate to actual or possible experiences, a moral is produced, and we are asked to *think* about the world differently as a result. Rather, *Earnest* unleashes a sort of epistemological rebellion through a pandemonium of iconoclastic laughter directed at the *ways* we think. It's not what we think that is undermined; it's how we think. So, the logical overridings of such Wildean lines as "If the lower orders don't set us a good example, what on earth is the use of them?"[9] are not social commentary but small tugs at our wiring systems. The play's unlikely resolutions are not commentary on the nature of the world or some peek at a utopian ideal but are momentary epistemological chal-

lenges to our assumptions about order. Rarely, if ever, is anyone successful at providing a thematic commentary of this play; rather, the laser
spikes directed at the soldered connections of our soft-wiring are what
become central. And they are clearly difficult analytically to explain.

If this process is apparent in *The Importance of Being Earnest*—
because, as I see it, that's all there is—it is likewise a process more subtly
apparent in all effective, that is, dramatic, works of theater. *Arms and the
Man* challenges the notion of faulty romanticism at the higher-order
level of conscious and discursively absorbed reflection, but it also works
in the theater through preconscious means to provide a pleasure that
encourages a rewiring of our soft, undedicated system. It's likely that we
don't actually "know" that the process is even occurring, as perhaps in
the case of a man never quite aware—except upon reflection—why his
reactions always draw his hand away from a flame. Indeed, in some cases
the seriality of mind and parallel preconscious operations may in fact be
at odds. Consider again the point that *Arms and the Man* discursively
assaults faulty romanticism but that the play, at a prediscursive level, has
nonetheless captured our imaginations in other ways and resulted in
spin-off romantic light operas endorsing the very flaws in romanticism
that this play discursively condemns. Consider also the case of an
antifeminist spectator watching *A Doll's House*. Despite walking away
from the play unconvinced by the discursive, serially conveyed message,
it's possible that some effective rewiring resulting from gathering sympathies with Nora may someday result in a transformation of this antifeminist's serial thought. Finally, the conscious awareness of the play's argument may have less effect than the preconscious sympathies (that is,
those developing below the level of awareness) of the common humanity shared by Nora and her perhaps resisting audience.

Here is where I feel Marc Robinson is on the right track. In his
defense of alternative nondidactic theater, Robinson observes, "Too
often, it seems, we limit our discussion of alternative writing to questions
of form (as though it could be isolated), and rarely venture into those
foggier zones where one must reflect on how form embodies thought"
(5). It's as if this alternative theater can be condemned for lacking
thought because it discursively fails to be didactic. Robinson, however,
argues that beneath the levels of conscious awareness the theater does
produce thought on an order akin to my earlier suggestions regarding
Oscar Wilde. But he misses the point (or fails to make the point) that the
agenda he asks us to follow here applies even to many kinds of didactic

theater, especially given the fact that we often overlook the level that inheres "beneath" the didactic when the didactic is overshadowingly present. In essence his point applies to Shaw and Ibsen as well as Wilde and Williams.

We need to extend Robinson's point to include, rather than exclude, didactic theater into the formalist agenda he advocates. Robinson very much supports a quote he provides from Robert Lowell: "Unrealism can degenerate into meaningless clinical hallucination or rhetorical machinery, but the true unreal is about something, and even eats from the abundance of reality" (5–6). I would argue that Robinson's and Lowell's point applies to realist and even didactic theater as well, though from a different direction. Note that realism succeeds when it does more than merely convey a sense of verisimilitude; as theater, realism is about more than surface matters because it also operates—in its un-degenerated form—beneath the surfaces of linear conscious awareness, that plane to which too much of our critical attention is often directed. Where formalist/"unreal" theater only has form to study, didactic and realist theater has form *and* discursivity. Unfortunately, as Robinson notes, the latter is often valorized as the place where meaning inheres, virtually to the exclusion of the former. It's time to adjust priorities.

The Russian formalists drew a distinction between what they called *fabula* (story) and *syuzhet* (plot), the *fabula* being the myth or story told and *syuzhet* the mode in which it is told. Sophocles' *Oedipus Rex* is not Cocteau's *The Infernal Machine,* for example, though the *fabula* on which they are based is the same. Concentrating on the *syuzhet,* the formalists asserted (in the words of Leo Jacubinsky) that "linguistic patterns acquire independent value."[10] It is through these patterns, significantly assisted by an audience's active engagement via assumptions and inferences, that *fabula* is revealed. In the drama that arose in reaction to realism/naturalism, however, revealing *fabula* became increasingly less important, and the patterns of the theater—linguistic and otherwise—became the subject of attention. But it need not be the case that in our pursuit of valuing pattern via *syuzhet* we need to create theater without *fabula.* It is possible to have both, provided we focus properly on that aspect of the theater that really matters. We can take this distinction one step further by recalling Roland Barthes's three levels of visual meaning: informational, symbolic, and the "third meaning," which "compels an interrogative reading" initiated by a "poetical grasp" rather than a rational pursuit.[11] Accepting these various distinctions, we can develop an approach to theater whereby content as well as process of "content acquisition" can be more appropriately weighted. Less concerned with uncovering *fabula,* we could better see that patterns retarding the rational, linear processes of consciousness should become the "content" of our attention. And, furthermore, of rising concern is the affect of the patterns as they build up and potentially effect a soft-wiring adjustment.

What must be highlighted here—and throughout the study of consciousness in science and the arts—is that issues of psychology, even dream psychology, are at best only incidental. Most of the theater that challenges the dominion of a mind-excluded positivist realism on the stage and that strives to enter the realm of theater of consciousness acquires at least some degree of dreamlike status. It is no surprise, however, that realism embraced Freudian psychology as wholeheartedly as it did, since Freudian analysis works to explain the real world through correlations to dream states, a top-down practice that deprives dreams "of any privilege as a specific form of experience," as Michel Foucault observes.[12] Studying dreams to unearth what they *tell* us about the physical world is not the same as entering the dreamworld to unearth the interactive experiences of consciousness as a phenomenological reality unto itself.

Dreams don't arise in some top-down manner merely to be used to interpret reality. Rather, they are themselves an extension of reality and consequently are themselves a form of reality. As with consciousness interpreted materially, dreams arise out of material reality and then loop back to become part of the material reality out of which they arose. Herbert Blau observes that Freud himself

> never overlooked that "A dream is in general poorer in affect than the psychical material from the manipulation of which it has proceeded. . . ." It is this material, the *dream-thought* to which both dreamwork and theaterwork are indebted for their staying power, to the extent they really have it. This is another way of saying that whatever the appearances (the manifest content) both play and dream are worlds which in order to appear must first be *thought.*[13]

To a great degree, Freudian psychology as exercised by modernist realists as well as clinical practitioners is a sort of study of *syuzhet* in order to arrive at *fabula,* the physical canvas of reality. For consciousness studies *syuzhet*—specifically the methods of pre- or subconscious "information" acquisition, what Blau reminds us are the processes of *thought* itself—

should more centrally be the point of concentration. This is where I see serious value as well as pleasure in Wilde's masterpiece. The dream-thought it creates leads to a neural meltdown, encouraging a recon-figuration of our soft-wired system.

So, indeed, if *The Importance of Being Earnest* can validly be seen as fundamentally unattached to rationalist fact-gathering activities—unat-tached to some central search for *fabula*—the dream states of numerous antirealist modernists work in even more rarefied conditions. But this argument should take the additional step. As with *The Importance of Being Earnest,* we can fruitfully work with such experimentalists as Gertrude Stein to see their value in their own right, but the exercise additionally enlightens us to events in more conventional operations such as *Arms and the Man,* for they, too, succeed at an awakening at some level of pre-linear awareness. And the result is that the conventional theater, by using both prelinear *and* linear awareness, directly utilizes the former to con-front the limitations of the latter. Speaking of the contemporary (1970s and 1980s) theater scene but acknowledging a connection to modernist forebears such as Stein, Michael Vanden Heuvel observes that such a theater urge moves "away from the monologism and anxiety that infiltrate thought built on rational dichotomies, toward a pluralistic investigation of less overarching and self-affirming narratives and perfor-mance."[14]

Robinson observes of Stein that, "like Picasso and Braque, she worked to bring out a new awareness of art as the work of imagination, not merely of disciplined observation" (11–12). In *The Autobiography of Alice B. Toklas* Stein herself observes (in her third-person way):

> Gertrude Stein, in her work, has always been possessed by the intellectual passion for exactitude in the description of the inner and outer reality. She has reproduced a simplification by this concentration, and as a result the destruction of associational emotion in poetry and prose. She knows that beauty, music, decoration, the result of emotion should never be the cause, even events should never be the cause of emotion nor should they be the material of poetry or prose. Nor should emotion itself be the cause of poetry or prose. They should be an exact reproduction of either an outer or inner reality.[15]

In her first play, *What Happened: A Play,* Stein deals with points of out-side observation, but, unlike conventional plays cluttered with narrative observation, the play's five acts fill only five pages, effectively reducing the observation to, as Stein herself observes, "the essence of what happened."[16] Argues Robinson, "What happens in *What Happened* is looking itself, a living process, the act of perceiving made as visible as the thing perceived" (14). Bonnie Marranca echoes this sentiment, observing: "What happened was the theater experience itself. In other words, the creation of an experience was more important than the representation of an event."[17] An agenda clearly anticipating the work of Robert Wilson and numerous current experimental practitioners, Stein's urge can nonetheless apply to much of theater, even conventional theater that forefronts exposition and other conventional modes of argument.

Theater is looking: it is self-consciousness in operation, which, with a re-sighted critical instinct, can be studied and perceived throughout the process of data accumulation. What we get, however, in the more conventional theatrical successes is use of a direct, didactic, and linear avenue to conscious awareness coupled with this more *seemingly* experimental approach, which targets the parallel soft-wiring of the neural system. This is what Robinson sees Stein as realizing: "Meanings weren't invisible or obscure, something to be dug from the granite of the play. . . . The 'meanings' were obvious to all who were patient enough to see what lay before them" (15). Better or improved critical *concentration* is not the goal; rather, it is opening up of alternative avenues that will allow a percolation of experience, perhaps even to the level of direct awareness, which is the focused goal of Stein's work. Marranca observes: "In every sense, the perceiving intelligence took precedence over the art object, whose status as an autonomous, self-contained totality was diminished. The observer and the art object were not separate but interdependent." Marranca adds that Stein's theater "placed supreme value on the experience of the mind, and therefore presence, or, in her sense, the continuous present" (6).

Of Stein's most memorable work, *Four Saints in Three Acts,* Robinson notes: "As acts and saints accumulate so do the spectator's perceptions of the play's world. Stein takes the spectator across the same terrain over and over, and with each circuit a new detail emerges for the watchful spectator" (15). "Terrain" is an important word here, for Stein virtually excludes efforts at directing a linearly conscious gaze, opting, instead, to present a landscape through which our nonlinear senses are permitted to wander without directed constraint and without any real fear of either missing something ("the point") or of not being able to take it all in by our linear mind before we move on to something else. Fuchs observes that these "non-linear spatial structures . . . are concerned not with individual character or a temporal progression, but with a total state or condition,"[18] which, of course, encourages parallel absorption at prelinear levels of consciousness. Rather than being digested and analyzed by our linearly restrained critical awareness, the accumulation builds within the prelinear faculties along the sensory neural system, rewiring synapses for more efficient future responses, which will eventually trickle up to affect our critical awareness of landscapes in general, away from didactic analysis and toward experiential satisfaction. The play's the thing, not its represented other.

The pragmatic upshot may very well be a backgrounding of factual knowledge in favor of a more visceral experiential gratification. Foregrounding such material and developing the necessary "skills" to receive that material may better prepare us for the long run up the fitness scale itself, perfecting us as Darwinian machines to be better suited to cope with our environment as we simultaneously allow our faculties of conscious awareness and self-awareness to function within their own appropriate domains.

Stein's agenda argues for placing humanity more proficiently within its natural domain rather than pursuing more rationally grounded conscious exercises demanding objectified outside-looking-in reflection upon our condition. We are performatively part of the experience, as the materialists argue, rather than, as mistakenly conceived by dualists in the past, merely or exclusively rational observers from beyond. We must forever remember that this latter rational "level" is an outgrowth rather than an exclusion of our visceral engagements with the world, and so its separate objective value should always remain suspect. Finally, it is from that visceral entrance into our neural system that we move to conscious awareness rather than from some notion that we must somehow remain, to draw again from *The Iceman Cometh,* "foolosophers in the grandstand" in order truly and finally to comprehend the world.

Indeed, Stein helps us to access even Eugene O'Neill's realist drama *The Iceman Cometh* in this regard. From Stein's perspective the ultimate pipe dream is the one that argues that maintaining abstracted distance from existence is the way to secure peace with the world. The old foolosopher's attitude that knowledge/wisdom comes from an idealist's (as opposed to a grounded materialist's) contemplation of abstract forms rather than engagement with concrete realities is humanity's ultimate pipe dream, at least since Descartes and more likely even since Plato. Truth, abstraction, consciousness, are grounded in the concrete.

Bernard J. Baars, in *In the Theater of Consciousness,* presents a thought experiment that seems to verify this materialist perspective. He asks that we consider the following "ideas":

bird

chair

animal

robber

woman

vegetable.

Concerning the list, Baars postulates:

> If you are like most people, these names for abstract categories will bring to mind, not an abstract definition, but a specific mental image. . . . The class of birds is represented not so much by an abstract description of birds, but rather by some particular bird we can visualize, like a Robin.[19]

Baars pinponts exactly the process of the theater Stein and O'Neill implicitly utilize: theater is a grounding mechanism, a reflection of the very process utilized in our neural system building up to consciousness. We are not equipped so much with top-down Platonic ideas toward which discrete reality conforms; rather, we build up from the concrete to the abstractions of mind. In a manner of speaking, even the homunculus we all feel we have within us is, in fact, merely the production of an accumulation of concretely generated neural data made abstract.

Here we can recall States's observation that "once realism had perfected the fusion of psychology and scenery—finding, as it were, the mind's construction in the environment—the next step was immanent" (83). That next step was expressionism. But to a perceptive eye the next step was less a leap than a shuffle or sidestep still grounded in the efforts of its predecessor. With realism mind and environment were interlocked, with environment being foregrounded; with expressionism we have more of the same, only this time with mind being foregrounded. In his foreword to Elmer Rice's expressionistic *The Adding Machine,* Philip Moeller observes:

> Now, if "expressionism" is objective seeing, as all observation must be, it is *subjective* projection; that is, all the self-understood "hinterland" thought, all the yearnings and unknown suppressions of the mind, are exposed, so to speak, in spite of the character, just as an X-ray exposes the inner structure of a thing as against its outer, more obvious and seeming form.[20]

Objective material is digested by the subjectivity of mind and presented accordingly onstage. Of course, the same can be said of all but the most journalistic of realist drama, and even then to some degree this same point holds. Internal/mental and external/physical are, finally, inseparable, the former invariably arising from the latter.

This matter of degree rather than of type helps to explain why, say, Strindberg's naturalist play *Miss Julie* feels so much like his expressionist work *The Ghost Sonata*. Julie (and the play as a whole) is haunted through metaphorical manipulations much as the student of *The Ghost Sonata* (and the whole play as well) is haunted by the Milkmaid apparition. Although *The Ghost Sonata* expands ontology to include the dead among the living rather than more simply using metaphorical specters, as in *Miss Julie,* the *tangible* haunting of particular consciousnesses is nonetheless parallel in both works.

So, too, is the sense that Ibsen's *Ghosts* is only different to his more expressionistic *When We Dead Awaken* by degree rather than kind. Harold Clurman says of Ibsen's later plays, including *When We Dead Awaken,* that they seem "to merge into a softer field in which the outlines fade and what remains is pure atmosphere. We are no longer in the realm of drama but of mood and mystery."[21] We are, of course, still in the realm of drama, though not the standard drama sighted as plot or character driven. Rather, we are in the presence of a theater of direct experience. To the degree we accept this gratification, Clurman's description easily applies to Stein's work as well. But, significantly, the same could also be said upon reflection of Ibsen's earlier plays, especially when experienced today, since those earlier works have lost much of their former social impact: they survive today without requiring the harsher lines of social critique to prop them up, the result being that we see more clearly the rising mood and mystery of the softer field beneath the formerly more prevalent, socially relevant scaffolding. Given this perspective—this suggestion to re-view the drama—is Ibsen or Strindberg so different from Stein?

Upon reflection we do distinctly benefit from expressionism in one crucial way: it highlights for us the fact that the Aristotelian notion of the possible and probable should be determined *within* the realm of the theater itself rather than from the perspective of determining probability from some external realm such as "real life." Often in realist drama the urge is to judge probability by whether or not the events could occur in the real world. With expressionism we are reminded that probability inheres *within* the confines of the theater itself, predicated upon the theater's givens, not the given of some objective correlative beyond the theater.

This reminds us of what States strives to remind us, that theater is phenomenologically complete, similar in numerous ways to the world itself as, say, our mind's constructs are similar to and even predicated upon the world. But it is not merely a reflection of that external reality. That is not to say that the theater is not real. Its very materiality belies such a conclusion. Furthermore, we cannot say that theater in no way reflects the world. Rather, manifest as it is in a fictive-yet-real other existence, it seems perhaps more valuable to see theater as that place where "mind-stuff" and "physical-stuff" intermingle in a manner precisely parallel to our growing sense of material consciousness. In the theater matters are just more focused than in the diffusion of daily existence.

Symbolist Transformations

Similar phenomenological happenings transpire when symbolism moves from the page to the stage. Styan observes that the symbolic, according to Kenneth Burke, "is associated with [the] idea of 'dramatism'" wherein the "realm of 'symbolicity' is one in which man finds himself in a middle area of sensory images somewhere between the purely physical and the purely abstract" (2:4). Here again we see a materialist, specifically biological, leaning when Burke himself observes, in defense of a notion of universally common experientiality, that "situations do overlap, if only because men have the same neural and muscular structure as men who have left their records from past ages. We and they are in much the same biological situation."[22] From this point, Burke observes:

> As regards the correlation between mind and body, we may note . . . that the poet will naturally tend to write about that which most deeply engrosses him—and nothing more deeply engrosses a man than his *burdens,* including those of a physical nature, such as disease. We win by capitalizing on our debts, by turning our liabilities into assets, using our burdens as a basis of insight. (84)

Styan, in turn, concludes:

> Watching a play, therefore, may be a fundamentally symbolic act in itself, and in discussing symbolism in drama we are dealing with an elusive sub-

ject, fraught with problems yet rich in possibilities. . . . It is not surprising that, at the time when naturalism was at its peak in Europe, the theatre was urgently seeking a justification in myth and ritual at another level for the visionary quality it had missed in realism. (4)

So, we have Artaud, Maeterlinck, Cocteau, and Jarry all moving beyond realism but through the medium of theater remaining embedded in the physical from which and out of which their abstractions and rhythms derive. Jarry's *Ubu* plays and O'Neill's *The Emperor Jones,* for example, stretch beyond the ontologies of straight realism into the subtler realities of the mind via techniques not accessible to the realist. But we must constantly remind ourselves that their works all are grounded in a materialism frequently overlooked when we study/view these works operating on the material-immaterial edge. The putative evanescence they strive to capture is a breath from the material world rather than something breathed from above into otherwise inert matter.

Even Yeats's attempts to reduce the physical via the dynamics of Noh drama or Craig's efforts to reduce the stage to a puppet theater were still grounded in the physicality of the theater. Even, much later, Beckett's notorious *Breath*—reducing the stage to a two-segmented birth-to-death bellows of human exhales—still grounds its sounds in the physical.

It is significant to note that the surrealism and dadaism that sprung from the symbolist urge in many ways anticipated recent advances in contemporary sciences. In these movements, according again to Styan, "The rational control of our perceptions was to be disturbed and questioned by whatever means could be devised, and to do so the surrealist artist would use elements of surprise, the involuntary and the unconscious" (2:52). Attacking the domination of logical thought and causal assumptions has become the very cornerstone of material consciousness thinking: we have now come to realize that logical thought, this "pinnacle" level of consciousness, is quite truly only the tip of the overall consciousness iceberg. And by the same path of analysis we have simultaneously confronted the point that such a conclusion *does not* lead to a confirmation of dualism, Cartesian or otherwise. Rather, processes occurring at the fully conscious level, preconscious level, and every state in between well up from material sources.

Burke, finally, is correct in spirit rather than in fact when he observes that the symbolic occupies some middle ground between the concrete and abstract, since he never quite articulates the direction from which the process unfolds: if he would confirm that it is the concrete that inspires the symbolic and abstract—in fact, if he would argue that the symbolic and abstract are actually levels of material truth themselves rather than some other "stuff" or some different reality—then he would align himself with the materialists and with the apparent processes of theater themselves. I am not entirely sure that the symbolists would agree with this assessment of their theater, but, finally, there is no reason for not casting their works into this light, given the fact that such an interpretation would in no way necessitate rewriting their art in order to have it reflect this vision.

Indeed, Cocteau (and others, too), had he lived into the late twentieth century, might have embraced the new materialism. In his preface to *The Eiffel Tower Wedding Party* he proclaims: "Here, I renounce mystery. I illuminate everything, I underline everything. Sunday vacuity, human livestock, ready-made expressions, dissociation of ideas into flesh and stone, the fierce cruelty of childhood, the miraculous poetry of daily life."[23] He continues: "The poet ought to disengage objects and ideas from their veiling mists. . . . In my play I rejuvenate the commonplace" (154). Ideas and objects seem to be of the same stuff; they certainly experience similar manipulation in Cocteau's thinking. Leonard Shlain has argued, in *Art and Physics*,[24] that abstractions inherent in modern art— the strange *patterns* and *forms* surfacing in that art—are now being revealed to inhere in reality after all, much as the patterns and forms inherent in such works as Cocteau's can be said equally (though strangely) to reflect material reality. And, as Tom Stoppard so aptly observes in his 1993 play *Arcadia,* referring to forms and patterns in Picasso's art: "Nature is having the last laugh. The freaky stuff is turning out to be the mathematics of the natural world."[25]

Styan draws a telling conclusion about Cocteau, which comments on art in particular but implicitly also on the complex interactions of the mental/physical life in general:

> While he declared his opposition to realism, he also considered that Jarry's *Ubu* and Apollinaire's *Les Mamelles de Tirésias* consisted at the same time of symbolism and a species of drama *à thèse,* that they had successfully merged symbolism and realism. It could well be true that a play which manages to draw upon both symbolism and realism is likely to be the more universal and durable. (2:60)

Cocteau's position that mystery inheres in the commonplace marks a sense of wonder deriving from the most unlikely sources. And Cocteau clearly anticipates the sense of wonder aroused by those in the scientific community who today assert that our material understanding of our environment (brain/mind included) increases for them rather than diminishes a sense of wonder in the world.

This sense of wonder via the physical-to-mental (and back again) development is, of course, a cornerstone of Pirandello's work, especially *Six Characters in Search of an Author*. Again, Styan makes a significant observation: "In the last analysis, the evolution of Pirandello's dramatic thinking can be explained only by the growth of his own consciousness of the world in which he lived" (2:77).

In his preface to *Six Characters,* written several years after the play, Pirandello explains the play utilizing concepts of consciousness strikingly parallel to contemporary ideas. Dennett and Flanagan state something of the obvious by observing that selfhood and consciousness, at their highest levels, entail manufacturing fictions of selfhood out of an actual pandemonium of discontinuity. Paralleling this idea, Pirandello likewise presents a sort of continuum of selfhood through varying degrees of consciousness among his six characters:

> The most alive, the most completely created, are the Father and the Step-Daughter who naturally stand out more and lead the way, dragging themselves along beside the almost dead weight of the others—first, the Son, holding back; second, the Mother, like a victim resigned to her fate, between the two children who have hardly any substance beyond their appearance and who need to be led by the hand.[26]

Not having actually rejected the characters themselves but, rather, their dramas, Pirandello places the characters in an existential dilemma that tests these varying degrees of consciousness: "In these six, then, I have accepted their 'being' without the reason for being" (368). Pirandello basically experiments with his characters' respective reasons for being, which will be contingent on their degrees of conscious evolution.

The Father and Step-Daughter, being fully conscious and therefore more full of a sense of selfhood, cannot accept that their newly acquired "reason for being" is to search for an external author whose larger "text" they are only part of. Still possessed of a Cartesian sense of dualistically charged separateness from their environment, they remain wedded to a belief that they exist purely as discrete autonomies, exclusive authors of their own stories. They tenaciously cling to their own current manufactured stories of discrete, independent existence rather than accepting the new identities as searchers for place within a broader context of consciousness. Pirandello observes:

I have taken the organism and entrusted to it, not its own proper function, but another more complex function into which its own function entered, if at all, only as a datum. A terrible and desperate situation especially for the two—Father and Step-Daughter—who more than the others crave life and more than the others feel themselves to be characters, that is, absolutely need a drama and therefore their own drama—the only one which they can envisage for themselves yet which meantime they see rejected; an "impossible" situation from which they feel they must escape at whatever cost; it is a matter of life and death. (368–69)

Their existences, or, more precisely, their consciousnesses of their existence, have no context, and drifting without grounding in their environmental place, they are frankly as good as dead. What they need is a twofold conversion: first, to reaffirm that their realities are naturally and materially grounded and, second, to realize that their current senses of discrete selfhood are creative fiction-making processes based on evolutionary necessity but necessarily open to renegotiation. What they need is opened to them by way of the search set before them.

Yet what they actually search for—an author to tell *their* stories as *they* have discretely and traditionally/centrally created them—will forever elude them because it is based on self-delusion of discrete, isolated identity. Indeed, a strictly linear and inflexibly firm consciousness of their own lives precludes accepting any other proffered function, no matter how contextually grounded it might be in the reality (materiality) placed before them. They've become too encrusted in a sense of discreteness rather than in an acceptance of integral flow and engagement with their context. Even when they are given the function of seeking a suitable context, this function for them is at best secondary and, indeed, not even fully realized by them to be a function. They essentially prefer to be narrative abstractions rather than entities grounded in a material context.

The Mother intrigues Pirandello, a woman less developed or encrusted (as a stage reality and as a conscious being) but who *feels* the torment of her driftlessness. This torment is something "she *feels,* without being conscious of it, and feels it therefore as something inexplicable: but she feels it so terribly that she doesn't think it *can* be something to explain either to herself or to others." This, Pirandello observes, is the condition his critics have cited to be "the true and complete 'human type.'" I would suggest that perhaps Pirandello senses through these critics what the materialist scientists see. That is, the Mother's pre-self-conscious, pre-full-awareness mode is quite possibly the level wherein experience, as yet unpolluted by serial self-conscious constructs of selfhood, can best benefit humanity. Experience at this level can affect a new sense of awareness in ways that it can no longer affect (without almost revolutionary difficulty) the Father and Step-Daughter who have already succumbed to errant conclusions about life and selfhood. The Mother's experience is directly felt experience, and this direct connection conveys to her a knowledge that has somehow bypassed rational consideration, in the process transferring decentralized truths about consciousness and selfhood as yet unfettered by centralizing mechanisms of serial consciousness itself. After all, says Pirandello, "Conflict between life-in-movement and form is the inexorable condition not only of the mental but also of the physical order," and our consciousnesses, predisposed as they are to overlay form onto experience, tend to lose track of unfettered experience as our urge to serialize experience analytically seeks dominion by ordering all before it (371). In order to short-circuit this domineering ordering urge, in order to rebalance the "conflict," drama must bring back an urge for experience at least only minimally polluted by our centralizing processors.

In many ways Pirandello's essay is as illuminating as the play, given that the essay is itself an after-the-fact conscious reflection of a work he concedes was written at a sort of preconscious level. He wrote, in essence, at the same fully open, nonlinear level that he created in the Mother, and only upon reflection does he see the order he rather preconsciously placed upon the experience of writing the play. Like a reflection upon a burn reflex, the essay is a reflection of exactly what he sees the Mother herself must achieve in her own search. His sympathies with the Mother exist because he is (or was) at that same evolutionary stage of consciousness when he wrote the play. And the critics, when viewing the play, reveal themselves to be at a similar sympathetic stage as well (a rare case in which the playwright approves of the critics!). Quite romantically, Pirandello concedes that out of some pre–fully conscious urge he has succeeded in creating an organic product that very likely would have been stillborn had he engaged his rational, self-aware skills—much as the realist dramatists he condemns do, or so he says—in order to produce the play he has now before him: "The poet, unknown to them [the characters and the actors], as if looking on at a distance during the whole period of the experiment, was at the same time busy creating—with it and of it—his own play" (375). And through that play Pirandello found his own context/grounding.

Working at a level unattached to self-conscious control, Pirandello's faculties succeeded at stringing together a work that, upon self-conscious reflection, embodies for him a perfect reflection of his own organic balance between linear/serial thought and nonlinear/parallel experience, generated from a bottom-up, experience-to-idea process reflective of the materialist process of mind itself.

Beckettian Consciousness

Samuel Beckett's work extends the efforts of the modernist assault on the problem of mind in numerous fruitful ways. Its incipient tone of despair notwithstanding—reflecting Hegel's "unhappy consciousness"—Beckett's theater takes full advantage of the physicality of the theater to probe the interconnections between nature and mind, suggesting as a result that consciousness arises out of nature, rather than being, metaphysically and dualistically, something other than nature. Beckett's art calls specific attention to the nature of human awareness in ways perhaps only incidentally true of its countless contemporaries, though (like Wilde) his art points to the incidental truths often backgrounded in many of his contemporaries' efforts.

Beckett's dramatic agenda can best be described as one that approaches consciousness by directing attention to the interplay between it and that which falls directly in front of the human gaze—and that is the landscape or geography of the natural world, no matter how denatured it appears on Beckett's stage. One could also argue that Beckett studies that which occurs "behind" the human gaze, if we take our cue from his set directions for *Endgame:* "Left and right back, high up, two small windows, curtains drawn."[27] Easily construed as eyes high up on the wall, the set literally becomes an "inside-of-his-head" arrangement, and *Endgame* becomes—as do all of Beckett's plays—a study of how the brain/mind works to reach out to the world before our eyes, even those eyes that are sometimes closed shut.

Take Winnie in *Happy Days*. The image of her being literally grounded in her environment speaks directly to the point of Beckett's interest in the interconnectivity of the physical and mental. Winnie is revealed through her response to the world, of which she is literally a part. Taken as a squarely phenomenological exercise, we see that mind can only reveal itself as consciousness *of something*. Her spare but very real possessions are literally her life supports. She would be nothing without them. And the fact that she is literally grounded in her world, nearly totally buried in her world, is an ontological comment on our need to realize our physicality as essential to our sense of self, being, and consciousness. In turn selfhood relies on some consciousness of being part of yet another consciousness, of having some other conscious context through which our existence leaves its trace. Winnie reveals this need in her monologue directed at her mate, Willie:

> I shall not trouble you again unless I am obliged to, by that I mean unless I come to the end of my own resources which is most unlikely, just to know in theory you can hear me even though in fact you don't is all I need, just to feel you there within earshot and conceivably on the qui vive is all I ask.[28]

This need is the same need experienced by Estragon and Vladimir in *Waiting for Godot.* Hell may be other people, as Sartre suggests in *No Exit,* but that assessment is moral and even aesthetic, not ontological. If hell is what we must expect of existence, at least existence is, ontologically speaking, a *living,* physical/material hell. For Beckett, however, it seems that hell is less a moral issue and more ontological, more a case of an existence lacking context. For Beckett hell is a world without other people; no matter how depraved or hollow those others may be, they are crucial to existence.

Beckett's Lucky and Pozzo (in *Godot*) and Hamm and Clov (in *Endgame*) make this point fundamentally evident by revealing the necessity of relational contact, even if it entails morally unappetizing behavior. Critics have frequently correctly observed that the relationships of Beckett's characters are of the master-servant, dominator-dominated variety. I would suggest that Beckett makes this choice not so much to comment on human brutality (a much-covered theme) but to observe that the basic human need for context overrides even the need for creature comforts and moral "niceties." At its most basic, context in and of itself is vital, regardless of any aesthetic or moral contingencies. It is not "goodness" that's needed so much as place. As David H. Hesla observes, "We might say that just as consciousness cannot be consciousness absolutely but must always be consciousness *of,* so mastery cannot be itself absolutely but must be mastery *of.*"[29] Moralizing aside, the issue of context, or, more specifically, of consciousness of context, is central.

Beckett even experiments with a further minimalized reality when he focuses on the possibility of isolated self-consciousness. But even in these "laboratory" situations context is crucial, for even self-consciousness is a matter that involves the "of." Sartre's own phenomenological observations conclude: "Every positional consciousness of an object is at the same time a non-positional consciousness of itself."[30] Even self-consciousness is a consciousness of a consciousness of something, engaging a sort of physicalized landscaping of the mind generally in relationship to an actual physical landscape. In this regard Beckett offers *Not I,* a reduction of a self to simply Mouth, which speaks to no one in particular, though Auditor stands by throughout. Mouth expels a halting list of miseries from birth to the present moment, interspersed with cryptic reflections on the brain:

> what? . . . the buzzing? . . . yes . . . all silent but for the buzzing . . . so-called . . . no part of her moving . . . that she could feel . . . just the eyelids . . . presumably . . . on and off . . . shut out the light . . . reflex they call it . . . no feeling of any kind . . . but the lids . . . even best of times . . . who feels them? . . . opening . . . shutting . . . all that moisture . . . but the brain still . . . still sufficiently . . . oh very much so! . . . at this stage . . . in control . . . under control . . . to question even this.[31]

Consciousness even of the conscious brain radiates out to consciousness of the physical. Mouth confirms for itself its own existence not through some Cartesian abstraction but through solid grounding in an awareness, no matter how minimal, of its environment. Likewise, the need even for minimal contact is also confirmed by the presence of Auditor. Indeed, Beckett's own existence (like Pirandello's) seems confirmed in a similar process, that is, through his art conveyed to his audience: he seems to argue, "I write (and have place); therefore, I exist." Even Beckett's decision to write for the theater is—as should be the case with all thoughtful theater practitioners—necessarily a concession that context is crucial to being. The stage demands it.

The text of Beckett's *Waiting for Godot* reveals an interesting contextual philosophical enterprise, encompassing a wide array of ontological speculations by two least likely of characters, Vladimir and Estragon. Vladimir observes, "What is terrible is to *have* thought,"[32] harking back to the Cartesian proof of existence. This statement is followed shortly by Estragon's insistence regarding another matter, "You don't have to look," suggesting the Berkeleyan assertion, "To be is to be perceived." This, in turn, is followed by Estragon's "We should turn resolutely towards Nature" (41b), a romanticist invocation that doesn't appease their concerns either, though the men shortly turn toward contemplating the tree. Vladimir then observes of a "little canter" that has now come to an end, "now we'll have to find something else" (42a), suggesting the existential tag, "To do is to be."

Waiting for Godot is full of many such allusions, either intentionally inserted by Beckett or merely textually evident to the peculiar observer. Through these pared-down allusions, however, Beckett has effectively stripped existence down to bare necessities of thought and the role place has in thought. Baroque opulence proves nothing; essentialist minimalism is where true, basic need is unearthed. The point, as I see it, is that Beckett advocates thought and specifically thought *of*—distinctly rejecting the Cartesian intransitive reflection of "I think"—as the *minimal* requirement for conscious existence. And this "thing," conscious existence, runs a gamut of degrees of awareness from something just above reflex to fully aware, linearly revealed self-consciousness. Stanton B. Garner Jr., in his study of theater and phenomenology, observes of Beckett, "The result, for this playwright of the image, is to etch the contours of performance even more in the spectator and to replace a theater of activity with a theater of perception, guided by the eye and its efforts to see."[33] Consciousness struggled with onstage has an additional stage on which to interact, and that is on the stages of the minds within the audience (a metaphorical observation, of course).

Turning to this notion of a theater of consciousness, Bernard J. Baars's *In The Theater of Consciousness* is particularly useful. Echoing something like Dennett's multiple drafts suggestion, Baars observes:

> Chances are that unconscious incubation makes use of all the highly practiced automatism that we have thought about over our lifetimes. Word search is an unconscious type of problem solving in the mental lexicon, but it can handle all the words we have paid attention to in our lives. It seems that the unconscious mechanisms that are quietly buzzing away before the answer is returned are themselves the working residues of earlier conscious thought. (50–51)

Baars adds later: "Children learning language don't consciously label the words they hear as nouns and verbs. Rather, they pay attention to speech sounds, and the underlying grammar is learned implicitly. We rarely become conscious of abstract patterns" (60). Baars's observations parallel the earlier suggestions concerning the effect of expressionist and symbolist art, that unconscious incubation arising from preconscious activities stimulated by the theater may ultimately rise up actually to affect serially/linearly conscious states via a sort of reconfiguring of the soft-wiring in the brain. This, too, is what I would suggest occurs in Beckett but also in virtually all types of theater.

What distinguishes Beckettian theater and the expressionistic/symbolist heritage from which it grew, however, involves yet another level. Beckett's is an art that strikes us "unexpectedly," which disorients our logical faculties and dramatic expectations. His art is, quite simply, strange. The result oftentimes is that students/audiences give up trying to "understand" Beckett, ill equipped as we all are on first inspection to comprehend what is placed before us. For others, however, accepting disorientation and at least determining to "see what happens" can be fruitful. Baars observes, "While we are usually unaware of their presence, unconscious contexts can become consciously accessible" (126), and achieving accessibility often occurs only when violations of our expectations occur, leading first to an uncomfortable "decontextualzation" but eventually to a new or "re"-contextualization. And Beckett's strangely staged world—for the "open-minded"—effects such a process. Baars interestingly notes that this process of decontextualization is the cornerstone of intellectual postmodernism of which Beckett is a beginning and through which our culture has consciously come to witness (through numerous "violations") formerly unconscious decontextualizations inherent in our thought processes.

Clearly, Beckett's stage presents numerous creatures who experience such decontextualization. The violations, of course, do not simply occur to the characters onstage; they occur to an expectant audience as well, traditionally trained as it is to expect conventional elements of theater that Beckett intentionally abandons—though they are perhaps less violent today given our culture's decades-long exposure to them. Nevertheless, resistance to Beckett's dramaturgical violations parallel the resistance experienced by the plays' characters (and Pirandello's Father and Step-Daughter), victims of depersonalization striving to reconstruct/reconstitute selfhood through linking fabrications/narratives that reconnect "self" to reality. Part of that reconnection, when violently violating, generally necessitates a reformulation of a sense of reality and identity itself. Beckett's characters suffer through this process, generally unsuccessfully, as does Beckett's audience suffer violations of theatrical expectations, hopefully more successfully.

Such violations, despite any initial conscious resistance by our serial awareness, may initiate a rewiring and eventual conscious inclination toward reevaluation. Perhaps our culture may have already benefited from exposure to the violating spirit of Beckett in ways still unaccounted by our linear faculties. Finally, it's Beckett's theater as much as, if not more than, his drama, that engages the theater of the mind. Perhaps, in fact, through exposure to Beckett's countless violations we may, as a culture, already be better equipped to adjust our vision of the Cartesian Theater itself. While all theater arguably bridges the mind/matter gap, leaving preconscious traces of the bridging, only through violation of our preconceived prejudices—flashing directly before our resisting, conscious, serializing eyes—can we come fully to realize the fundamental illusion of our prior assumptions. Theater is far more than dramatizations of stories placed before passive spectators. Theater is interactive engagement, made clear by the very violations Beckett—and his other nontraditional predecessors and successors—has made manifest on his stage.

Baars agrees with the materialists that awareness inheres in numerous regions of the neural system. His suggestion is that all these "actors," "designers," "directors," of the neural network coordinate their inputs to create on the stage of the brain a theater of the mind. As with the others, this "theater of consciousness," actually like real theater, is an intangible thing, a place belonging to no necessary place but occurring quite simply whenever and wherever it does. Baars correctly implies that there is no literal need for actual scaffolding in order for theater to occur, as there is no real need for a physical Cartesian Theater in the mind (recall Descartes's pineal gland). We need not have a literal stage with ticket-holding spectators before it. It occurs everywhere. And, even then, even when theater *is* placed before us literally on a stage, we barely see the whole operation under way. So, too, by analogy, in the theater of consciousness we are not fully aware of all that occurs. Says Baars, "Thus, whatever we experience is shaped by unconscious processes, just like a theater in which we see only actors onstage, but not all the people *behind* the scenes who make it all work" (180). What goes on behind the scenes of final, polished, linear constructs is ultimately more important than we formerly believed.

To go one step further, one can see how Baars and this sense of theater parallels an awareness reflected in the recent proliferation of performance studies programs among American universities. To tweak the *theatrum mundi* trope, theater/performance occurs beyond the institutional controls and confines of actual theaters, unfolding in any number of venues, from political rallies to "happenings," even to activities in the lives of private citizens daily placed in public situations. Rather than there being some centralized cultural Cartesian Theater consciously presenting reality to a cultural consciousness, theaters erupt all along the cultural neural network, no longer—if ever—centrally controlled, censured, or limited. Such theaters erupt in nature, as Baars argues, as well as within cultures and among individual consciousnesses themselves, altering neural networks and making us aware of what "makes" us. To borrow a term from the modernist Marcel Duchamp, existence that includes some/any aspect of consciousness is, basically, a theatrical "ready-made."

Chapter 4

Logic, Creativity, Etc.

In the process of attempting to rewire the human neural network, playwrights and scientific theoreticians both are integrally challenging our
notions of logical progression and striving to place us in a situation to
reevaluate logical premises inherent in our current thought processes.
The logic that seems to escape those who are attempting emergently to
jump from the material physical world to the material mental world may
become accessible if one considers a reassessment of logic itself, something that implicitly inheres in the playwrights already discussed and that
more directly inheres in the sometimes "illogical" works of such playwrights and artists as Robert Wilson and Sam Shepard, among others.

"Fuzzy" Logic

To better understand alternatives such as Dennett's multiple drafts model
of mind, one must turn to "fuzzy" logic. The science of fuzzy logic is
not a new development in Western thought but, rather, a development
that has taken on recent cultural relevance. In 1926 Jan Christian Smuts
observed:

> The science of the nineteenth century was like its philosophy, its morals
> and its civilization in general, distinguished by a certain hardness, primness
> and precise limitation and demarcation of ideas. *Vagueness,* indefinite and
> blurred outlines, anything savoring of mysticism, was abhorrent to that
> great age of limited exactitude. The rigid categories of physics were
> applied to the indefinite and hazy phenomena of life and mind.[1]

Dominated by a sense of either/or—the rigid law of excluded middle—
such a world as Smuts describes translates reality into black and white,
ignoring the fuzzy, or gray, nature of reality that dominates a vast terrain
between the two extremes of precise *is* and *is not*. This tight perspective

on reality is a revered Western perspective perfected by Western science, reaching its zenith in pre–World War I Victorian/Edwardian Europe, though by no means extinct following the Great War. The alternative logic that Smuts was implicitly endorsing in 1926 (but which was in the main largely ignored until recently), supporting a view of understanding the world as something more than a world of excluded middle, is a logic of multivalence (multiple values) challenging the bivalent (either/or) tradition of Western culture, a distinction best epitomized by the philosophy of Confucius over that of Aristotle.

Aristotle, the cornerstone of Western thought, is credited with seeing all experience in terms of exclusive categories. Something was either good or bad, tall or short, hot or cold, dead or alive. Yet measure, morality, and life itself often fail to follow this bivalent principle. Things, events, descriptions, often incorporate qualities of both extremes, are both/and to such an extent that either/or is accurate for only a relatively few actual conditions in the real world. Nevertheless, Western culture has remained wedded to systems of bivalent thought.

Eastern thought, on the other hand, has operated from a multivalent perspective since at least the time of Confucius. The recent Western phenomenon known as fuzzy logic—the logic of multivalence—takes Confucianism to heart while bringing it into the Western fold. Consider the concept of tallness as a simple example. If one chooses to define tallness among humans as anyone 6' tall or over, then we clearly have an either/or proposition. But this arbitrary assignment artificially reduces the complexities of the concept. Is 5'0" as "not tall" as 4'5"? Is 6'1" tall in the same way 7'2" is tall? Even embracing a four-tiered multivalent continuum (in this simple case, short, shortish, tallish, tall) significantly increases the accuracy of description. The more values included, the more precise the description. Instead of a single point of demarcation, a line of gradation far better explains the concept of tallness. The more values we acknowledge, the closer we come to achieving and acknowledging fuzzy logic, fuzzy because it challenges reductive and oversimple categorization but far more precise/logical as a descriptive process than mere bivalence.

Bivalence has become virtually synonymous with *serial processing,* especially with the rise of computer technology, committed as it is to traditional logical processes. Truth is a matter of either truth/fact or non-truth/falseness, with the vast matter of that which falls in between the two extremes often rounded off to its nearest bivalent value. "Mostly true" is rounded off to "absolutely true." Assignments in bivalence of the numbers "0" or "1" are the central processes in computer language. The statement "Either someone is married or not" can accurately be reduced to 0 or 1. But, as Bart Kosko suggests in *Fuzzy Thinking: The New Science of Fuzzy Logic*,[2] what about the matter of whether or not someone is happy with her or his career? Couldn't someone be in part happy and in part unhappy? Can 0 or 1 accurately reflect that state, or should various "between" values be included, say, 0.24 or 0.5 or 0.96? The idea of multivalued systems has recently resulted in the development of "smart computers" that can produce "gray" reactions in response to gray data, relativizing reality as facts about reality are themselves relative.

If we adapt Dennett's point, the mind likewise has evolved (with crucial Western cultural enforcements) to organize brain data bivalently, creating crisp lines between concepts rather than accepting the blurry reality of data and of reality itself. Reality has been reduced to a system that for the most part unnecessarily fictionalizes reality except in radical cases of, say, impending fight/flight decisions that require almost instinctive either/or responses. The more we accept multiple values, however, the more accurately we begin to depict reality. And, in survivalist situations, we even begin to see the growing multivalent, or gray, possibility of negotiation as an evolving survivalist strategy. Here we see an invitation to attempt a culturally predicated evolutionary step. If nature originally evolved our serial minds to cope with the prompt necessities of basic survival, then perhaps, given our (putative) triumph over nature, we should now consider staging another alteration of our concept of reality, namely, consciously striving to alter our vision of epistemological necessity/reality. While bivalence and seriality have led to significant human advances over our environment, they have also led to numerous dead ends and near (as well as actual) catastrophes. Perhaps we now need to consider consciously created advances over our (mainly) biologically produced mind in order for even further human advance. This culturally and consciously produced effort could very well effect a biologically material alteration—a neural rewiring—of our brain/mind functions, a tantalizing thought, indeed.

Three values are better than two, four are better than three, etc. We begin here to accept a rich multivalence that approaches parallel/brain processing, accepting a pandemonium of possibilities and a resulting liberating opening-up of higher-order conscious mental considerations. We should reevaluate the filtering and reductionist mechanism of mind and adjust to the possibilities of a more full-bodied creativity. Here, however, we must once again be forewarned about the potential limits of this liberation. Too great a degree of multivalence may better reflect reality, but it can also result in informational overload. Too much multivalence settles into pure pandemonium, a chaos-as-disorder phase of existence of unmanageable proportions leading inevitably to Prufrock-like decision-making paralysis. Finding a balance between too much order (bivalence) and too much disorder (radical multivalence) seems a pervasive necessity.

Establishing a more flexible order within the disorder of our existence is necessary. Thus far, our evolutionary leanings have progressed toward increasingly refining the amount of the brain's serial output that survives to levels of mental awareness, increasingly—and perhaps habitually—limiting that which we evaluate as we have evolved a more restrictive sense of what is relevant and what is mere noise to be disregarded. Freeing ourselves of these ever-tightening shackles will require a cultural rather than biological evolution, a change promoted by self-awareness coupled with an ability to modify behavior. G. L. Stebbins utilized a concept of genetic and cultural templates to explain the idea, observing, "A safe generalization is that genetic templates transmit *potentialities* or *capacities* rather than adult behavioral traits, which is for cultural templates."[3] In essence Stebbins is arguing that we have the hard-wire/genetic capacity to engage a soft-wire/cultural transformation. Adopting a concept of multivalent cultural templating is an apparently crucial transformation, and our genetic templates, in fact, predispose us to do so.

We are not talking here of an intriguing though only nominally valuable transformation, for in many ways our continued survival demands it. It is obvious to most that challenging the difference inherent in racism, sexism, and nationalism by instituting their bivalent opposites—homogeneity, androgyny, globalism—is not a satisfactory option. Failing to acknowledge a need to find a balance between difference and commonality in matters of human ethnicity, gender, and nationality will likely result in still other unforeseen failures. Universal advocacy of sameness seems every bit as unsavory as militant advocacy of uniqueness. In the theater we see such matters addressed by such practitioners as Caryl Churchill, who in *Cloud Nine* problematized issues such as gender, race, and nationality by inserting multivalent options into all categories. And in *Top Girls* Churchill observes the problem of what she would doubtless call the pseudofeminist urge of women confronting male domination either by beating males at their own games (in the form of

Marlene) or by accepting a subordinate "feminine" role (in the form of Marlene's sister, Joyce). Surely, there are other options to Victorian bivalence, as confronted in *Cloud Nine,* and to the contemporary, male-structured either/or structured universe erected in *Top Girls.*

As diversity and adaptation are crucial to natural progress, so are they likely crucial to cultural progress: too much order/sameness or too much disorder/difference are both to be avoided. Rather than operating under a continued delusion that middles should be excluded in favor of the triumph of one "bad" extreme over the other "good" extreme, humanity seems in need of embracing a fuzzy logic, a nonlinear conception and parallel processing mechanism that considers degrees of both extremes (of whatever categories we choose), a true sense of multivalent ecologicalism, embracing an integrated whole rather than selected parts.

The Question of Creativity:
A Quantum Suggestion

Encouraging a wider range of options (multivalence), the mind (or a computer) can potentially allow interrelated possibilities to move beyond strictly linear calculations to derive subtle and often unexpected conclusions. Material generally considered irrelevant surfaces to take on an unexpected centrality and groups together with other elements to produce essentially unique ideas. This vision of creativity feeds well into Dennett's own suggestion of a pandemonium of input being somehow sorted into multiple drafts in the mental stream of consciousness to produce original thought.

Roger Penrose, however, suggests in *Shadows of the Mind* that Dennett's theory model may be incomplete.[4] Basically, Dennett's model (and others like his) still subscribes to a fundamental computational, even mechanistic (though this term is no longer bound to linear bivalence) model of the mind evidenced by the various computer allusions forwarded by such models. Penrose suggests that no computer technology—at least no computer as we currently design or conceptualize them—could ever precisely duplicate human thought, that the human mind is far more than the computer (as we know it) could ever be. While computers may eventually come *close* to duplicating human thought, they will forever remain fundamentally computational regardless of either serial or multivalent advances. Penrose centrally argues that "the human faculty of being able to 'understand' is something that must be achieved by some non-computational activity of the brain or mind"

(48). Understanding is a basically *creative* element and must have a non-computational source in order to break out of an otherwise inescapable cycle of basically same, finite results.

Even chaos theory paradigms, Penrose argues, are likely to be insufficient because they, too, are fundamentally computational in nature:

> Can it be that it is *chaos* that provides the needed answer to the mystery of mentality? For this to be the case, there would have to be something completely new to be understood about the way in which chaotic systems can behave in appropriate situations. It would have to be the case that, in such situations, a chaotic system can closely approximate *non-computational behaviour* in some asymptotic limit—or something of this nature. No such demonstration has, to my knowledge, ever been provided. Yet it remains an interesting possibility, and I hope that it will be pursued thoroughly in the years to come. (178)

Chaos theory argues that out of the apparent disorder of nonlinear events clearly emerges new and unexpected *combinations* of results. Perhaps, eventually, chaotics will be discovered to be central to the creative processes of the mind. But the set of possibilities remains limited, for the chaos paradigm suggests that nothing is new except in the way it is arranged. Producing new relationships between that which is already known would be the chaotics definition of *creativity*. This definition is intriguing and perhaps even accurate. But Penrose suggests that being itself computational—even if nonlinearly or fuzzily or pandemoniously computational—chaotics will likely fail *fully* to describe the creative processes, though it may succeed at explaining certain levels of creativity.

The ancient Greeks recognized what seemed to be either a non-computational or a chaotics aspect to creativity but conceded an inability to explain it and therefore credited the muses with having fed their artists/thinkers the necessary "spark" from the top down. But, as with all the other mystical questions put before the materialists, there is no need in this case to invoke a dualist necessity. We can either accept the chaotics model or move to embrace something like Penrose's suggestion.

Penrose suggests that noncomputationality is actually a fundamental cornerstone of science (despite traditional scientific claims to the contrary) and that by extension all creative human thought is potentially noncomputational as well. He observes that math is the apparently perfect manifestation of all our computational efforts, working to confirm the computational nature of reality itself, albeit in ever-increasing complexity. And, while math can be used to derive seemingly ingeniously new ideas, Penrose suggests that it fails fundamentally to explain its own sources of the truly and inspirationally new. Penrose observes that mathematics succeeds as it does only to the extent that it proves itself one step at a time; it cannot explain the basic sources/causes of its own success. Why is math "true"? This is Gödel's theorem at work, which Douglas Hofstadter translates as, "All consistent axiomatic formulations of numbers theory include undecidable propositions."[5] Basically, math has no way of proving *itself* to be true: there is a human, noncomputational, inspired leap of faith, essentially, that accepts the computational accuracy of the whole of our mathematical knowledge. For Penrose this is a central verification of the noncomputational inclining of the mind and therefore of the necessary incompleteness of *any* computational model of thought. If even math is noncomputational at its root, surely other forms of creative thought are likewise at heart noncomputational.

Should we credit the muses, the gods, a homunculus, or something else with providing us with the noncomputational spark? Should we, as Penrose rhetorically asks, look more closely at Platonism or mysticism? Penrose proposes that we turn to quantum physics, that strange submicrocosmic world of counterintuitive activity where quantum material can be both here and there (superpositioned) and where traditional expectations of linear, deterministic behavior are consistently undermined. "Brain action, according to the conventional viewpoint, is to be understood in terms of essentially classical physics—or so it would seem. Nerve signals are normally taken to be 'on or off' phenomena, just as are the currents in the electronic circuits of a computer, which *either* take place *or* do not take place." But Penrose disagrees with this traditional bivalent perspective, seeing quantum physics as rising up from its microcosmic source actually to effect the macro-machinations of the brain/mind. He argues that the conventional viewpoint fails because it allows for "none of the mysterious *superpositions* of alternatives that are characteristic of quantum actions"(348). Penrose is making the unique and encouraging argument (a theory sketch) that the noncomputational irregularities of the quantum world are not activities restricted to the subatomic quantum world but that they rise up to integrate with macro-cosmic events, marking those events with their own noncomputational processes (one could say, with their own "quantum-leapability").

What Penrose is suggesting is a holistic union of micro- and macro-cosmic phenomena, uniting subatomic studies to neural studies to macro studies of integrated mental behavior. The ancient world argued that separate laws existed for the operations of the heavens and of the earth. Over the last few centuries we have come to understand that laws governing the heavens and earth are the same. Of late, however, scientists have sort of slipped back to the past, arguing that separate laws govern the subatomic and the visible worlds. Penrose suggests otherwise, observing,

> It is my own opinion—an opinion shared by a sizable minority of physicists—that this state of physical understanding cannot be other than a stopgap, and we may well anticipate that the finding of appropriate quantum/classical laws that operate uniformly at *all* scales might herald a scientific advance of a magnitude comparable with that initiated by Galileo and Newton. (307–8)

While admittedly in the minority,[6] Penrose argues the minority perspective quite convincingly.

His first step in uniting the two worlds comes with the mind, making the traditionalist's point that, "whilst it would be admitted that, at *underlying* levels, quantum effects must have their roles to play, biologists seem to be generally of the opinion that there is no necessity to be forced out of the classical framework when discussing the large-scale implications of those primitive quantum ingredients." Penrose suggests that noncomputability in the mind, leaps of creativity and even of basic understanding, are the result of the "strange *superpositions* of quantum theory, that would allow *simultaneous* 'occurring' and 'not occurring'" (348). Seeing quantum activity at work, Penrose observes further:

> The unity of a single mind can arise, in such a description, only if there is some form of quantum coherence extending across at least an appreciable part of the entire brain.
>
>   Such a feat would be a remarkable one—almost an incredible one—for Nature to achieve by biological means. Yet I believe that the indications must be that she has done so, the main evidence coming from the fact of our own mentality. (372–73)

The leaps and bounds revealed by quantum mechanics in the microcosmic universe may ultimately be the part of the process that helps the brain *emergently* to overcome the plodding inevitability necessary in the traditional models of brain activity. The thought is intriguing, since it brings together all the formerly discussed necessary conditions of true human consciousness.

Michael Frayn, in his 1998 play *Copenhagen,* introduces a unique phrase, *quantum ethics,*[7] into his dramatic conversation between physicists Werner Heisenberg and Niels Bohr (and his wife). In a curiously dramatized twist the play discusses matters of personal responsibility for mass murder in regard to the creation of the atomic bomb during World War II. These two quantum physicists become almost literally superpositioned elements by play's end, each simultaneously innocent and guilty in their past actions. Echoing in many ways the same use of a quantum metaphor as Tom Stoppard used in his 1988 play *Hapgood, Copenhagen* shows the value of quantum potential as a postmodern metaphor. Interestingly, Penrose suggests that quantum physics is more than metaphorically relevant to our conscious lives.

An Organic Suggestion

In this materialist pursuit of consciousness reductionist science still has its place, though it seems limited to describing more or less linearly computational nonfuzzy elements of mind. And a vision of multivalent pandemonium further explains some of the more complex creative albeit still computational levels of consciousness; chaos can show how mind unites elements of thought into potentially unique combinations. Yet noncomputational levels of consciousness—sources of even higher-order original thought—may require quantum considerations. We are witnessing what Stuart Kauffman has called "the incessant urge of complex systems to organize themselves into patterns" as the scale of complexity progressively increases.[8]

We are witnessing, in essence, a growing scientific and cultural awareness that consciousness has emergent qualities that may appear mysterious but are far from mystical events. Increasingly, distinctions between materiality and immateriality no longer hold except in cases of extreme (obviously bivalent) comparison. Thought/consciousness, we now see, is not an isolatable event; it operates throughout the neural system, and it has myriad material manifestations. These two points reveal the impossibility of determining some point of demarcation between thought and nonthought. They even suggest a certain degree of difficulty in determining animate from inanimate reality. Certainly, the problem of distinguishing material from immaterial becomes a multivalent issue rather than the bivalent one we frequently thought it to be. It is quite probable to conclude that very few elements in reality are either/or animate-inanimate or material-immaterial

Summarizing the field of complexity in science, M. Mitchell Waldrop observes: "Thus, molecules would form cells, neurons would form brains, species would form ecosystems, consumers and corporations would form economies, and so on. At each level, new emergent structures would form and engage in new emergent behaviors" (88). We see now that we can escape our quasidualist illusions/self-delusions, arriving as we have at the verge of achieving materialist certainties about consciousness and its interrelatedness with myriad other material realities. But how do we go beyond the verge?

Matter and that which we have formerly called nonmatter appear *materially* to interact. That's the process that Crick, Dennett, and Penrose argue. The process is explained, but we still haven't dealt with the question of what that matter that is nonmatter actually is. F. David Peat and David Bohm have pursued such questions in various books, including Peat's work *Synchronicity: The Bridge between Matter and Mind* and Bohm's *Wholeness and the Implicate Order*.[9] Two illustrations suggest Peat's and Bohm's perspectives on what Penrose has introduced by way of quantum physics. (Actually, their philosophical musings predate Penrose's study.) Peat discusses the phenomenon of solitons, quoting an 1834 report by J. Scott Russell on its first recorded sighting. While riding along a narrow canal, Russell observed a solitary wave that "rolled forward with great velocity, assuming the form of a large solitary elevation, a rounded, smooth and well defined heap of water, which continued its course along the channel apparently without change of form or diminution of speed" (74). Solitons have since been sighted in many wavelike forms, including by satellites that have sighted single waves rippling for thousands of miles in the ocean. They are self-organized, self-generated entities that force their ways through otherwise random material bodies. The soliton is not the water per se, since this wave event only utilizes the water it locally runs through. But without the materially existent water we would never know the existence of the soliton itself. Perceiving the material reality of the rising/falling water allows us to see the effect of the force that is the soliton. What we have is a materially real event that seems in its essence to articulate forces buried/hidden beneath its surface materiality.

Solitons and like phenomena exhibit the strange self-organizing quantum behavior that Penrose ascribes to mind. Mind is pattern sighted only by the traces it leaves in material reality while at the same time being the product of that materiality via quantum potential. The rising quantum-based connection between these forces and their visible, material manifestations are not mystical phenomena. They are, in fact, quantifiable, but they require a different kind of sighting than our reductionist, linear perspectives have heretofore encouraged.

Along this line we may use another illustration to depict a changing way of understanding our connections between mind and universe: the hologram. Taking any organized conglomeration of parts as a collective entity, the standard assumption would be that the parts add up to a whole. For example, photons are organized in a slide show to create a picture. The parts add up to a picture.

In the case of a hologram, however, if we secure only a part of the total hologram source—say, the leg of a hologram image of a dog—and then isolate and rebroadcast it, a strange phenomenon will occur. As Bohm reports, the result is *"we see the whole structure,* but in somewhat less sharply defined detail and from a decreased range of possible points of view (as if we were looking through a smaller window)" (146). In the part (the leg) inheres the whole (the dog). We do not simply get an enlarged leg; we get the whole reconstituted from the simple part we've isolated. In this regard, too, Bohm argues, we can see the mind as a sort of hologram of the universe, attuned to the patterns and rhythms that organize the universe. It can be ventured, in fact, that our minds are attuned to the energies out of which matter actually derives, to follow the thinking of "big bang" astrophysicists. Mind, after all, is an extension of that universe, quite possibly a holographic part of the whole.

Peat and Bohm advocate what Bohm calls *implicate* wholeness, the order that underlies all visible, *explicate* reality. This theory sketch, however, is not some rehashed idealism. Rather, with the nonlinear triumphs of chaos, quantum, and complexity theories, we are now able holistically to sight the very complex, interconnected implicate patterns that our reductionist and linear thinking has so long blindered itself against pursuing. Knowing mind is knowing materiality operating at its most profound levels—and vice versa. Quantum mechanics, it turns out, may not be merely so much unrelated "knowledge-for-knowledge's sake" study of the unperceivable; rather, its very operating schemes may reveal structures and operations that inhere in and influence the entire universe.

This idea of patterns governing the universe makes sense when one considers the notion of natural selection. The universe is actually too young to have generated life in a truly random way, as inert Darwinism suggests: there has not been enough time for truly random selection to have blindly gone through even a fraction of the nearly infinite options that would have been required for the generation of life. Yet, if patterns and rhythms within the universe *controlled* the selection process and, soliton-like, organized units of inert reality, then the odds of life evolving slip into the realm of possibility, even likelihood. An infinity of possibilities has been reduced to a manageably finite realm of options within a stream defined by these patterns and rhythms. Kauffman suggests that inert nature and these active patterns *must* have operated together to create life: "The precise genetic details of any given organism would be a product of random mutations and natural selection working just as Darwin had described them. But the organization of life itself, the order, would be deeper and more fundamental."[10] Nature is a combination of blind materiality controlled by some orderly, ordering element, an unseen pattern—at least unseen until now. If this theory is accurate, Kauffman concludes, then "life is not We the improbable, but We the expected.[11]

Here we move to the next question of what to do with these theory models. Peat rather intriguingly suggests seeing Carl Jung's concept of the collective unconscious as the human mind's trace of this implicate order in the universe. He further suggests that the mind has been constructed not only by evolutionary factors of a biological nature but also by cultural evolution, which has helped adjust our collective unconscious as it has been handed to us from our more primitive ancestors. This suggestion echoes Stebbins's template theory, which leads to a theory forwarded by Richard Dawkins and further developed by Dennett that warrants brief explanation.[12]

Evolution of "Memes"

Attached to Dennett's overall theory model is the intriguing element—borrowed from Richard Dawkins—that, Dennett observes, involves the potential for a "speeded-up" human evolution. Whereas nature has used relatively vast chunks of time and natural selection to evolve inorganic matter into organic matter and then into complex thinking units such as the human species, there is the human potential today to speed up the evolutionary process in a way that our human ancestors may also have to some degree helped speed up the process. Dennett's brand of evolution is an epistemological one that involves what Dawkins called "memes," units of *information* rather than actual units of matter, each of which parasitically strives for survival in the mind/brain, engaging in a coevolutionary process with its animal/organic host.

Take an idea. It must attach itself to a brain/mind for survival. Weak ideas/memes die out as their host determines their limited appropriateness in dealing with the environment surrounding the host. Stronger memes, however, contribute to stronger hosts and "infect" still other hosts/brains/minds through communicative transmission. If these memes contribute to the continued or extended health of their animal/organic hosts, the memes' "lives" are more fully guaranteed. If they harm their hosts—encouraging actions that may jeopardize the host's survival—they die out along with their hosts or are abandoned by the host in favor of more beneficial memes.

Memes at their most basic level have likely contributed to evolution even at some of the earliest stages of consciousness development. For example, a primitive meme suggesting that the colors red and yellow signal danger may be a beneficial meme given that sunrise—and its red hue—signaled danger to nocturnal hosts. These hosts escaped the dangers of daylight and lived to evolve more capably into diurnal creatures. That humans still have such a meme may be a simple residue of this early beneficial meme. As brains developed among life forms, other memes became more complexly influential in the evolutionary process until humans exploded onto the scene many millennia ago and evolutionary development likewise exploded. Says Dennett of the more complex variety of memes, they "could not get started until the evolution of animals had paved the way by creating a species—*Homo sapiens*—with brains that could provide shelter, and habits of communication that could provide transmission media, for memes" (202). The result is that "human consciousness is to a very great degree a product not just of [biological] natural selection, but of cultural evolution as well" (203).

Significantly, Dennett observes, "The meme for faith exhibits *frequency-dependence fitness:* it flourishes best when it is outnumbered by rationalistic memes; in an environment with few skeptics, the meme for faith tends to fade from disuse" (206). The faith meme has within it the Cartesian Theater meme and, generally, the meme for the disembodied soul. Memes can be valuable even when their truth is suspect. The meme of suspicion, for example, believing a potential friend to be an enemy, may promote survival, but a trust meme may be even more beneficial, though the opportunity for its parasitic growth may never arise, delaying or preventing opportunities for interactive advancement.

The Materialist Search for Soul

Along that biological and cultural evolutionary path it may be possible to see where we can appease Dennett's faith meme while undermining its fitness mechanism of surviving best under greatest rationalistic assault. Although Crick merely teases us in his book with a claim to be searching for soul and Dennett never addresses the matter of soul, one can see a hint of where soul lies and what it might be. Traditionally, soul is thought to be that immaterial, immortal *thing* that is essentially "me" (or you), the thing, or homunculus, within our material bodies that allows us to distinguish our selves from our bodies and the rest of creation. It is for most of us, quite simply, mind. I would suggest that the soul, in Dennett's model and in materialist models in general, does exist, but there is first the need to make several memic adjustments away from our commonsense conclusions. We need to restrict what we include and envision when we use the term.

First, I would suggest that soul is not a "thing" so much as it is like the soliton. This suggestion does not itself challenge traditional concepts, since soul is generally conceived of as spirit, or "no-thing," unlocatable and empirically unverifiable. Rather, it should be looked at in the same way that Dennett suggests mind should no longer be considered a thing, a point that also parallels the soliton image. Mind and soul both appear, soliton-like, to inhere within material existence. But, as mind should not be considered synonymous with brain (or soliton with ocean), neither should soul be considered synonymous with mind, as some would suggest. Rather, mind should be recognized, as described earlier, as the rough manifestation of the empirically verifiable *processes* that manipulate data into awareness or consciousness.

Extending this point, soul is not mind, and it is not some other thing, either. Instead, soul can be considered the *accumulation* of awareness—another evolved level of consciousness—that rises beyond the materialist self-awareness Dennett or Penrose describe. What this heightened, evolved awareness is—what soul is, I suggest—is a sort of meta-awareness, an accumulation that floods into an awareness of the discrepancy between our mind's linearized awareness of the explicate world around us and our brain's data that houses an implicate reality of underlying forms and patterns. Soul is that awareness that falls between the memes and sensations we are aware of in the materially processed world of mind and the fluttering data within our brains that our minds have subdued as noise (or that mind simply fails to grasp) in favor of other heightened data that have risen to the level of mind.

Awareness of the gap between what the mind knows and the brain offers the mind is the "floating thinglessness" we call soul, that awareness we can never fully grasp but that is holographically or soliton-like attuned to the organizing patterns and rhythms of existence. The knowledge that we can know more than we do know is the trace that we call immaterial soul. And, just as with the fallacy of the Cartesian Theater, we must come to realize the error of the rather understandable delusion that soul is a thing. It is not a thing but the "trace," a thing that is really a no-thing, as consciousness is also a thing that is a no-thing. This conclusion is not necessarily a new one; after all, in 1739 the empiricist philosopher David Hume concluded in *A Treatise of Human Nature* that the idea of a substantial self, an organized single entity called "me," really did not exist. The difference today is that science—empirical and materialist—has virtually drawn the same conclusion, namely, that self, rather paradoxically, is a material reality that is pattern and awareness, physical (as patterns are) though not concrete (as patterns are not): the thing that is a no-thing.

And we are likely correct in concluding that other animals have not evolved to this meta-awareness, a memic awareness of the process of awareness of its incompleteness. On a mystical level finding our souls has typically been seen as a process wherein we escape consciousness in a pursuit of deeper truths. Materially, we likewise can see that this gap-awareness operates in a way that makes us long for that deeper truth or reality unmediated by mind, an awareness that something exists that lies beyond the realm of linear consciousness.

Possession of that gap-awareness we call soul gives us the longing to strive to move beyond the linearity of mind/consciousness, moving into a world of trance in an effort to come in contact with the raw data that our brains constantly try to slip through the editing processes of the mind, memically coerced to edit as it does in order to create optimal survival conditions.

If we choose to search for soul, we have found it in our longings to converse more directly with reality; soul is the forever lingering trace in our brains/minds that acknowledges a sense of the implicate patterns of reality but fails fully to perceive them, given our mental training virtually exclusively to sight explicate, concrete reality. It acknowledges a fundamental urge to get closer to nature than our overriding minds allow.

From this perspective the mind can be seen as a veil, though without mind we, of course, would be absolutely nothing except an undistinguished part of nature, a thing little better than an undifferentiated no-thing. We obviously need minds to function as autonomous individuals, but that need paradoxically restricts our full engagement with nature. Yet, perhaps by evolving a meme that allows us holographically to tap into the patterns and rhythms of mind and perhaps more directly into the pandemonious operations of the brain as well, we could then better allow ourselves to sense the subtle patterns in reality ignored by our current memically enforced bivalent, linear, serial, and quasidualist prejudices.

One scientist, albeit a scientist who admittedly chooses to stand outside the scientific community, is Bart Kosko, who has suggested that God is Information (279), the kind of information, as I have suggested, that is not an information/god of facts or things but a god/information of processes and patterns. Kauffman, too, observes that his sense of patterned order can be seen to "rank as one of the secrets of the Old One," "the Old One" being Einstein's term for God.[13] The notion of patterns of reality among the apparent pandemonium of nature leads us exactly to that possibility. Can these patterns possibly be sorts of "radio waves of God" that we have lost the ability to interpret though we still have the mechanism to receive? Soul, in essence, is a steady reminder of our lost contact with the rhythms of the universe, reduced as they are to linear and fictional simplicity. Recovering that contact in turn may return us to a sense of contact with God-as-rhythm-of-the-cosmos.

While traditional Western versions of God portray "him" as an anthropomorphic reality, other versions concede an omnipresence and omnipotence of this being that belies anthropomorphic reductions. If we accept the concept that this being is no being at all—in the same way that consciousness itself requires no homunculus—then God is universal nonbeing life pattern. And, if we accept recent theories placed under the headings chaos, complexity, and quantum theories, wherein science has engaged a search for patterns of reality permeating all existence, then perhaps God, this beingless being, is the patterns of reality that science has begun to uncover, even as it begins to shake itself of its linear, serial habits of truth searching.

Science has begun to realize its delusions about the nature of consciousness and has begun to unravel itself from its bind with mind. And science has likewise begun to see the universe in ways freed from the prejudices of mind's seriality. In the process, is science perhaps inadvertently revealing to us that soul exists and that God exists (given the memic reconsiderations of the notions of soul and existence), that they have both been within our grasps all along but that our meme systems have deluded us into searching in all the wrong places? The patterns Fuchs sights in the theater seem to be working in this direction. Perhaps the arts have something to offer the sciences in that feedback loop that is becoming increasingly crucial in the pursuit of higher order, be it consciousness, soul, or god.

Theater's "Fit"

What place does the theater have in this effort to effect a memic paradigm shift? Crick has made a solid suggestion:

> The abbreviated and approximate shorthand that we employ everyday [in the sciences] to describe human behavior is a smudged caricature of our true selves. "What a piece of work is man!" said Shakespeare. Had he been living today he might have given us the poetry we so sorely need to celebrate all these remarkable discoveries.[14]

Amid the new scientific breakthroughs it might well be that theater can contribute by capturing these new visions and triggering an explosion in the cultural imagination. What could be considered the goal of this new theater is to reflect a sense not only of what science is telling us but also of what we need to relearn in order to live in this increasingly complex world. The new theater could assist in demonstrating how memically to be infected by this necessary, new paradigm shift. And it can do so in ways that satisfy and even transcend the discursive celebration of science that Crick is suggesting as part of his agenda. Theater could help to promote the shift by giving us a place to experience its possibilities.

First, one must realize the nature of language itself in this process. Language arises from the linear mechanisms of the mind, structuring thought in ways that both reflect serial mental processing, generally of a bivalent nature, and that very likely feed back to crystallize the processes themselves. Roger Lewin reports the following interview with Daniel Dennett, who observes that

> Wittgenstein once said, "If a lion could talk, we could not understand him." I don't think that's correct. I think we would be able to understand the lion, but we wouldn't learn much about the life of ordinary lions from

this talkative one, because language would have vastly transformed his mind.[15]

Language molds perceptions of reality as it fashions and refashions the circuitry of the mind.

Given its influentially transforming potential, language is a crucial point of attack in this effort to attain a new cultural paradigm that escapes the nearly total dominion of bivalent linearity/seriality. We can, as Crick suggests, use our old language to explain our new perceptions, but the very process would mire us in the processes we are, in fact, striving to overcome. Or we could work to create a new language and allow the feedback process to strive to remold the mind to a potential multivalent, parallel emergence that steps beyond our currently sophisticated but still limited use of our brains/minds. While Crick chooses to examine the brain and explain what we have and what we are, another possibility is to take what we are learning—what is new in these new settings—and strive to achieve a new potential.

This new potential is what Antonin Artaud himself sought to locate in the theater. His theater is a theater that replaces discourse as the center of activity with the language of the stage, a language that in parallel and multivalent fashion captures raw the rhythms and patterns of the thing (that is no-thing) that lies beneath the levels captured by the serial and bivalent discursive stage. As Derrida observes in reference to Artaud, "A stage which does nothing but illustrate a discourse is no longer entirely a stage. Its relation to speech is its malady. . . . To reconstitute the stage, finally to put on stage and to overthrow the tyranny of the text [and its restrictive underpinnings] is thus one and the same gesture."[16]

Intellectual, discursive insight provides valuable information, but, without a fully experiential, parallel, and multivalent dimension working beneath surfaces, that information promises little or no significantly creative memic growth. Creativity and growth can come, however, if we allow the processes of emergence to be experienced, untethered by discursive reduction, and then use those emergent experiences from the stage to refashion human experience beyond the stage. Ultimately, it's not nature that is being altered; it's how we perceive and experience nature. And, since the experience rather than the thing experienced is our object (the phenomenological enterprise), much of what can be said of a future theater can also be said of the past theater, namely, that the reforging of our vision of reality via an altered vision of consciousness may/should present insights into the past theater (discursively perceived/received masterpieces included) not previously highlighted or fully experienced. We need not alter that which we observe—Shakespeare and Ibsen are not dead to the new theater—but, rather, alter how we see that which we observe. So, while aesthetic adjustments may in part be needed—creating new masterpieces—we are perhaps more fundamentally looking for critical adjustments to how we see what is offered, a new way to look at nature and a theater perhaps fundamentally unchanged but currently re-visioned and therefore restaged for reemphasis.

Ontology remains the same; it is epistemology that must alter. In that regard I see the avant-garde/experimental theater described so well by Elinor Fuchs to be a sort of critical means to an end rather than an aesthetic end in itself. As she says, "The postmodern artist longs for a vanishing natural world, and sometimes a vanished world, existing before history, before culture."[17] But this longing to regain a paradise lost can be expressed as much by a new directorial and/or critical sense applied to the extant theater as it can by a new art form. This stage, Fuchs observes, is becoming "post-anthropocentric" (106), a term similar to other currently valid critical terms such as *post-humanist, environmental, ecological*. It calls for an erasure of individual, serially constructed bivalent (me vs. other) identity derived from singular isolated (me) criteria and a rising sense of parallelly constructed, multivalent (us) identity deriving from some larger experiential field. If the stage can serve as that experiential field, whatever is placed upon it (or in it) can be accordingly redefined.

Here is exactly where I suggest that the vast multivalence of theater could be of help, in the form of new theater pieces, yes, but also in taking the theater (and culture) into a new age through critical and directorial de-emphasis of our "old language" and placing heightened emphasis (reemphasis?) on the stage's language of *rhythms* of consciousness. As noted earlier, this suggestion is more than a veiled call for an empty theatrical metaphor, for what this new theatrical vision emphasizes is a validated material vision of reality through consciousness itself.

.

Chapter 5

Theater of Complexity,
Past and Present

Before we turn to theater, consider first the following ambitious but ultimately unnecessary option, unnecessary at very least because the theater option already exists. Quantum physicist David Bohm's Implicate Order theory sketch involves an embracing theory of organic order, including mind *and* environment/nature. As noted in chapter 4, Bohm is not unique in advocating this integrated ecosystemic approach, but he adds a significant linguistic twist to his argument.

All nature enfolds into a single reality, according to Bohm, from subatomic quantum realities to those massive realities described by relativity. Speaking of the traditional mechanistic, linear vision of order, Bohm observes:

> The principal feature of this [traditional view of] order is that the world is regarded as constituted of entities which are *outside of each other,* in the sense that they exist independently in different regions of space (and time) and interact through forces that do not bring about any changes in their essential nature.[1]

This system suggests that "each part grows in the context of the whole, so that it does not exist independently, nor can it be said that it merely 'interacts' with the others, without itself being essentially affected in this relationship" (173). As noted earlier, the difference involves a distinction between what Bohm calls "explicate" reality and "implicate" reality. Explicate, distinct reality is the reductionist scientist's foregrounded subject of interest. Echoing the agendas of Gertrude Stein and others in the theater, Bohm proposes for the scientific community that the implicate, thus-far consciously backgrounded, reality is the reality we should be in search of. He concludes: "The more comprehensive, deeper, and more inward actuality is neither mind nor body but rather a yet higher-dimensional actuality, which is their [mind's and body's] common ground and which is of a nature beyond both" (209). Distinctly antidualist, Bohm sights consciousness actually at a place beyond the material and the non-material, in a thus-far unperceived dimension.

This emergent theory is not altogether distinct from such material-ists as Penrose, Dennett, and even Crick, when they observe the emer-gent qualities of mind/brain. And it does strike particularly close to Pen-rose's quantum coherence theory sketch, which proposes an as-yet unverified new dimension in physics.

What is unique about Bohm's perspective, however, is that his attendant ideas of language go far beyond Crick's limited perspective and even moves beyond Dawkins's (and Dennett's) memic proposition, because Bohm actually proposes "a *new mode* of language" to capture the essence of this new level of reality, which he calls the *rheomode, rheo* derived from the Greek verb meaning "to flow" (30–31). Challenging the tacit and implied stability of our object-based language systems, Bohm proposes a language that calls attention to the dynamic, not static, nature of reality. He observes that in the rheomode

> truth and falsity have, like relevance and irrelevance, to be seen from moment to moment, in an act of perception of a very high order. Thus, the truth or falsity *in content* of a statement is apprehended by observing whether or not this content fits a broader context which is indicated either in the statement itself or by some action or gesture (such as pointing) that goes together with the statement. (42)

Our current object-identity system fragments nature into a compilation of discrete units. On the other hand, process- or flow-identity creates a sense of wholeness that Bohm (and the others, too) argues is a more accurate depiction of reality.

Bohm offers the concept of "*truth in function*" as an alternative to truth as some discrete and abstract universal (42). As such, Bohm asks:

> Is it not possible for the syntax and grammatical form of language to be changed so as to give a basic role to the verb rather than to the noun? This would help to end the sort of fragmentation indicated above, for the verb describes actions and movements, which flow into each other and merge, without sharp separations or breaks. Moreover, since movements are in general ways themselves changing, they have in them no permanent pat-tern of fixed form with which separately existent things could be identified. (29–30)

Bohm follows these points by outlining just such a language reemphasis. His system of language transformation is rather complicated (and need not be outlined here), but his keen sense of awareness of our need for reevaluation is clear and simple. Much like the dynamic multivalence of fuzzy logic, Bohm asks that we take in a wide range of data to determine how to assess the vast gray areas of reality. Rather than reducing outside noise to a point where absolute truth/falseness can be determined, language/logic/thought should work more fully and flexibly to embrace the full interactive complexity of a reality in flux, not to reduce it to static and bivalent possibilities but to embrace the essence of multivalence, that place at the edge of chaos.

Bart Kosko, as noted earlier, sees the bivalent/multivalent dilemma stemming from Western cultural Aristotelian indoctrination.[2] He strongly suggests a Western movement toward Eastern, Confucian thought, which rejects the bivalent reductionism of current (and past) Western thought and opens up an expanse of possibilities that may, like the speaking lion (but more positively sighted), succeed at transforming humanity to a heretofore unrecognizable species of superior intellect. "Smart" (that is, creatively thinking, multivalent) computers are the product of fuzzy programming; imagine the possibilities of a fuzzy humanity. To exact this change among humanity, however, would require new logic and a new language to embrace that new logic, new perspective, and new worldview.

Kosko, unfortunately, makes a crucial error in his argument but one that is correctable and that pushes us into the realm of theater. While he argues that Aristotle is fundamentally bivalent and ultimately the source of Western culture's delusions, he fails in his own argument to make the multivalent distinctions he advocates in that he bivalently sets up the choices as either Aristotle or Confucius. He claims to understand Confucius, but he never quite says the same about Aristotle. And here's the flaw. Much of Aristotle's writings are, in fact, fundamentally bivalent. But one very significant way of viewing Aristotle's canon involves a multivalent perspective that concedes Aristotle's rhetorical bivalence in matters rhetorical and political, while his canon engages a multivalence in matters aesthetic. In his singular discussion of theater/tragedy, the *Poetics,* Aristotle fundamentally acknowledges that nonlinear data processing is central to the stage, and he concedes that a multivalent perception of reality results. The theater, claims his *Poetics,* transcends the limited bivalence of rationality and infects its viewers with an emergent knowledge of truth more complex and precise than mere rationally foundationed discourse can present. The multiple elements of theater emergently cohere to transcend mere bivalent discursive exchange.

So, while much of Aristotle's overall canon is linearly procedural—seeking the proper form for law, argumentation, and social policy (including ethics)—the *Poetics* suggests that the ultimate reflection of truth engages more than linear, bivalent activities. Theater offers greater truth than rhetoric, greater even than the empirical process Western culture has gleaned from Aristotle's many teachings. In the *Poetics* Aristotle concedes the emergent nature of reality and suggests it is best reflected in the human artifact of theater, which we must concede does use linear language and empirical enquiry, but the true power of theater lies in the fact that the total theater process also accumulates phenomenological data unpolluted by rational manipulation and presents that data in a non-linear parallel process that exceeds all linear and serial efforts.

Fuchs reminds us that plot, or action, is Aristotle's central concern, not the fragmented reality or imitation of character. Flow is the central concern of theater, even for Aristotle. Theater is a vast emergent enterprise rising beyond the sum of parts placed in a soup of action virtually indivisible. Richard Schechner reminds us that even "the 'Stanislavski system' is largely devoted to training the actor so that flow can be generated through a conscious process."[3] Even that "method" style, heralded as the triumph of discrete understanding through characterization, is dedicated to flow when done right. In turn, the audience, too, must be engaged in process and flow for anything like the Holy to make its presence felt. Peter Brook observes of an audience the need for each member to fall into a sympathetic rhythm: "An event will occur only if each one of these individual instruments become attuned. Then all you need for something to happen is for a single vibration to pass through the auditorium."[4] This flow of energy placed in tune is a "first step in a performance, . . . a process of gathering and focusing the dispersed energies of the audience, which in turn reflect the dispersed energies of the actors" (108). We have orderly disorder at work, complexly emerging into patterns that transcend linear and serial comprehension, embracing reality as something necessarily requiring more than linear/serial comprehension. We have in this complex interaction the essence of Bohm's rheomode at work. And we see it in the theater, from Wilde to Stein and at all points in between.

Theater multivalently invades multiple sensory ports and enters the human consciousness through myriad receptors. *Explaining* a play, after all, never does justice to the *experience* of a play (a good one, at least). So, if Aristotle had a failing, it seems to have been in his own rhetoric of conveying the singular importance of his aesthetic undertakings in the *Poetics* by subdividing the whole in his explanations. The failure, it seems, stems from his dissection of the theater and his failure to bring the parts together in his final assessment. Or we might fault Western culture itself, which, like Kosko, has grasped at crucial parts of Aristotle but not at the complete Aristotle to be considered in sum. Our general (mis)reading of Aristotle can ultimately be seen as a summary of Western culture's more far-reaching misreading of the world at large, theater certainly included. Finally, it is not Aristotle who is at fault; it's Western desire for fragmented, discrete understanding. Going back to Western roots very likely will reveal other unfortunate misreadings (consider the Bible) and necessary revisions. Western theater seems a very good starting point.

This point is not to say that Western culture could not learn from the East. In fact, Western theater has many times tried to do just that. Yeats experimented with Noh theater, and Artaud was intrigued by Balinese theater. But perhaps our own traditions, given our culture's current rising efforts to call special attention and validation to advances in scientific thought, can do precisely what Kosko encourages and what Dennett, Bohm, and others seem to want. In the bargain these Western adjustments may possibly satisfy even Crick's reductively discursive assessment of the value of art. Multivalence rather than bivalence, the flow of performance rather than the stasis of object-language, and parallel rather than serial reception all operate in the theater.

Bohm acknowledges the following point concerning our current uses of language: "We are, of course, often able to overcome this tendency toward fragmentation by using language in a freer, more informal and 'poetic' way, that properly communicates the truly fluid nature of the difference between relevance and irrelevance" (34). Add to this Brian Swimme's call for a "cosmic creation story" suitable to our postmodern world:

> *A cosmic creation story* is that which satisfies the questions asked by humans fresh out of the womb. As soon as they get here and learn the language, children ask the cosmic questions. Where did everything come from? What is going on? Why are you doing such and such anyway?[5]

Science is now piecing together evidence to support a new, postmodern cosmic creation story. I suggest, agreeing with Crick, that the theater can serve well to present this cosmic creation story, but it can do much more than "tell" us a story. It can add to Swimme's wish and Crick's charge by including a cosmic creation *dance* and an integrated cosmic creation *experience* as well, both of which *emergently* engage reflect rather than merely discursively tell what we are to learn from the story.

The implicate rhythms and patterns that underlie explicate reality are the very things that theater and its multivalent languages of the stage capture. As Aristotle implied centuries ago, the theater is the place where numerous languages of the stage (verbal as well as other modes) can explode our general dependence upon the one verbal language that has deluded us into a sense of serial and bivalent actuality, revealing patterns that do much more than accumulate parts and add them up to some (incomplete) whole. In the process we are focusing both on an altered epistemology and an attendant revised sense of ontology.

When theater works, it presents vast amounts of information in numerous forms and engages parallel distribution, disrupting serial and linear inclinations feeding our static, object-focused visions of the world. Theater beyond the written text presents a flow and inundation that alters our serial predispositions. I would, in fact, suggest strongly that these new scientists, advocating a new paradigmatic adjustment to science, may do well to spend some time in the theater to see their various visions actually at work at any number of levels significant to their own studies.

The Theater's New Materialism: Artaud as Early-Twentieth-Century Antecedent

As suggested earlier in regards to modernist drama, it is not the case that the endeavors outlined here have only recently surfaced. As also noted earlier, Jan Christian Smuts approached the issue with a great deal of philosophical insight and sophistication in 1926 with his work *Holism and Evolution,* in which he argued:

> Nineteenth-century science went wrong mostly because of the hard and narrow concept of causation which dominated it. It was a fixed dogma that there could be no more in the effect than there was in the cause; hence creativeness and real progress became impossible. The narrow concept of causation again arose from a wider intellectual error of abstraction, of narrowing down all concepts to hard definite contours and wiping out their

definite surrounding "fields." The concept of "fields" is absolutely necessary in order to get back to the fluid plastic facts of nature.[6]

Here we clearly hear the first steps of fuzzy logic, of Bohm's implicate
order, Dennett's stream theory sketch of consciousness, and Penrose's
quantum coherence. Smuts would work without the empirical support
and technological backing afforded these later thinkers, but the general
turn toward what we now see fast developing in the contemporary scientific community is clearly evident in his early effort.

Significantly, however, science was not the only field to have
developed an interest in assaulting nineteenth-century rigidity. In the
modernist theater of the early twentieth century significant first steps
were taken as well. Perhaps the most vocal opponent of such nineteenth-century tyranny was Antonin Artaud, a man who was in many
ways certifiably mad but whose madness frequently exhibited great sense
and method. Particularly appropriate to Artaud's case is Kenneth Burke's
observation that "nothing more deeply engrosses a man than his burdens, including those of a physical nature, such as disease. We win by
capitalizing on our debts, by turning our liabilities into assets, by using
our burdens as a basis of insight."[7] Artaud's suffering physical body fed
into his metaphysical thinking in ways that even today still escape full
comprehension. But the new sciences offer us a valuable new approach.

Among the many ideas advanced by Artaud is one that parallels
Bohm's "rheomode" concept wherein language is to effect and facilitate
flow rather than to be an instrument of object identity. This is the cornerstone of Artaud's insistence that masterpieces must be undermined,
masterpieces being the things that prescribe static attributes to what
should be dynamic processes of flow and change in the theater. In other
words, Artaud assaults Brook's Deadly Theatre and Crease's mechanical
and standardized performances. The theater succeeds when its *vitality*
affects its audience; the thing called "theater event" is not an event until
it actively and dynamically interacts with an audience, becoming something more than an imitation of an event, or of life, and becoming an
experiential life event itself. True theater, Artaud argues, elevates to the
portals of higher serial consciousness that which the "lesser" parallel consciousness "has been able to collect (or conceal) of accessible everyday
experience."[8] It is an incantation drumming up a heightened reality out
of the occluding mists of daily experience. When it succeeds, theater
"doubles" life, in fact *is* life, though of another, heightened order than

daily life itself. It embraces flow and reveals patterns underlying the events of life.

Theater awakens the processes of consciousness previously operating in a sort of unaware, automatic pilot mode, and it reveals the complex location of consciousness within the materialist spectrum. As Eugenio Barba notes: "Just as there is no vocal action which is not also a physical action, there is no physical action which is not also mental. If there is physical training, there must also be mental training."[9] Barba continues on the subject of actor training: "The long daily work on physical training, transformed over the years, has slowly become distilled into internal patterns of energy which can be applied to a way of conceiving or composing a dramatic action, a way of speaking in public, a way of writing. Thought has a physical aspect" (55). For Barba, and for Artaud, mind and body interact, are essentially inseparable in the process of awakening us to the integrated nature of our existence. Seeing *how* body and mind connect, however, is the maddening part of the agenda.

The doubling function of theater is crucial to Artaud's thoughts on the theater. The term is part of the title Artaud gave to his collection of essays, *The Theater and Its Double.* Though that collection remains surprising silent on the nature of *double,* Artaud does cryptically observe:

> To make use of his emotions as a wrestler makes use of his muscles, he [the actor] has to see the human being as a Double. . . . It is this double which the theater influences, this spectral effigy which it shapes, and like all specters, this double has a long memory. (134)

In a 1936 letter to Jean Poulhan, Artaud provides an aphorism for his followers to digest: "If the theater is the double of life, life is the double of the true theater."[10] Timothy Wiles explains the complexity of the concept:

> If we ask what is affected, and by whom, the aphorism about the double responds that engagement in theater is one means of authenticating life, and that the achievement of authenticity is a means of discerning that which is "true" about theater. Each affects the other, and the operation is simultaneous not progressive.[11]

Wiles continues:

> The fact that this conversion of affectivity into authenticity must be instantaneous accounts for Artaud's maddening, circular argument, his nearly

solipsistic form which serves as a concrete embodiment of a nonlinear process (at the expense of violating the linear quality of syntax). And since the process is instantaneous, it immediately falls into inauthenticity and must be renewed. (123)

Wiles's observations are significant and hint at a certain frustration that he and other Artaud scholars experience when trying to comprehend Artaud's writings. But what we have outlined here about recent scientific processes actually helps break through certain of Artaud's circularities and apparent solipsisms.

That Artaud longs for the theater to convert the ineffable into the concrete initially seems an alchemical (a term Artaud liked to use) and gnostically unattainable goal. If, however, we come to understand from the new materialists that what we once conceived of as immaterial, ineffable top-down vitalist processes are, in fact, empirically comprehensible bottom-up potentialities, then we aren't very far from actually achieving Artaud's impossible theater, albeit coming from an unexpected, materialist, rather than mystical, direction.

Here we approach, though in a slightly different manner, what Derrida has called the element that "distinguishes the affirmation of cruelty from romantic negativity; the difference is slight and yet decisive" (233). Elaine Scarry makes the traditional observation of Artaud's agenda when she observes:

> The self-flagellation of the religious ascetic, for example, is . . . a way of so emphasizing the body that the contents of the world are cancelled and the path is clear for the entry of an unworldly, contentless force. It is in part this world-ridding, path-clearing logic that explains the obsessive presence of pain in the rituals at large . . . that partly explains . . . why in the brilliant ravings of Artaud some ultimate and essential principle of reality can be compelled down from the heavens onto a theatre stage by the mime of cruelty.[12]

From the materialist's perspective, however, while a path-clearing logic should, in fact, be the goal of cruelty, this goal is not designed to urge anything "down from the heavens"; rather, the loosening up of mind's imprisoning logic opens the path for material body to convey its presence and essence to mind. We're talking about a bottom-up rather than, as Scarry and others assume, a top-down process. From this altered perspective we can see Artaud's alchemy as a process of materializing a heightened reality rather than rarefying and mystifying mundane reality, as many have assumed. Finally, there is nothing really mystical about Artaud at all, unless we redefine the term *mysticism* (not an altogether fruitless option to consider).

While Artaud may have approached the theater from a mystic's, alchemist's, gnostic's perspective, this option makes sense only given that at the time it appeared to be the only option for an antireductionist to pursue. Today, however, scientists who have likewise targeted the terrain Artaud confronted but from an empiricist's base offer us an out from Artaud's circularity without needing to dismantle the heart of Artaud's agenda. Consciousness *may* appear ineffable and mysterious, and Artaud's theater *may* strive to make it concrete through a twist of magic. But science now argues Artaud's agenda can be realized through concretely comprehensible processes, freed of a need for magic (unless, again, we consider a redefinition). The realization comes in ways not fully envisioned by Artaud or his early-twentieth-century contemporaries. If we accept the new science proposition that consciousness is a process derived *from nature,* then there is no need to look elsewhere when attempting to connect mind to nature. Artaud's vision of the interconnectivity of the two worlds of mind and world is validated, though from an unexpected direction.

Consciousness is a natural wave rather than either discrete material corporeality or some immaterial other, as many have until now presumed. Barba again provides a valuable insight, referring to the material body of a performer as a "dilated body":

> The dilated body is a hot body, but not in the emotional or sentimental sense. Feeling and emotion are only a consequence, for both the performer and the spectator. The dilated body is above all a glowing body, in the scientific sense of the term: the particles which make up daily behaviour have been excited and produce more energy, they have undergone an increment of motion, they move further apart, attract and oppose each other with more force, in a restricted or expanded space. (54)

In the theater we see a middle-ground world of massless energy visible only inasmuch as it affects materiality. This is the site of Artaud's concentrations, looking for the place where consciousness best can be sighted. Artaud's agenda actually parallels a physical scientist's efforts to understand a soliton. We have evidence of the existence of this force in the material that consciousness influences, but we must understand that consciousness itself lies beyond the material in which it is sighted. As with the soliton, despite the materialist characteristics of consciousness, it cannot be placed or located as other material entities can. It is a sort of immaterial materiality.

Artaud suggests the theater can be the materialization of that place-less place to search for consciousness, but, as consciousness is itself not a thing, the best we can hope for is to sight its trace, for, like the living theater itself, once sighted—the instant we are aware of it—it moves on in time, vanishing from sight (or transforming into something else) and leaving only its residue upon our data-gathering apparatuses, like an image captured on film (a poor replication). Strangely reminiscent of quantum physical assessments of subatomic superpositioning (being here and there as well as not here or there, both simultaneously), Artaud's conceptions anticipate trends that clearly undermine the strict object-based causal linearity Smuts has identified as the foundation of nine-teenth-century progress, and Artaud also undermines the false dichotomy of thought somehow being either only material brain or mystical/immaterial mind. Thought/consciousness somehow occupies both realms, though we now come closer to knowing how.

Comprehending the ineffable and trying to sight/locate/capture the essence of consciousness (based on traditional expectations) are likewise concerns that science and Artaud seem to agree upon. Once conscious-ness is initially comprehended or fleetingly sighted, traditional thought tries to bottle and dissect it, reductively looking at it as if it were a linear, serial sequence of memory bits. This perspective, of course, instantly saps the life out of our original comprehension of consciousness because the parallel bombardment of brain data is necessarily molded into something that the societally affected/infected mind identifies. In the process con-sciousness is molded into an idea/concept that ultimately bears little resemblance to that which it actually is (or was). Like Wittgenstein's lion, we've striven to teach our minds to speak a serialized language, and the result is we hear only what we have molded mind to tell us rather than to free mind to tell us what is *really* out there. And as I've suggested earlier, this discrepancy often leaves us with a fleeting awareness of incomplete awareness, which may best be considered the process we have traditionally concretized into the term *soul*. Seeking soul is a possi-bility, but, once it's found, it's lost through our rationalist efforts to snare its essence, and the process must begin anew in order to regain contact with it.

This suggestion that authenticity must be instantaneous and not cumulative or storable speaks to the inadequacies of the serial mind and all the products derived from such human seriality, including the vast human archives of masterpieces. As with the theater event converted to masterpiece status, the search for consciousness ends when reductive reasoning tries to quantify it—to pin it down—rather than to allow for its quantumlike multivalent superpositioning.

Artaud speaks of the language of the stage as a concrete reality and observes that it "is addressed first of all to the senses instead of addressed primarily to the mind as in the language of words," adding, "This does not prevent it [language] from developing later its full intellectual effect on all possible levels and in every direction" (38). Language of various sorts must speak to our prelinguistic faculties, including the emotions; then and only then can it precisely address the emergent and ineffable qualities of reality "on all possible levels and in every direction." Bettina Knapp observes of Artaud's understanding of discursive language, "The *term terminated* the thought . . . rather than described or represented it,"[13] a point that accounts for what Wiles observes to be "Artaud's obsessive refusal to define any key terms like 'cruelty,' 'plague,' and so on; instead, in additive fashion, he expands the variety of metaphoric meanings the term may have" (128).

Is there a way of capturing this parallel instantaneity, of in some way holding onto and prolonging its affectivity? One suggestion could be to develop or exercise our dawning parallel potential to override our serial prejudices, the very thing Artaud's theater strives for in capturing its double via metaphoric/nonlinear, rather than purely discursive/linear, ways. Life is parallel explosion captured in the theater but only as a flash of light is captured in the eye, fleetingly and impermanently—and only when we look at it indirectly. The more our "light-gathering" mechanisms improve, however, the longer perhaps we can glimpse that impermanence. The sciences are now suggesting, it appears, exactly what Artaud's theater advocated, but while Artaud considered his theater an "impossible theater"—while he considered his goals ultimately unattainable—it now seems that Artaud's theater, at worst, may only be *practically* very difficult and not conceptually impossible, as he concluded. It is, at least, not something that should be written off as the lunatic ravings of a madman.

Artaud advocates two key qualities in his theater: that the immaterial be made material and that linear language be supplanted with a nonlinear language of the stage. We have what Wiles calls a "sense in which language 'materially' occupies the stage and becomes a 'poetry in space'" (129). Susan Sontag identified Artaud as "one of the great daring mapmakers of consciousness *in extremis*,"[14] to which Jane Goodall adds, "It was madness (sometimes more specifically schizophrenia) that, having fractured the constituted subject, opened the way to ideas of subjectivity as multiple or heterogeneous, as *en procès* [in process or on trial]."[15] Finally, it is the physicality of the body (in torment) that opens up awareness to the mind.

Goodall viably approaches Artaud's pursuits of an understanding of consciousness through the extreme dualism of Gnosticism. While such an approach succeeds at underlining numerous often contradictory Artaudian observations, its description of Artaud (understandably) stops at the solipsistic dead end Artaud seems to have created for himself. His mystical dualism, his essential Gnosticism, paints him into the same corners that all dualism paints itself into, namely, the dilemma of reconciling the interaction between the material and immaterial (the failings of which Dennett earlier describes). But, rather than striving to move the dualism into a realm of either/or—either ultimately material (realism) or immaterial (idealism)—we now have the alternative of an "emergently complex materialism" that embraces that which was formerly dichotomized as *either* material *or* immaterial. The new paradigm may have been exactly what Artaud sought but never found, a materialist description of formerly ineffable material such as consciousness.

Artaud, of course, chose to move into realms of immateriality, alchemy, and Gnosticism because the materialist sciences of his day followed the reductionism of nineteenth-century thought and really offered nothing of a paradigm sophisticated enough to include the highly complex nature of the interaction between reality and consciousness that Artaud envisioned. Here, perhaps, is where it is best to acknowledge Artaud's central value as inspiration rather than as model maker and to turn to Jerzy Grotowski, who used Artaud as inspiration in his efforts to materialize an Artaudian stage.

Grotowski Reads Artaud: Materializing the Immaterial

In his essay "He Wasn't Entirely Himself" Grotowski observes of Artaud:

> We realize he was after a theater transcending discursive reason and psychology. And when, one fine day, we discover that the essence of the theater is found neither in the narration of an event, nor in the representation

of life as it appears from outside, nor even in a vision—but that theater is
an act carried out **here and now** in the actors' organisms, in front of other
men, when we discover that theatrical reality is instantaneous, not an illustration of life but something linked to life **only by analogy,** when we
realize all this, then we ask ourselves the question: wasn't Artaud talking
about just this and nothing else?[16]

Against discursive explanations and favoring concrete, instantaneous
realizations of a greater reality, Grotowski sees Artaud as the beginning
of Grotowski's own project in the theater. Artaud allows mystery its
broadest path, as traditional religion and mythology have done; Grotowski, however, like the materialist scientists, has striven to reduce the
terrain that mystery governs and to comprehend material intersections
between that which is materially comprehensible and (perhaps as yet)
incomprehensible. Unlike Artaud, Grotowski's actors—which include
both actual actors and audience-as-actor—populate the empty spaces,
concretize what has been assumed to be the ineffable, and work to discover the precise though forever fading boundaries between the phenomenologically knowable (the material) and the seemingly mystically
unknowable (immaterial) realms of human consciousness.

For Grotowski the theater is a place of authenticity where the serial
restrictions of mind are assaulted by a process that opens the parallel
brain to direct contact with parallel, multivalent levels of consciousness.
Grotowski sees mythologies and archetypes buried in rigid cultural traditions, leading to a life (or acting style) of aping the fashion rather than
grasping its essence. These patterns of habitual behavior may have been
consciously learned or unconsciously transferred, but, whatever the
input process, they have clearly become rigidified within our mental
networks to the extent that we are virtually unaware prisoners of their
rigidified constructs rather than liberated by their flow, as we should be.
This is the site of Brook's Deadly Theatre and Crease's mechanical repetition of performance. To liberate serialized processes of the mind captured in these forms, to free humanity to a potentially wider scope of
possible options/actions, we must once again become conscious of our
limited/limiting underlying memic constructs and then work to tran-
scend/escape them. This is Grotowski's agenda, and it appears to be validated by the new sciences of consciousness given that they support
Grotowski's perspective on current levels of human consciousness and
encourage such efforts as Grotowski's to move beyond the current. We
are not in an inescapable Artaudian pit of gnostic despair but on the
material verge of quantum leaping beyond our self-imposed limitations.

The actor and actor-audience can leap beyond these limitations through a complex process Grotowski, in *Towards a Poor Theater,* calls the "**via negativa**—not a collection of skills but an eradication of blocks."[17] He explains:

> The process itself, though to some extent dependent upon concentration, confidence, exposure, and almost disappearance into the acting craft, is not voluntary. The requisite state of mind is a passive readiness to realize an active role, a state in which one does not "**want to do that**" but rather "**resigns from not doing it.**" (17)

Again, we have an almost mystical characterization of higher attainment wherein we must escape the linear, serial, bivalent shackles, not by replacing them with some other regimen but by eliminating the nature of regimentation itself. As Grotowski adds, "We find that artificial composition not only does not limit the spiritual but actually leads to it" (17).

But Grotowski need not necessarily be read as a traditional mystic. He is more significantly a materialist in mystic's clothing. Grotowski's agenda is materially to free ourselves from the need for formal and restrictive (generally linear) patterns of behavior/thought; tellingly, he strenuously works not to provide a regimen to undertake such a transformation. The *via negativa* is a nonlinear pathway that acknowledges the role of "chance, inspiration, and belief," according to Wiles (147), elements that can quite easily be materially described by emphasizing, for example, the noncomputational function of quantum mechanics in the brain that frees us from limited linear computational interactions most fully manifest in the discursivity of our language. The *via negativa* also suggests an avenue of liberation that can lead us to engage the patterns of new symmetry, engulfing ourselves in them rather than resisting, standing outside of, or trying to manipulate them.

The acting techniques Grotowski advocates mandate awareness of our physicality and encourage a wide spectrum of techniques loosely (and unpredictably) designed to eliminate the culturally inscribed devices that repress our inner impulses to conform to nature's rhythms and patterns. There is a physical/*non*physical interactivity at work, which at first suggests dualism until the materialist theory sketches of the new sciences are invoked, at which point the table is turned. Again, we can take Scarry's observations on the body but must adjust them anew:

> The body is able not only to substantiate itself but to substantiate something beyond itself as well: it is able not only to make more amply evident

its own existence, presence, aliveness, realness but to make ever more amply evident the existence, presence, aliveness, realness of God. (193)

The standard assumption that the body can become a sort of antenna to pull in the signals from God presumes an unfortunate dualism. But, instead of accepting Scarry's assessment and seeing the purified/scourged physical as a conduit to the mystical realms of immateriality, we have an alternative possibility. We now have access to seeing a process whereby apparent immateriality comes to us *through* the physical from the bottom up, a process that acknowledges its interconnectedness with materiality through the activities/processes of the brain and mind. The materialized immaterial world as well as the generally accepted material realm conjoin to rise materially to a sense of consciousness at all its various stages along the neural path. Finally, there's nothing mysterious about the mysterious.

There are two crucial assumptions behind the ideas of system that Grotowski assaults and that interconnect with this new science of material consciousness. Put in contemporary terms, the first is that the physical blockings of our minds restrict full human potential, even, ironically, as it once succeeded in its early evolutionary stages at promoting human potential. The second is that, by breaking now from these mind blocks, we will put our minds in contact with the more direct and less mediated data of the brain—since that is the repository of what we call "forces outside ourselves"—and free us to new potentialities.

There is yet another instance of validly reinterpreting Grotowski from a new materialist perspective. Unlike Artaud, Grotowski places a good deal of emphasis on text, though he concedes that texts are constantly reborn, never fully recovering their original meanings but always recreating new—though similar—meanings as they are themselves recreated through time. Recapturing textual truth is a task that forever reveals the discrepancy between human desire for full awareness freed from serial constraint (of which time is instrumental) and the human realization that this goal is unrealizable, presumably no matter how fully we succeed at reconstituting ourselves through Grotowski's *via negativa*. Here we once again have that almost spiritual sense of the permanent discrepancy between what we can know and what we desire to know. Our various potential successes at breaking through mind-brain barriers—a potential epistemological success—will nevertheless reveal an even more daunting ontological barrier involving a spatiotemporal reality we may never be able to overcome. In other words, if the mind-brain block can be overcome, the now-then barrier will still remain insurmountable, though perhaps only arguably so. Or perhaps the best and most we should hope for, given our material (and spatiotemporal) essence, are fleeting moments of escape—via the theater?—to levels of awareness unfettered by spatiotemporal constraints.

The point is that here, at this (these) crucial juncture(s), we return to what was described earlier as a sense of soul, the inescapable sense of our awareness of the inevitable incompleteness of our awareness. Like the scientists of consciousness, Grotowski, too, has come upon this meta-awareness. But, perhaps also like these scientists, Grotowski need not move to a sense of mysticism to explain that meta-awareness; rather, like them, he can escape dualism by conceding the need to complete a Western hermeneutical perspective, as his highly physical/material theater seems to be attempting, despite frequent turns to mysticism and Orientalism. Perhaps, after all, the very process of breaking through blocks will lead to a breakdown of the epistemological meta-awareness. And perhaps pursuit of physicality may reveal means of transcending spatiotemporality via the quantum potential (of being both here and there) Penrose hopes to see evolve. Maybe we will, in fact, locate soul—if we redefine *location* and *soul,* as earlier—or at least we will come as close as possible to that task through this process and thereby at least locate the trace of soul, which in turn may minimize the extent to which we suffer the "unhappy conscious" Hegel (and Beckett) cites as central to the human condition. As with Gödel's theorem, which asserts math cannot prove itself, perhaps mind/soul, too, will ultimately be unable to prove itself. But the materialist agenda will at very least shrink the parameters of the current realm of the unknown/unknowable and the extent of our "unhappiness."

Clearly seeing the current unattainability of universal awareness through current linear thought processes, Grotowski undertakes what Wiles describes as a "kind of encounter which results in the audience's recognition of the actor behind the character he performs, of the man behind the part, of the nature of man which compels him to mask, play roles, and act at the same time that he most wants to break down defenses, narrow distances, and unmask" (156). Wiles sees Grotowski's theater events as reaching for the stars but coming up somewhat short of its goals, achieving a fusion in the process, however, that brings us closer to our inevitable goals. If we haven't found soul, we have nonetheless come one step closer to it by coming one step closer to ways to feed our desires and at least achieve a sense of community while searching for our answers. Full Hegelian "happiness" may not be attainable, but we may be able to approach it more closely than we had previously imagined.

Grotowski's important 1968 "spektakl" piece, *Apocalypsis cum figuris,* is a collage text of Christian scriptural passages and interwoven excerpts from Dostoyevsky, Simone Weil, and T. S. Eliot, fraught with self-contradiction and ambiguity, disrupting the very notion of coherence and linear expectations. What may be the central event in this piece, however, has little to do with text, always a suspect element of Grotowski's agenda. Amid the myriad intertwinings and underminings of conventional Western mythology (including Christian and Polish peasant traditions, among others), Grotowski undertakes what Jennifer Kumiega describes as a literalizing of myth:

> The most fundamental and universal of religious myths became incarnate in a brutally literal manner. Indeed, the opening words of *Apocalypsis Cum Figuris,* taken from the traditional Christian ritual of the Mass, presaged both physical acts undertaken in the course of the production, and the underlying spiritual parasitism of the theme: "He who eats my flesh and drinks my blood will have eternal life". Similarly the central Christian miracle of Godhead, for love of humanity, becoming incarnate in Christ, was portrayed literally in the physical acts of love between Mary Magdalene and the Simpleton.[18]

In a reversal of the traditional material-to-immaterial/spiritual/symbolic process of Christian practice, Grotowski converts the symbolic to the literal and almost ghoulishly concrete. Wine, for example, literally becomes the blood of Christ. And the Christ figure is variously made material by turning his involvement with Mary Magdalene into erotic rather than spiritual love, by presenting Christ's scourging of the temple as a nearly sadistic whipping of the moneylenders and by depicting the ritual washings and baptisms as actually a physical cleaning. Lazarus' resurrection, furthermore, is depicted as a spiritual violation of a material right to death.

All these sacrilegious ritual reversals may at first glance appear to be mere sensationalist assaults on the mystical properties of Christianity, befitting the atheistic inclinations Grotowski himself adopts. But they can also be seen as a revitalization of the rites, moving them away from the ossified abstractions of mysticism and toward a reconcretization of their ultimate significance. Concrete, real events replace the symbolic; materiality takes on a "spirituality" that dispenses with the need for some immaterial transcendence. The material reality of human existence takes on a holiness and even respectability that Christianity has traditionally obviated in favor of valorizing an otherworldliness toward which we should aspire. In Grotowski's theater worldliness itself is a spiritual reality.

That Artaud never quite comprehended the *completeness* of this perspective is evidenced by his early belief in certain forms of mysticism that he felt he could capture through his concretized theater and is further evidenced by his eventual turn away from the theater. Grotowski, likewise, seems to have sensed his own incomplete or limited success in the theater. Ironically, the new sciences suggest that what these men espoused and accomplished in the theater is precisely what humanity needs to realize about its existence, that the rhythms of life are empirically verifiable, concrete entities, as evidenced by chaos theory, quantum physics, and the materialist hypotheses concerning emergence and consciousness. Metaphor is less necessary than a literal belief in the implicit spirituality of the material.

But it's not a simple case of modifying or reversing the mystic dualist's epistemological processes and ontological conclusions. We must realize that the very terms we use in these pursuits—and the ways we use them—must be redefined. The fact that these realities cannot be bottled/labeled is the very point that Artaud and Grotowski make when they assert a certain ineffability, that the reality they grasp vanishes the instant it is comprehended, that a sidelong glance allows us to perceive deeper-level materiality, and that a fully linearized conscious stare frightens it out of our field of vision and scope of comprehension. Unfortunately, the *fact* of this reality's fleeting staying power has led both men either to seek nonmaterial options in their pursuit of truth or to give up on the enterprise altogether. The fact is, they introduced the agenda that captures at least the traces of the spiritual life force they so long sought. The flaw has been that they did not know precisely what they had captured.

Perhaps tragically, their limitations here are the ironic result of themselves subscribing to a dualistic cultural predisposition that asserts there need be something more to life than the physical and concrete. Despite being so violently opposed to being products of their cultures, they were nonetheless bound to a deep-rooted bivalent hermeneutics predisposing them to look for something where that something was not. The something they sought was entwined with the physical reality they sought to liberate. It could be said that they were defeated by their own quasi-dualism. Beneath the superficiality of contemporary cultural visions of reality—the superficiality they sought so vigorously to expose—was the reality they sought, though their search was misdirected by an incipient, centuries-old insistence that mysticism held the true answers. Looking closely at what they revealed may, in fact, have satisfied a hunger that their misguided longing for mystical answers prevented them from seeing. The impossible theater is actually materially there, before their eyes.

Yet maybe their respective enterprises were too compact, too concentrated, for them to perceive fully the value of their results. Or maybe their dissatisfaction stems from the possibility that they did not have a viable tradition—other than Christian, gnostic, or Eastern mysticism—to point them toward a profitable viewing. The new sciences have now directed us to attempt a less resistant gaze into the spirituality of materialism.

Chapter 6

Theater of Complexity, Present and Future

Numerous contemporary theater avant-gardists have actively engaged the realm of consciousness, among them Richard Foreman, Elizabeth LeCompte, Lee Breuer, Richard Schechner, Joseph Chaikin, Julian Beck, and Judith Malina, all finding sources of inspiration to one degree or another in the 1960s Happenings of Allan Kaprow. Among them must be highlighted Robert Wilson, whose theater provides a fruitful link between contemporary culture and earlier modernist assaults exemplified by Gertrude Stein. Perhaps more than anyone else, Wilson addresses the concern articulated by New York video artist Bill Viola, speaking in terms formerly most unbecoming an artist, allied as they are to the world of science: "The classic 'mind-body' problem, the inability of western science to reconcile the physical external world with the immaterial inner essence of the human mind, is reaching a climax on an unprecedented scale, with unprecedented consequences."[1] This convergence of attempts to reconcile the two worlds is occurring through what Bonnie Marranca calls "theater of images,"[2] and its most spectacular practitioner is Robert Wilson.

Wilson, Glass, and the New Consciousness

Robert Wilson's theater is distinctly informed by his training as a painter and architect, resulting in onstage compositions using total theater to produce haunting scenes of impressionistic visual effect virtually void of narrative structure. Marranca observes of Wilson's theater: "Now, at the approach of another century turning, the symbolist impulse foretells once more the new frontier of consciousness and creativity, this time the union of spirit, art, and science."[3] She adds: "The subject of this theater is not history but memory. It lingers in myth and dream, the liminal zone between literature and history" (37).

I would suggest, however, that the zone Marranca identifies lingers not between literature and history but between consciousness and the preconscious in the realm of parallel activity prior to serial transformation. But Wilson's work is even more than that, especially given the broad evolution evident in his massive productivity. Wilson presents material crafted by a self-taught preconscious, multivalent, parallel, and nonlinear logic, equivalent to that which we now know to be fuzzy logic. Wilson's work encourages us to accept/absorb that fuzzy logic, in turn leaving audiences to absorb and inherit the process as they inevitably shift to their serial existences amid inescapably linear consciousness. Theirs becomes a consciousness that has been altered by the parallel, nonlinear, premental experience in Wilson's theater.

Describing Wilson's monumental *the CIVILwarS* (1984) but making a point relevant to most of Wilson's work, Arthur Holmberg observes:

> The eye goes immediately to a bright spot, especially if it contrasts with a darker surrounding area. By exploiting this physiological reflex, Wilson gives his stage pictures a strong focus, guiding the eye and letting it take in the composition. Wilson avoids visual confusion by allowing the spectator sufficient time to explore his images.[4]

The eye is directed, and time is allotted for thorough absorption, leading to a process operating in the reverse of standard causal procedure; as Wilson himself observes, "Get the effect first, a million causes can be found later" (qtd. in Holmberg, 147).

Speaking of *Einstein on the Beach,* the 1976 collaboration between Wilson and Philip Glass (among others) that was twice remounted (1984 and 1992), Glass observes:

> It was truly more radical in 1976 simply because the language was not generally known, both the visual, dramatic language—the theatre language, if you will, and the musical language. [In the later productions] there was an ability to hear it, not just a willingness but an ability to perceive it that simply wasn't there before. In fact, in just ten to fifteen years we begin to find a way to listen, to hear, and to see. And it becomes simply the language of our time, the theatre of our time, the dance of our time.[5]

Although perhaps overstated, the point is that over time Wilson's theater has encouraged a significant shift in the way we look at theater and, by extension, the way we look at our world.

Einstein on the Beach is arguably Wilson's signature piece, revealing much of Wilson's general agenda. The piece (not easily classified drama, dance, painting, or any other standard "type" but referred to as opera inasmuch as it is an "opus") is what Wilson has called a poetic interpretation of Albert Einstein, a "mythic-god" of our age. Einstein is an ideal subject for a Wilson creation, given Einstein's almost omnipresent influence in twentieth-century Western culture and his popular, virtually universal recognition. The result is that Wilson could dispense with any efforts at creating a discursive, serially created history or linear biography about Einstein and could move, as he prefers, into the parallelly created imaginative realm of association. We don't need to know his story, since it is already part of our common cultural awareness. So the use of Einstein minimizes—if it doesn't entirely eradicate—one of the charges generally levied at avant-gardism: *Einstein on the Beach* escapes the sense of solipsism so easily leveled against consciousness-centered art by encouraging full and active interaction between the Wilsonian images onstage and the ideas/images Wilson's audiences bring to the theater. Einstein is already "in us," to be brought to the theater experience and refashioned accordingly.

If meaning wells up at all, it will ultimately be less the result of the "interference of a conscious artist," as Stefan Brecht observes,[6] and more the result of a process engaging cultural constructs uniting the consciousness of artist and audience. The associational nature of the work, furthermore, eliminates any real possibility that some rational, linearly formulated narrative meaning will overshadow Wilson's intended highlighting of "subtext." As Glass observes:

> To me what something meant wasn't important. What was important was that it was meaningful, and that's a very important difference. If you're looking at the haystacks of Monet, what do they mean? You don't know. . . . The conviction of meaningfulness is all that was necessary for me.[7]

The "what" is the welling up of serial mind, overtaking the parallel input offered by a Wilson work. This process of searching for a what may be inevitable—and by no means necessarily bad—but it is not the point through which Wilson strives to enter our system. *Einstein on the Beach* enters prior to that process level, reminding us of the following observation by Holmberg: "Mistrusting the senses, criticism rates thinking higher than perception, not realizing that perception is thinking." Holmberg adds:

Wilson challenges the dominant tradition of western drama, grounded in idolatry of the word. Wilson changed the way theater looks and sounds. By refusing to flirt with the corpse of Naturalism—tied to ordinary language—Wilson wakes the audience from its stupor. But to appreciate his dramaturgy, one must learn to read images. (76–77)

Glass suggests that the ability to "read" these images has begun to develop among those who follow Wilson.

Indeed, anyone who knows Wilson's work knows of his interest in nonlinear association rather than linear narration, of his interest in time not measured by the clock on the wall but by the biological clock of a fly or, more often, the geological clock of a glacier. Single actions—such as crossing a stage—frequently take up to thirty minutes to complete, encouraging audience reflection and absorption of the spectacle typically beyond the spotlight and into the shadows beyond center stage. Consciousness is given free rein to develop its own sequence in absorbing the entire landscape; Wilson may tightly choreograph even the most minute event in a production, but nowhere does he dictate meaning, process of absorption, or comprehension. He simply insists that the audience exercise its nonlinear, pre-serialized apparatuses of perception. Wilson insists: "The body moves faster than the mind, and the body doesn't lie. The body says things that have nothing to do with what the tongue is saying" (qtd. in Holmberg, 97). Discursivity becomes at most a secondary consideration, minimizing its structuring, ordering effects in favor of receiving the prediscursive parallel input and encouraging chaotically/quantumly inspired creative efforts at reordering what is absorbed.

If one chooses to search for a discursively presentable meaning in *Einstein on the Beach,* it may best be found in the title, that image of a great thinker physically placed in a venue of playfulness. While Holmberg suggests Wilson is "pitting Einstein the dreamer against the scientist" and thereby investigating "two diametrically opposed ways of knowing the world: art and science" (11), I would suggest that in *Einstein on the Beach* we see the fusion and creative interplay of both "halves" at work, something of a multivalent challenge. The bivalent law of excluded middle we rationally serve is replaced by a multivalent suggestion that art and science are variously interwoven (at countless intersections) by the threads of imagination we confront in *Einstein on the Beach.* Einstein as subject succeeds as nexus between these two realms; after all, art that merely apes the fashion is little better than science in a box. It's the truly imaginative and even playfully generated science of Einstein—as it is the truly imaginative work of those artists we recognize as paradigm makers—that advances human culture. We might recall that the revolution of thought inaugurated by Einstein began with a childhood thought experiment: what would the world look like if we were riding on a rocket at the speed of light? And we must be reminded of Einstein himself, who observed, "The most beautiful experience we can have is the mysterious. It is the fundamental emotion which stands at the cradle of true art and true science."[8]

The mystery here is something of a wonder at the orders of the universe reflected in the orders of the mind. It is at once the lifelong subject of Einstein's studies and the subject of Wilson's art. And this connection is more than metaphorical because both men pursue(d) the mysteries in concrete, physical ways: Einstein approached mystery through the world of physics, while Wilson pursues it through the concrete realities of the stage. Michael Vanden Heuvel makes the key observation here, one that distinguishes Wilson from many of his contemporaries: "Wilson . . . was not interested in the Dionysian body mysticism preached by Schechner and other experimental theater artists of the sixties."[9] Vanden Heuvel then calls attention to C. W. E. Bigsby, who observes that Wilson's

> emphasis on physicality is not just an assertion of the primacy of instincts or the suspect nature of rationality. It is the assertion of clinical theory, the suggestion that rational processes may be restored through a deliberate programme of physical stimulation. The body redeems the mind by quite literal and physical means; it is not an article of spiritual faith.[10]

The connections between the physical world and the formerly-believed-to-be nonphysical consciousness are literal. The mysterious for Wilson and for Einstein has been relocated through a bottom-up engagement with the physical rather than top down through the shadowy realms of mysticism.

Significantly, this bottom-up enterprise, as Bigsby notes, remains wedded to a recognition that the rational is *not* devoutly to be avoided. That much of Wilson's recent work has shifted to text-based theater—drawing on Heiner Müller as well as works from Shakespeare and Ibsen—is clue that he has either shifted directions toward a recognition of the significance of the rational and linear or that he had never fully abandoned seeing such interactive enterprises as crucial to human existence. I would suggest that the latter option is the case. While his earlier

work was clearly indebted to alternative, nonverbal modes of communication, even they seemed to be of an interactive linear-nonlinear, dis-
cursive-nondiscursive nature that resists any general avant-gardist tendency merely to move beyond rational language.

Wilson's later forays into text-based productions still concentrate on
the visual and even the haunting (as in Ibsen's *When We Dead Awaken*),
revealing a lack of patience with mere discursive revelation. Wilson forever reminds us that, as Holmberg observes, "Language, a public con-
vention, cannot capture the individual in all its particularity" (68). Here
is where theater can introduce us to other forms of communication, the
place, in fact, where we can be trained to see beneath, beyond, and
through our discursivity. Holmberg offers a telling example in Wilson's
production of *King Lear,* appropriately a play about "seeing." Conflating
three scenes in the later acts of the play, Wilson sets up three simultaneous acting spaces contrasting the speeches of a Goneril fearful that Regan
will win Edmund's love, a Cordelia thinking only of her father, and a
Regan doting on the vain Edmund. Separately, the speeches are telling,
but, united as Wilson unites them, they add up to more than the parts
themselves explain. The decision, and such decisions all directors make,
utilizes the stage to tell more than is offered when the speeches are rev-
erentially delivered in "appropriately" discrete, linearly digestible order.
We cannot escape the fundamental fact of our linear mental predispositions, as evidenced by our discursive propensities, but we can enhance
our understanding of our environment by moving beyond mere discursivity, by seriously qualifying the assumed preeminent value of the discursive, and by learning the interactive potential of discursive and
nondiscursive understanding beneath which we see the value of multivalence and parallel receptivity so frequently discounted.

In Wilson, finally, we are *not* seeing traditional theater. But what is
offered is also less a theater of simple aesthetic novelty than a theater of
creative imagination, in some instances chaotically uniting the familiar in
uniquely new combinations while in others actually quantum leaping
into emergently new levels altogether (depending in each case upon the
receptive talents of the audience to Wilson's landscapings). Wilson's theater is, to remind ourselves of Brook's charge, a Holy Theatre created
from the physical that supplants the mystical via an idiom digestible by a
postmodern consciousness. But, while Glass is correct in observing Wilson's success at creating a "new language of the stage," there must
nonetheless be reservations placed on the observation. In 1986 *the
CIVILwarS* was nominated for but ultimately denied the Pulitzer Prize.

And, though initially commissioned to be produced at the 1984 Los Angeles Olympics Arts Festival, it was deemed unworthy of such a venue and canceled. Wilson's work is, indeed, important, but its audience remains limited. What seems crucial to this overall agenda is to make it accessible and digestible to as wide an audience as possible.

The Growing Anatomy of Awareness

Richard Schechner's 1982 work *The End of Humanism* echoes the pain many practitioners and theorists have felt about the work of avant-garde American theater during the 1960s and 1970s, a theater whose early vitality promised much but unfortunately soon dissipated. Schechner notes that this vitality centered around a political agenda, one particularly focused on the Peace Movement of the 1960s and opposition to the Vietnam War. But, as Schechner argues, "Once the war ended and the recession of the mid-seventies hit, artists fell into a formalist deep freeze. Great work was done, but it was cut off: it did not manifest significant content. Instead a certain kind of 'high art obscurity' took over."[11] Having lost its target, avant-garde American theater consequently moved rather listlessly away from efforts to produce a politically conscious, culturally uniting forum. Avant-garde theater turned isolationist and narcissistic, introspective to an almost barren extreme. A new agenda of engagement was necessary, but finding it amid a general and often vague discontent proved rather elusive.

In *The Eye of Prey* Herbert Blau similarly notes the rather empty turn toward isolationist undertakings. Reflecting on his own work in the theater, he describes this transformation from the 1960s to current practices "as a deviation from Brecht through Beckett into a highly allusive, refractory, intensely self-reflexive, ideographically charged process in which we were trying to understand, *to think through,* at the very quick of thought—words, words, unspeakably in the body—the metabolism of perception in the (de)materialization of the text."[12] Blau is basically observing that earlier efforts to fathom broader issues of community have been replaced by the pursuit of understanding discretely individual means of perception. He adds, "As with the Conceptual Art of the late sixties—particularly that strain of it which jeopardized the body in the self-reflexive activity of thought—the subject of our work, and the danger of its becoming, was *solipsism*" (xxvi). Such work approached a productive goal of confronting the processes of consciousness, but the results led to increased isolation from self and environment, a likely consequent of incipient quasi-dualism. A modification of assumptions and possibilities, it seems, would be needed in order to shift to more integratively productive results.

Blau goes so far as to argue that the activist work of this period was solipsistic, in that its dream of paradise was naive and little more than an enfeebled attempt at political and idealistic awakening. The theatrical "recession" of the 1970s and 1980s merely brought greater attention to the fundamental flaws of the politically motivated ideologies of the previous decades. As Blau notes, "What seemed to be left in the recession, along with the new conservatism, was the dispossessed *subject* of the postmodern, reviewing the disenchantments, as if through the solipsistic orifice of a needle's eye" (3). For both Schechner and Blau the unfortunate result of this "high art obscurity," with its attendant "dispossessed *subject,*" was that avant-garde theater lost its contact with material reality, closing its eye to the reality around it and consequently failing to establish contact with this critical base or to learn the essential lessons to be gained from that contact. While speaking particularly of the avant-garde theater, Schechner's and Blau's comments speak to our culture in general, one that has lost its ability to see its place in the world because it has lost its ability properly to see the world at all, except mistakenly as some objectified other out there for us to manipulate for our creature comforts.

The results in the avant-garde world have become manifest in what Blau observed in *Blooded Thought* as a sort of "advocacy of confession in acting," of which "there is also the offshoot of explicit autobiography, more or less disciplined, more or less confessed."[13] He notes that the best of this self-reflexive genre among the avant-garde are Spalding Gray's Rhode Island trilogy (formally entitled *Three Places in Rhode Island*) and Lee Breuer's *Animations,* but he adds, "Originally, the impulse had something devout about it, a kind of penance, as in the monastic period of Grotowski" (41). Although he acknowledges that self-exposure is essential to powerful theater, Blau insists that "it is not mere authenticity we're talking about . . . the self-indulgent spillover of existential sincerity"; rather, it must be "a *critical* act as well, *exegetical,* an urgency in the mode of performance . . . part of its *meaning,* that the Text be *understood,* though the meaning be ever deferred" (42). Blau complains that too much of such work has thus far failed to go beyond documenting a sort of contentless Artaudian "authenticity." Exegesis of such events, or of the *presentations* of the events, has yet to be pursued to Blau's satisfaction.

The disenchantment that Schechner and Blau feel, however, is not shared by C. W. E. Bigsby. Bigsby agrees that the American avant-garde "became an expression of intensely private experience, moving from the gnomic tableau of Robert Wilson and Richard Foreman to the heavily autobiographical pieces of the Wooster Group (the Rhode Island trilogy) and the monologues of Spalding Gray."[14] Bigsby further agrees that the work of the isolated subject often "concern[s] itself with the nature of perception and consciousness" (34), which on the surface may do little to establish community and more to increase isolation. But, though the works may turn inwardly rather than reach outwardly in any direct way, Bigsby points out that "it may well be that in requiring audiences to offer their own completions, in provoking a degree of aesthetic complicity and imaginative collaboration, such theater practitioners may be reminding them [audiences] of their capacity to act and to imagine a world beyond the banality of appearance" (35). Such art as Robert Wilson's, for example, subtly requires an audience's "imaginative collaboration," which may engage a growing awareness of the need for epistemological revisions, which, as noted earlier, may catalyze a reenchantment of the world and a fundamental ensuing adjustment of human goals and motives based on these newly developed procedural mechanisms of self-awareness. We are seeing here a sort of nonlinear pandemonium of performance, a process of chaotics or quantum experimental combinings and recombinings out of which we may be approaching the more complete, integrative urges felt by those who have become disenchanted looking for reenchantment. That these experiments increasingly reflect assessments made by the new sciences is no mere coincidence.

Recalling again the observation that soul may be a heightened, meta-awareness of the gaps between our parallel and serial mental processes helps to clarify Elinor Fuchs's point regarding Richard Foreman's Ontological-Hysterical theater:

> In Foreman's theater . . . there is never an expectation of realizing the mystery, or becoming present enough, as in Julian Beck's aspiration, to make God present. . . . In Foreman's cosmogony, God is in the "cracks in our . . . system of discourse," but will never pass through them. We are not waiting for God. We are waiting for the cracks. Thus the liveliness he hopes the spectator will attain through opening herself to perception is always penetrated by the absence whose mark is the mark, or notation, whether of presence or absence.[15]

Through the insights offered by contemporary science we see here the *appearance* of mysticism—Foreman is frequently identified as a cabalist—transfigured into a contemporary idiom, utilizing what may at first appear to be solipsistic methodologies, but through that apparent solipsism we arrive at a larger conception of humanity's means of contacting at least the trace of some cosmic essence. We first need to see consciousness as materially embedded in its physical environment. Then the serial consciousness is required to be *aware* that this ontological adjustment must be blended with preconscious parallel "hysteria" to arrive at something far more than the sum of any accumulated parts. Awareness of existence unadulterated is impossible, but awareness of its existence via parallelly absorbed traces is not.

Kate Davy observes of Foreman, "His goal was to replace the theatre of confrontation, emotion and 'ideas' with what he terms a 'mental,' non-emotional, yet sensuous theatre."[16] She adds, "The functioning of the consciousness became his preoccupation, resulting in work that deals directly with the nature, process and activity of thought itself" (ix). But, as Susan Sontag tellingly reports, "I don't believe in consciousness-as-such is Foreman's subject. Or, if it could be—and I don't think consciousness-as-such is really a subject at all—that it could be very engaging."[17] Indeed, Foreman's work remains embedded in a process that contextually engages a phenomenologically informed "consciousness about"; that is, he is grounded in an environment or geography of the theater, as his influence Gertrude Stein would have it. He refuses merely solipsistically to subscribe to the abstract Cartesian "I think; therefore, I am" argument, choosing instead to argue/perform an "I have context; therefore, I am" epistemology. Selfhood and consciousness are literally physically grounded.

Of course, not all recent avant-garde artists aspire to reach such a sophisticated level, and even when they do they are often lumped with the mass of less-sophisticated contemporaries, and the significance of their work is missed. For example, what Schechner particularly confronts in his *The End of Humanism* assault on the lost theater is the work of the auto-performers that has dominated much of theater recently. Schechner argues that the work is "brilliant, but not enough; personalistic rather than concerned with the polis, the life of the City, the life of the people" (53). He concludes: "With this personalism comes a passivity, an acceptance of the City, the outer world, the world of social relations, economics, and politics, as it is" (54). Schechner focuses in particular on the evolution of his own splintered Performance Group, turned

Wooster Group, and the further splintering of that group by the individual efforts of Spalding Gray.[18] As Bigsby notes, "For Richard Schechner this work [Gray's] and that of others implied a regrettable shift not merely from a public to a private art but from a concern with subject to a concern with subjectivity." In fact, Bigsby notes the obvious conclusion to such thoughts when he observes of Schechner, "As the title of his book, *The End of Humanism,* seems to imply, he saw this as in some sense a betrayal" (34–35).

Gray, however, disagrees that any betrayal occurred, arguing in his own defense: "Often, what the audience saw was the reflection of their own minds, their own projections."[19] In other words, the private art reached the public, though in subtler ways than Schechner might have advocated. Instead of direct surface confrontation at the level of the political, undercurrents began to play a central role, initially pushing through a sort of *via negativa* agenda but then moving beyond that inevitable isolationism. Speaking of Spalding Gray, Una Chaudhuri argues that he "stands against postmodernism's entropic dissemination of ideas and images; it is a theater of *gathering together,* and its modes are those of an ecological imperative."[20] In Gray both modernist psychology and postmodernist de-characterization are adjusted through a post-psychologizing, materialist reconstruction.

Spalding Gray and a Physically Emergent Eye/I

In the realm of theater and consciousness a particularly vital point of convergence occurs in the theater career of Spalding Gray. His dramatic monologues, especially *Swimming to Cambodia* (1985) and *Gray's Anatomy* (1993), present an emergent, postmodern consciousness attaching itself to its own physicality. These works engage the matter of comprehending the nature of consciousness, distentangling the ego-centered, psychologically constructed self/character from that process and challenging both traditional epistemologies and their various nontraditional "opposites" in an effort to appropriate a multivalent physical awareness in line with a postmodern, Western frame of mind. Despite the fact that Gray's art is centered in language—literally telling his life's story onstage—as Gay Brewer notes, Gray's success lies in his performance as he tells the story, a centering on a physical *performative* presence that "reveals the body to be as crucial as the voice to his artistic quest."[21]

In his works Gray creates a sophisticated theatrical persona that reenacts a physical awakening onstage designed to sensitize the audience to its own potential for modifying its physical mechanisms of awareness. The awakening comes over a very conventionally minded onstage persona (Gray the performer) bound up by all the conventional radical Judeo-Christian phobias concerning the pleasures of the body. In fact, Gray struggles from an even more radically Cartesian anti-body perspective than the typical Westerner, having been raised a Christian Scientist: "Growing up a Christian Scientist, it took so long for me to realize I had a body."[22] In *Swimming to Cambodia* and *Gray's Anatomy* he has singularly succeeded in coming to terms with his body—its pleasures and pains—on the stage and before an audience perhaps less "hung up" than Gray himself but likely suffering to some degree from the same dualist dilemma.

Gray's focus is upon consciousness not as some mystical other but as an extension of materially explicable reality designed to work integrationally with whatever it is that appears to be outside of itself. As Gray himself observes, he works against the "idea of paradise being a place outside the mind."[23] Brewer adds that for Gray the perfection of that external paradise is replaced by "a release from the restrictions of Gray's hyperactive mind. The integration of mental and physical then approaches a rare spiritual gratification" (237). Without grounding in the body, mind is lost, and so is the body. Performance, a concretization of physicality itself, has becomes Gray's recuperative avenue, the means by which he (and we) can reconcile the Cartesian mind/body split. Gray admits, "I fantasize that if I am true to art it will be the graceful vehicle which will return me to life."[24] He chooses not to transcend physical existence dualistically but, rather, to ground himself firmly in his own (and the world's) materiality.

It is often assumed that Gray's theater is no theater at all, since it merely entails having a man sit before a crowd and tell his story. But Gray's minimalist mode of presentation is more: its simple fusion of words spoken by a physical presence grounds the ineffable (though still physical) breath to its materially physical source. Less successful either as written text or even as filmed product, Gray's work *requires* a living presence before an audience. Actual presence, like Wilson's physical theater, becomes itself a cornerstone of Gray's overall "meaning," coupled as it is with his language. "The body," asserts Brewer, "centers the performer and offers itself to be witnessed and adored. Without a foundation in the physical, 'perfect moments' sought by the mind/voice cannot be sustained" (238). Indeed, Gray's pursuit of the perfect moment, primarily sighted throughout *Swimming to Cambodia,* and his pursuit for spiritual well-being in *Gray's Anatomy* "devolve" from metaphysical pursuits and are more closely encountered (if perhaps never fully gratified) through the body.

There's an additional twist to Gray's performance agenda, a self-defining one probably relevant to most performers. Brewer notes that Gray "continually defines and grounds himself in the context of others, in being 'perceived' more than in 'perceiving'" (238). Gray the artist—the actual man—finds himself not by some Cartesian exercise but by placing Gray the performer in a physical performative context and having him reveal to his audience this sense that identity is physically grounded in body and that body is grounded in environment. So, even though, as Vincent Canby notes, "it would be a coup de theater if he [Gray] just stood up,"[25] it is imperative to remember that Gray's physical presence is nonetheless central, as, say, even the minimal presences of Beckett's characters (and even character parts) are central. And that presence needs to connect to audiences even as the presence is connected to language/mind. It's a string of interconnectedness that succeeds only in the theater: written texts cannot capture this crucial physical ingredient, and film blurs or encumbers the purity of the connection.

Looking for a "perfect moment" is one of Gray's central pursuits in *Swimming to Cambodia*. Amid all the revelations of past suffering and death Gray experiences while working in Thailand on the film *The Killing Fields,* looking for a perfect moment nonetheless remains his central obsession. An unintentional secular baptism (leading almost to drowning) in the Indian Ocean is the result. This immersion of the body is repeated in *Gray's Anatomy,* resulting in Gray's recounting of an image of a bobbing, disembodied Spalding Gray head, a parody of the famous movie poster and book cover of *Swimming to Cambodia.* This comically described and parodied physical immersion (reminiscent of Winnie in Beckett's *Happy Days*), of course, parallels exactly the kind of physical immersion into the world that Gray perpetually and phobically resists yet is constantly—and correctly—attracted to. And it images a sense of mind-body separation that needs to be overcome. In fact, overcoming his phobias about his body is the cornerstone of Gray's work, the reason why it is sited in the theater. Although Gray the naive performer remains unaware that this is, or should be, his goal, Gray the artist, the actual man, is fully aware of this goal.

Even though *Swimming to Cambodia* incorporates a process of growing awareness with an essentially political agenda—asking that we take responsibility for our personal and cultural acts—I would suggest that the work's strength (though not likely the reason for its popularity) derives from its presentation of epistemic mechanisms of contemporary Western culture, including those dualist predicates that mislead us to a sense that we have succeeded at, or need to continue to strive for, achieving dominion over nature, the ultimate other. This epistemic arrogance virtually destines our culture both to tyrannize over our environment as well as to all but block our culture's ability to sight realities about existence that fail to conform to our culturally prescribed vision of right behavior. And that right behavior, in the final analysis, often is little more than self-interest cloaked in the guise of truth seeking. What Gray realizes is that he is inescapably physically part of that world, and what he does to it he does to himself. It's the sort of self-destructiveness that can only be seen when one adjusts one's vision from hovering above the physical world to crawling in its brambles. It is a vision that has Gray observe in the piece, "I suddenly thought I knew what it was that killed Marilyn Monroe."[26] Epiphany is a first step, of course; what one does afterwards, however, is crucial to our future.

In *Gray's Anatomy* Gray moves even closer to the essence of Western society's ills by placing his performance persona—that personification of Western, open-minded, liberal urges hung up by spiritual illusions regarding separation of mind/soul and body—under the microscope in a process that at first glance appears to be some 1970s-like return to unadulterated solipsism. But *Gray's Anatomy* is once again more than a therapy session with Gray, for as Gray-the-performer goes—as this postmodern Everyman goes—so goes dominant Western thought. The combination of self-identity established through context—first via the audience and then via the physical world itself—replays itself, but this time even more obsessively, given the tellingly ironic title of the work. To understand the spiritual Gray entails studying the physical Gray. And this physical pursuit becomes for Gray a Westernized pursuit of those mystical elements of selfhood standardly pursued by Eastern or New Age alternatives.

Gray's Anatomy documents Gray's search for a cure to a growing left eye ailment diagnosed as "macula pucker," described by his ocular specialist as

> a distortion of the interior limiting membrane secondary to the posterior hyloid face contraction. But the posterior hyloid, which was attached to the optic nerve macula, and major vessels of the retina, have remained attached and intact.[27]

The full description here is significant, for Gray is setting up a fundamental distinction between the advances of contemporary, reductive scientific process and a variety of alternative procedures he will attempt throughout the tale. Furthermore, this cold analysis belies the significance of the eye for the human "I" trying to maintain or establish connections with the physical world. Essentially, Western procedure has dissected Gray's eye/I, analyzed the condition, and determined a solution: to operate in an effort to fix the functional deficiency, devoid of any attempt to understand the complex whole. The eye operation reflects the operation Gray reductively undertakes to restore the "I."

Potential causes for his ocular degeneration abound, most of them of a physical nature. But at least one possibility is *meta*physical, namely, that his current work project has left him vulnerable to infection, a novel-in-progress being written in the first person that Gray concludes "was too much *I, I, I, I, I I I I I I I I I I I I I I I*" (11). He fears that it may be writing this autobiographical novel that threatens to blind him. Of course, this self-obsession is evidence of his metaphorical blindness (or myopia), but *Gray's Anatomy* chooses to move beyond metaphor to something closer to grounding itself in actual materiality. The fact is that this possible blinding literally threatens his very existence, given that, without his eyes, he can't see to observe and can't observe to report, which means that, without perception, Gray will no longer be able to perform. And if he will no longer be perceived by an audience, he will essentially cease to exist. Furthermore, the experience of Gray's novel writing is, in fact, destroying him at another level—whether or not he goes blind—since it is a process that physically disconnects him from the world outside (writing in his little room) as well as from his theater context, written as it is in isolation rather than performed onstage. Simply put, Gray must see and be seen to be, and without the theater—by being exclusively a writer—he increasingly becomes less "real." A long string of associations leads to the point that without the physical grounding/experience of the *eye,* the *I* will cease to be. There is, ultimately, no transcendental self beyond physical grounding.

Not satisfied with the cold analytic certainty of the first doctor and moving quickly to a second opinion, Gray locates a Chinese-American M.D., who announces that Gray's condition is "idiopathic," explaining the term to mean "no known cause" (12). In this encounter Gray has moved from a rigid, unaccommodating reductionist Western diagnosis to one that allows for uncertainty, for the uncontrolled and uncontrollable to become part of the descriptive universe.

This is the beginning of a long, humorous string of recounted encounters that, according to Brewer, "symbolize the refusal . . . to acknowledge the whole notion of chaos and fuzziness—that is, uncertainty—that the subject of failing eyesight produces" (254). Gray longs to find some immortal part of himself beyond the contingencies of physical mortality, only eventually to realize that the immortal part of him is either unattainable altogether or—more fruitfully aligned with the bottom-up perception of existence—is attainable via recognition of his physical interrelationship with his universe, from Richard Nixon (ironically) to his girlfriend. Gray's therapist insists:

> All things are contingent, and there is also chaos. . . . In other words . . .
> shit happens. Give up on this magical thinking and this airy-fairy Disney-
> land kind of let's pretend and your Hollywood la-la fantasy, please. Do the
> right thing. Get the operation. Hmmn?

The therapist appears on a sort of verge, acknowledging uncertainty, but then he falls back on Western reductionism, recommending the operation. This engagement leads Spalding to ponder why he should let someone "cut into the window of my soul," adding a certain wonder that the ailment centrally limits his ability to see detail (19).

Here are two crucial glimpses into the crux of the performance piece. Gray's reliance on reductive detail is, in fact, the thing Gray needs to transcend, for, while detail produces entertaining stories, Gray himself must move away from a personal, discrete obsessiveness about the details of his life and search for the larger patterns into which his life fits. (From "ego" to "eco" might be the charge.) This move suggests a larger cultural need to move beyond the fragmented and fragmenting reductionism of detail and toward the integrationist path of pattern sighting so often ignored as we pursue material discreteness.

Life may be lived through serially defined detail, but experience is gained through parallel absorption enriching patterned comprehension amid existence. This absorption includes an interaction of both parallel physical input and conscious/mental absorption leading to an adjustment of our serial conclusions and their obsessions with discrete identity. Gray is unwittingly accurate in his throw-off observation that his search for an ocular cure will affect his "soul's window." This material search for a physical cure *will,* ironically, lead to a material revelation about his self, consciousness, soul—terms the choice of which are virtually interchangeable in this monologue.

Idiopathy, a term that has stuck in Gray's mind for some time, implies a faith of sorts not in some mystical force beyond the domain affected by causality but in the seeming mystery of emergent material causes which are too complex and intertwined fully to be comprehended, at least not in a linear, predictive, and controllable fashion. A notion of material religion seems to have infected Gray's consciousness. Upon his return to New York and at another visit to his doctor's office, Gray sees Richard Nixon leaving the examining room, which triggers a rapid string of events: "It was seeing Richard Nixon come out of my doctor's office that gave me the faith and courage to have the operation." *Faith* seems at first an ill-placed word, for this brief encounter hardly explains its use, and the encounter even less convincingly explains Gray's determination to have the operation. In fact, immediately after Gray's point about Nixon, he adds "I also couldn't have done it without Renée," Gray's girlfriend (71). The operation, finally, neither helps nor hurts Gray's condition, but, very surprisingly, Gray doesn't grieve over this material stalemate, where Western science neither triumphs nor exactly fails. Miracles will not occur, neither spiritual nor medical; existence continues, and selfhood remains intact. But he has calmed down; his paranoid near-paralysis has left him: "I'm happy to have right eye vision," an ability to see patterns more clearly than occluding detail (74).

Significantly, Gray summarizes: "I began to realize that there are tricks in the world, and there's magic in the world. But there's also reality" (74). Seeing the combination of detail and the fuzzy outlines and patterns out of which the details grow, Gray has found something of a sense of larger order, not of the rigid linear, bivalent Western sort he has striven in the past to locate or of the freer non-Western options but something more "of nature" and less mystical. Gray almost literally emerges recognizing his place in a world that is real but that also holds in it the material magic that produces consciousness and makes life worth living. Although the operation doesn't restore Gray's failing eye, the production/performance itself has, in a parallel, multivalent, nonreductive fashion, restored Gray's failing "I," no longer obsessive and resistant to the changes of life but responsive and accepting of change, of immutable patterns of a larger existence sighted in the mutability of life itself.

With an adjusted vision, self-awareness, consciousness/soul may be attainable via a material pursuit of the emergent reality of existence. If metaphysical soul is unreachable—because it doesn't exist—a legitimately viable alternative to that thing-as-no-thing exists nonetheless, and Spalding Gray has striven to give us a sense of its attainability within our traditions, which require/necessitate essential re-visioning themselves, as Gray himself has been re-visioned. Brewer observes that Gray's central conclusion is that "the body and mind will not be separated" (256). If Gray's told tale relates that fact, his performance grounding in his audience and in his body further illustrates the fact, supporting exactly what Gray's words relate.

In the final analysis we see no endorsement of current Eurocentric practices, either dualistic or materially reductive and linear, as might at first be expected. In fact, the greatest expression of Eurocentrism—the traditional psychology of self—is replaced by a more inclusively contextualized ecology of selfhood within a whole. Within this frame we also see a reluctance merely to embrace the bivalent alternative of non-Western options. What we see is a new faith in the renewed potentials of our materialist pursuits of the issues that really matter: a faith in the productive nonmystical though emergent pursuit of consciousness and, through that pursuit, of the good life. A new religion stripped of mystical trapping may be precisely what our world needs.

"I, I, I, I" Kushner: Attacking Encrusted Angels in America

If one literally applies the concept of Fuchs's death of character to Tony Kushner's *Angels in America*,[28] the result is a rather macabre reflection on the carnage of AIDS in the late twentieth century. Kushner's work, however, operates at more subtle and valuable levels in the general assault on the notion of discrete individuality/consciousness hovering above an inferior nature awaiting manipulation by that discrete and superior consciousness. Kushner himself observes in his afterword to the play, "We pay high prices for the maintenance of the myth of the individual," adding a point echoing Schechner and others that among "the list of the evils Individualism visits on our culture are previewing playwrights suffering paroxysms of mortification and rage, caught up myopically, claustrophobically, sometimes catastrophically, in the dramas of their selves" (2:150). Kushner is not guilty of this charge (numerous critical assessments notwithstanding), though, like Gray, he begins work from the position of *seeming* to attempt to salvage the myth of the Individual.

But, like Gray, too, Kushner replaces an initial longing for a return to individual ideals with a growing awakening of the need to see the individual placed in a larger context. Producing something of a hybrid between Wilson's total theater and Gray's minimalist performance art, Kushner incorporates Wilson's epistemologically altering experience with Gray's journey of discovery. The result is a consciousness adjustment aligning itself with the materialist concepts presented by the new sciences.

Part 1 of *Angels in America* generally presents a cast of characters looking for individual regeneration. Central to this presentation is the issue of homosexuality in America, which can at first glance appear to be little more than Kushner "caught up in the drama of his own self." But matters go much farther than that. Confronting the othering promoted by gay issues is, of course, a first concern. The play asks that we assess the degree to which we are all different and compare it to the degree we are all the same. But, more centrally, this "Gay Fantasia on National Themes" opens us to a larger crisis revealed to us through our responses to AIDS. AIDS is sighted as establishing a plaguelike condition of cultural disruption in our world parallel to the idea of plague pursued and studied by Artaud. Plague disrupts and destroys, but, as Artaud celebrates, it also provides opportunity for breaking through personal and cultural encrustations, opening up a pandemonium of new options and opportunities in the process.

Kushner sets his play up to see AIDS as providing cultural opportunity amid personal crisis. In this regard Kushner has at least intuitively picked up on Artaud's equation of plague with theater. Theater is itself a sort of plague to that culture that it visits—a disrupter of the status quo—and so what better place to present plague as concept than in a venue that itself offers plaguelike process and plaguelike results? Here we see hints of a Wilson influence in that Kushner offers a realist script about the AIDS plague but then, Wilson-like, creates a disruptive, antirealist, antidiscursive, plaguelike total theater performance overlay onto that script.

That overlay, says Kushner, is intended to create "moments of magic . . . [that] are to be fully realized, as wonderful bits of *theatrical* illusion—which means it's OK if the wires show, and maybe it's good that they do, but the magic should at the same time be thoroughly amazing" (1:5). As such, incarnations such as the play's Angels become theatrical phenomena emitting complex and even conflicting signals. They are "angels" with a message, but they are also obviously and clearly "stage props" that intrigue us beyond the message. Discursively designed to positively convey a generally negative late-twentieth-century spirit of entrenching self-interest, they are attractive and even appealing sirenlike apparitions that draw us to themselves even as we are at least mildly repelled by their message. This discursive/prediscursive conflict is further complicated by the fact that these nonrealistic Angels flutter about on an ostensibly realistic stage, undermining performative expectations themselves. Realism and nonrealism tantalizingly clash, conflict, and confuse expectations. It is important for a production of *Angels* to accept these various conflations of formerly either/or propositions into a both/and performance agenda. In Kushner's theater serial mind functions compete with parallel brain operations to create a confusing pandemonium of events not easily discursively deciphered.

The confusion, I would suggest, is crucial and intentional. Consider even the level of plot. Even the apparently linear journeys of the characters are disrupted and undermine the expected message of such journeys as typically presented by the realist form. Walter Prior's terminal illness is a brutal refutation of any idea of progressive and universal order or justice prevalent in our culture. And it's a refutation that destroys Walter's lover, Louis, who aptly summarizes our illusions as he explains why he must abandon Walter:

> Maybe because this person's sense of the world, that it will change for the better with struggle, maybe a person who has this neo-Hegelian positivist sense of constant historical progress toward happiness or perfection or something, who feels very powerful because he feels connected to these forces, moving uphill all the time . . . maybe that person can't, um, incorporate sickness into his sense of how things are supposed to go. Maybe vomit . . . and sores and disease . . . really frighten him, maybe . . . he isn't good with death. (1:25)

Progress, that serialized and serializing assumption ingrained in our individual American consciousnesses, is countermanded by natural reality, the parallel bombardment of natural input, vomit, sores, and disease included.

Here lies Kushner's spark of genius, in his creation of the *super*natural Angels who are so utterly difficult to understand. They are manifestations abandoned by God and stuck in an orbit doomed to repeat the mantra, "I, I, I, I." Our current individualist-inspired dualist illusions about power and dominion are turned confused and desperate by the previously cited plot twists and then are made attractively manifest onstage by these emanations curiously hanging from wires/supports we can actually see. Essentially, the message is enhanced by the package. In one regard these Angels *are* capable of magic, for what they inspire in us has been an urge to transform the world into a progressive something it was never necessarily intended to be. And then, even as this world falls apart, the Angels encourage us to continue our quest for control. Seeing the negative results of the free rein given to humanity, the Angels argue we need to effect yet another transformation that is actually only a logical, entrenching extension of our current agenda:

> Forsake the Open Road:
> Neither Mix Nor Intermarry: Let Deep Roots Grow:
> If you do not MINGLE you will Cease to Progress:
> Seek Not to Fathom the World and its Delicate Particle Logic:
> You cannot Understand, You can only Destroy,
> You do not Advance, You only Trample,
> Poor blind Children, abandoned on the Earth,
> Groping terrified, misguided, over
> Fields of Slaughter, over bodies of the Slain:
> HORRIBLE YOURSELVES!
>
> (2:52)

The Angels, seeing the disorder of personal freedoms turned only to destructive turmoil, invoke the law of excluded middle and propose a turn toward static, unchanging order as the only way to preserve humanity and as a way to get an absentee God to return to His creation. The play's curious mixture of futility (offered by Louis, for example) and hope (offered by the Angels) is seemingly resolved by the ultimately overarching presence of the superior Angels into a seemingly simple answer of hopeful, conservative entrenchment.

But Prior, the Angels' hoped-for appointed prophet, sees things differently, asking these "mixed-up, irresponsible" creatures, "Did you come here to save me or destroy me?" (2:53). Given the opportunity to choose between an eternal but static, unchanging existence offered by these Angels in heaven or the self-destructive mortality humanity seems to be pursuing on earth, Prior sees a third option. His is a hopeful vision of a humanity converted by "plague" to accept an uncertain mortality in exchange for dynamic life and vitality. For Prior the world need not be as miserable as the Angels describe, nor is the option of a heaven of unchanging order as appealing as the Angels presume. Life even with inevitable death is worthwhile if for no other reason than that conditions *may* eventually change for the better.

Walter Prior's decision to choose the uncertainty of life may at first glance seem a trivial conclusion of a romantically heroic sort and hardly worthy of a play of such repute. But the choice is merely a discursive reflection of a deeper potentially parallel epistemological transformation. Prior sees a world he is part of and, through the pandemonious experience of AIDS/plague, has adjusted his own serialized consciousness (once so similar to Louis's) to adopt a newly integrating paradigm, neither embracing the discretely generated disorder of our current cult of individualism nor its logical opposite, the Angels' right-wing corrective of static, dis-inspired conformity and sameness. Rather, Prior chooses a mortal life at the edge of chaos, full of risk and even, likely, disappointment but also full of opportunity. And so does Kushner.

But Kushner actually takes matters a step further. Prior has, of course, literally rejected the metaphysical (immortal) in favor of physical (mortal) existence. But Kushner adds a twist to this point—what I see as his spark of genius—by creating Angels as high-wire parodies of our theistical expectations that salvation will come from above. Having salvation fail to come from above, Kushner fills the expectant void by offering an alternative to this deluded longing, in the form of Belize, the drag queen nurse sensitized to individual suffering and willing even to help ease the pain of an "enemy" like Roy Cohn. Suffering also brings the opportunity for compassion, very likely at least part of the reason Prior chooses life on earth rather than stasis in heaven. We get a vision that, if heaven exists, it will be found rising out of the materiality of nature, potentially in the form of compassionate human consciousness. The true "Angels in America" are material, human incarnations aware of the power of collectivity and communal empathy, rather than individual isolation and self-interest. Incarnations such as Belize are an advanced guard potentially pointing the way to a tangible paradigm shift, a material alteration of both personal and cultural consciousness. Perhaps out of the death of the "I, I, I, I" will come the consciousness of "we." And to get to God—if that's the goal—we must go through nature and its natural outcrop, human consciousness. Angels are not, finally, manifestations of some disembodied other world. They are grounded in the real world, and, if they fly, it's not because they defy laws of natures. The wires are there to be seen, and no one should be fooled by any attributions to them beyond what they really are.

If this materialist activation of consciousness is the play's discursive message, the play's performance experience works in complementary fashion to effect our transformation to minimize illusions of authority handed down to us from on high and to trust the grounded validity of our own senses. The discrete sense of isolated individual autonomy grown out of our confident manipulation of serial mentality is regularly assaulted in the play as serial processing is regularly undermined by the parallel bombardment of contradictory, seemingly discursive clues about what the play *means*. What viscerally appeals to us often is the very thing in the play that discursively repels us, and vice versa. Roy Cohn is an attractive villain, and the Angels are impressive though, finally, misguided. Belize appears at first entrance to be anything but a savior, but he ultimately is the one who "flies" in the play, unassisted by wires but bolstered by material compassion. Serial as well as parallel processing finally adjust our experiencing of this play, not one or the other, and, necessarily, the process must remain materially grounded. Finally, if we feel correctly ambivalent toward these staged Angels in America, perhaps we, too, can see our Founding Father Angels in the same light, revisit what have become sacrosanct, abstracted ideals propounded by these Angels—such as Individualism—and reground those ideals in the substantial reality of contemporary necessity.

Arising from such theatrical conflict—performatively neural and dramatically interpersonal—comes a sense of the necessary interaction between parallel and serial response to the world. The result is an awareness of the need for personal engagement with the world out there from levels neural to interpersonal. Kushner and Gray and Wilson are dreamers hoping for transformations of human consciousness. But their dreams are clearly materially grounded, and they are therefore facing the right direction.

Chapter 7

Multivalence and the Move
toward Emergence

In the wake of advances in the contemporary avant-garde theater world, popular, commercially viable contemporary theater is often overlooked even as it strives to digest similar advances for broader community consumption. Armed with both the insights of the new sciences and guided by similar avant-garde advances, however, it becomes clear that overlooking the commercial theater is a mistake, especially given any ultimate goal of establishing a broad cultural adjustment of any significance. In fact, it seems clear that the commercial venue must be engaged precisely in order to exact the shift in thinking advocated by both the scientific and avant-garde theater communities. With *Angels in America* Tony Kushner has become one such success, but others have succeeded as well.

Perhaps foremost among those other successful commercial practitioners is Tom Stoppard, whose 1988 play *Hapgood* actually entered the realm of quantum mechanics, reminding us of our cultural dependence on linear rational thought, hinging as it does on the bivalent illusion of excluded middle. Using the logic of quantum physics as an alternative paradigm, Stoppard assaults our currently encrusted thought by first reminding us of what needs to be reassessed. Stoppard voices his thoughts through one of his play's characters:

> Yes-no, either-or. . . .You have been too long in the spy business, you think everybody has no secret or one big secret, they are what they seem or the opposite. You look at me and think: Which is he? Plus or minus. If only you could figure it out like looking into me to find my root. And then you still wouldn't know. We're all doubles. Even you.[1]

Stoppard provides us with the concept that discrete individuality could/should be replaced by the notion of quantum superpositioning, namely, that we are often less either/or personalities (like good or bad) than some combination of both/and.

Stoppard, however, is by no means alone in confronting bivalent mental processes. Equipped with Stoppard's assault and further informed by advances in the works of such practitioners as Robert Wilson, we can see the problem of bivalent thought surfacing in any number of commercially successful playwrights. Much like Stoppard with *Hapgood,* Michael Frayn utilizes the notion of quantum ethics to problematize issues of responsibility and blame in his play *Copenhagen.* Less indebted to science but no less on target, Caryl Churchill has weighed in with numerous plays as someone who challenges the bivalence inherent in our current approaches to matters of race, gender, and nationality. David Henry Hwang, with *M. Butterfly* (1988), is yet another good example of a successful commercial playwright pursuing such an agenda by presenting the complexities of self-identity and endorsing a multivalent alternative. Hwang's bivalently minded Gallimard is almost literally blinded by his either/or mental constructs, leading to brief successes and advancement but ultimately to humiliation and suicide.

But Peter Shaffer is perhaps the perfect example to study in this regard, a successful commercial playwright often misread as reductively bivalent but who clearly assaults the bivalent mode of rational thought. He assaults bivalent consciousness by first appearing, through rational assessment, to endorse the bivalent orthodoxy but then, through his performance mode, insists on a pervading though subtle multivalency.

Peter Shaffer's Assault on Bivalent Consciousness

Peter Shaffer's career in the theater has been one of spectacular popular success as well as notable critical reserve. Shaffer has often been attacked for reducing complex and important sociocultural ideas to simple either/or conflicts that sacrifice the full complexity of a given situation in favor of digestible "formula plays." If the mass of critical opinion were correct in seeing Peter Shaffer's works as outlining dialectic oppositions between, for example, the primitive and the civilized or the sacred and the profane, then perhaps those critics would be justified in attacking Shaffer for pandering to the reductive urges of popular audiences. Upon reasonably close scrutiny, however, Shaffer's work, virtually without exception, belies such interpretation. Like many critics, Gene A. Plunka is typical in seeing Shaffer pursuing the "concept of the divided self, which unfolds into the dialectic between the Apollonian and

Dionysian."[2] While on the surface Shaffer appears to pursue some Hegelian dialectical agenda on the frontiers of psychology, the conflicts he presents are far more complex. In fact, I would argue that his unique blend of popular digestibility and subtle complexity is just the blend needed to help bring to fruition the paradigm shift encouraged by the new sciences.

Shaffer's *Equus* (1974) is a typical case in point, a play that at first glance appears, as Plunka observes, to present the timeless struggle between Dionysian worship and Apollonian resistance. A lesser talent than Shaffer would perhaps have pursued such a case study, instituting a process of excluded middle to articulate the tragic human condition of inevitable human incompleteness in the face of impossible integration of these two conflicting urges. Alan Strang, the youth engaged in full-scale primitive worship of his "Equus" god, is converted by the analytic reductionism of the modern psychiatrist Martin Dysart ("Dice Heart") to the godless "religion" of contemporary society while himself coming to realize the price paid for pursuing the godlessness of traditional, conforming psychology. If this were, in fact, Shaffer's agenda (or the agenda his directors have chosen to highlight), then he would justly fall into the critical cross-hairs of Elinor Fuchs, who argues against the fruitfulness of popular obsessions with character and psychology. After all, as Kushner argues, character and psychology are individualist obsessions that encourage social fragmentation rather than reunion or reconstitution of cultural parts into a larger integrated whole.

Given the suggestions provided by fuzzy logic, however, one can approach *Equus* in the spirit it seems to have been created, for Strang is not the distillation of primitivism, nor is Dysart the personification of civilized order. And neither is the play either a treatise on tragic impossibilities or some thesis arguing from bivalence for some simple synthesis of two opposing doctrines. This process further moves to an end that circles around personal matters involving discretely constructed characters, using the characters, instead, as means to an end rather than empathic, psychologically validated ends in themselves.

Looking at the two main characters of the play as multivalently cast protagonists rather than bivalent antagonists, one can find the first hints of a fuzzy logic at work. At first glance we see that Alan Strang worships his primitive equine god with a passionate fervor ultimately abhorrent to his Western culture. If this assessment is accurate, it would place Strang at one extreme of a Dionysian/Apollonian dichotomy, and Dysart's psychology credentials and institutional position would place him at the other, culturally endorsed, Apollonian extreme. A closer look, however, reveals Shaffer to be asserting that the dichotomy is a false one and that significant overlap occurs between the two representative positions.

Strang's religion is, indeed, a passionate, primitive, nonmodern, noncivilized one. This primitivism is clouded over, however, by constrictions and psychoses that are anything but the result of his primitivism. The crisis in Strang's world that leads to the horrific horse-blinding episode reveals a more complex relationship. Strang's assault on his stabled pantheon—blinding his Equus god—is not the result of primitivism organically gone awry, as the dichotomy posture would suggest. Rather, it is the result of Strang's own actual apparently inescapable immersion in the phobias of contemporary society. After all, it is his impotence when confronted with his first human sexual encounter that begins the string of events leading him to blind his horse-god, a combination of personal guilt and a pervading belief that his god is a jealous, vengeful god pettily demanding unadulterated worship. Ultimately, Strang has been influenced by a contemporary socialization process that actually helps to mold what Dysart himself incorrectly considers primitive contact with an essential reality. Finally, Strang is not some primitive opposite against which a civilized Dysart is pitted. Rather than being a type representing this unadulterated primitive urge, Strang is part of a vast webwork through which we see a complex and multivalent consciousness arise at several levels.

Even at the process level of Strang's preadolescent and ill-fated socialization, fuzzy logic arises as overlapping influences unravel the cultural symptoms leading to Strang's "condition." These multivalent symptoms are personified by Alan Strang's two parents, though at first glance we may see bivalence at work. His mother is a god-fearing fundamentalist puritan, while his father is an atheist socialist. Frank Strang, the father, adopts an atheism of meaningless materialism leading to an interpersonal, pseudointellectual bitterness that has left him to find minimal fulfillment through pornography, symptomatic of his inability to make contact, sexual or otherwise, with other humans. Dora Strang, the mother, is equally incapable of "normal" human contact—in the natural as well as social sense—opting to bury herself under a stern, retributional religion rather than to seek interpersonal fulfillment. While on the surface appearing to be representational opposites, they more accurately appear as points along a continuum, less part of some either/or proposition than cultural products along a continuum of dysfunctionalism.

In turn this fuzzy logic of dysfunctionalism rises up in its own fuzzy logic manner to cloud the easy dichotomized extreme Alan initially seems to represent in contrast to Dysart. Alan experiences guilty obsessions inherited from his upbringing, reflections of contemporary cultural dysfunctions, and he inserts them into his "primitive" Equus religion. The sources of Alan's personal, primitive religion ultimately are anything but naturally pure, corrupted as they are by culturally informed puritanism and guilt. While appearing to be half of a natural/healthy versus cultural/sick dichotomy, his character unfolds too complexly—too multivalently—to anchor itself as such an oppositional point. Alan is the product of a fuzzy system that belies either/or alliances.

And, if Alan is a multivalent adulteration of one extreme, so is Dysart. While Dysart's institutionalized cultural normalcy extends to a comfortable existence wherein he tolerates a completely sexless marriage, he nevertheless longs for engagement with the primitive, symptom of his own (fortunately) incomplete socialization and his ultimate unwillingness fully to resign to sterile cultural normalcy advocated by his modern-world upbringing.

So there are valuable points of fuzzy overlap between Alan's parents, between urges found separately in Alan and Dysart, between Alan and Dysart as an apparently dichotomous pair, and between (and within) the various positions they all at first glance appear to represent. The dichotomies that critics standardly see in Shaffer's work appear only at some imprecise level of generalization.

What we see in the critical literature on the play is the creation of an interesting human paradox. As there is within us (spectators and critics) a rather sophisticated urge to criticize easy dichotomies (to assault the law of excluded middle), there is also a critical urge supported by cultural prescription to seek out such bivalent, linear dichotomies even as we feel at least the urge to assault them in favor of multivalent nonlinearity. We as audiences and critics have standardly been socialized to see life's dilemmas through polarizing lenses and are at least initially pleased when life/art/existence reveals such simple bivalently symmetrical patterns. That seems, at least initially, to be what attracts us to Shaffer's work.

Yet, when further scrutiny reveals the necessary imprecision of this symmetry, we attack the craft, arguing for more sophisticated patternings. After all, the more precise the patterning, the better the art and the closer we approach "nature" and "truth." It's virtually as if the parallel nature of the brain is at war with the serialization of mind (to use an equally unacceptable dichotomy, for, as we now know, these operations are not mutually exclusive but overlap all along our complex neural network). Ultimately, our reductive mental searches for simple symmetry—which we seem to resist even as we have been acculturated to search for it—should perhaps give way to the more complex, emergent symmetries of chaos, complexity, and multivalence. This, I suggest, is Shaffer's actual goal, to present complex emergent symmetries amid appearances of more desirable simple symmetries. In the process Shaffer reveals that this desire for bivalent symmetry is delusional, running contrary to even deeper desires for and incipient recognition of complexity.

Even as we are alternatingly torn between attraction to and repulsion from Shaffer's apparent dichotomies, the apparent confusions and conflations within Shaffer's characterization, which undermine Shaffer's superficial symmetries, are sometimes themselves criticized. The reductive patterns are attacked as too tidy, and then the ironic sightings of their lack of neatness—their complexity, actually—result in a sort of paradoxical critique, first, that the dichotomies are too simplistic and then, in the face of their unraveling, that they need to be more rigorously articulated. Shaffer's primitivism-modernism dichotomy is at once too simple *and* too sloppily outlined, too full of apparently inconsistent clutter. Unfortunately, rarely do we hear charges against the nature of dichotomy itself, charges that would, in fact, lead to a defense of Shaffer's craft.

As this summary suggests, Shaffer's seeming dichotomies are neither merely too simplistic, nor are they too sloppily asymmetrical. They beg to be seen *ironically,* not as dichotomies to be endorsed so much as a sophisticated webwork—engaging a more complex symmetry—which belies the very notion of dichotomy perhaps sighted at first glance from a culturally inscribed (prescribed?) mental prejudice. The thought process that leads critics to see dichotomies and that Shaffer teasingly allows us to search for is precisely the thing Shaffer is assaulting even as he *appears* to capitalize on such a formula. I would suggest that Shaffer introduces such formulas in his works precisely for the reason of challenging them, extratextually undermining them, and then hinting at the complexities beneath tidy patterns of symmetrical thought as he further undermines additional particulars in each of his works. In essence Shaffer uses his characters to undermine the traditional notion of psychologically cohesive characterization itself.

If this process has been less than fully successful at critical and popular levels of reception, it is more the result of a sort of audience schizophrenia, working to move beyond traditional psychological positionings while being ill equipped to do so and thereby aggressively returning to the old forms. Shaffer offers us (audience, critic, director) the opportunity to move forward. What we do with it is not for him to dictate. The opportunity for an awakening of a multivalent consciousness clearly exists, but the hoped-for rewiring cannot be discursively dictated. Rather, performative, experiential exposure and at least *eventual* absorption is the goal, and Shaffer provides us with numerous opportunities to absorb his theater's experience.

Recall that it is the scientist/psychologist Dysart in *Equus,* the mediocre Salieri in *Amadeus,* and the parasitic Old Martin in *The Royal Hunt of the Sun* who tell Shaffer's plays' tales, and it is their consciousnesses that are ultimately the central objects of scrutiny in the plays. We are seeing their mental constructs materialized onstage. And it is their "normal," "mediocre," "parasitic" thought processes—bivalently, serially, and psychologically grounded—that are the objects of scrutiny and ultimate critique. As we come to see these men's mentally predicated shortcomings, so should we come to sense their systematic flaws as they fail, for they all suffer from the general patterns of oversimplified linear symmetry and reductive consciousnesses that are mirrored in the plays' seemingly dichotomous structures themselves. They are, finally, the *creators* of these dubious, dramatically structured sets of dichotomies. Shaffer does not advocate the bivalent structure he presents; rather, the structure is a reflection of the thought processes of each of these incomplete narrators and a manifestation of that which he attacks. We are looking at the landscapes of their minds as mapped out onstage, seeing material manifestations of their thought process manipulations.[3]

The fundamental failings Shaffer reveals through his narrators/characters and through *their* play structures are epistemological. The theme is that the narrators can't/don't *think* properly. In fact, their tragedies (if that's the proper term) derive from a growing awareness of their failed epistemologies (an awareness that belatedly awakens them to life itself), of the incompleteness of their socially/personally/psychologically molded consciousnesses and the bivalent, serial processes through which they activate and engage their incomplete consciousnesses.

So, if we would like to concede that the critics are right in seeing a too-reductive "Shafferian" format, we need then to add that these critics missed the major point that the flawed and over-reductive formats reveal *character* flaw and, through these characters, a reflection of a larger culturally enforced epistemological flaw. We are not witnessing a playwright's flawed craft. Rather, we are experiencing the playwright's talents at work, utilizing dramatic structure to present and undermine mental structure. Even more than anything found in the stories of these failed characters, the plays' structures are the central sites of the dramatic tension. Each play's story merely fills the stage space on which the real drama unfolds. What washes over the audience is much more than the reductive discursivity of story often seen in the play. The entire event becomes the experience, striving to undermine the very thoughts we bring to the viewing.

Seeing failure among the central protagonists—especially given the depth to which that failure actually goes—is one thing. But, as these characters fail, we also see something "emergent" in the plays, something that moves beyond the drama/melodrama of Shaffer's characters' narratives. Here is where Shaffer comes closest to being the "Artaudian" many have labeled him to be. Back to *Equus,* we can first consider the Dionysian/Apollonian split that is so often misinterpreted by students of Nietzsche's *Birth of Tragedy* yet seems actually accurately depicted in *Equus* not as mutually exclusive urges but as fuzzy, overlapping harmonies. For example, if primitivism merely *triumphs* over cultural forces, we sink to the oblivion of a savage mind. And, of course, when social constructs of guilt and puritanism invade, override, and triumph over primitive religious urges, the result is the horses' mutilations. However, if Alan Strang's primitivism were somehow allowed to *influence* his social behavior, we would see a healthy, culturally integratable primitivism at work. The point is that accepting degrees of both/and interaction rather than either/or exclusivity is what constitutes vital existence.

Nietzsche equates Dionysian primitivism with dreams and intoxication. Quoting from poet Hans Sachs, Nietzsche agrees, "All poetry we ever read / Is but true dreams interpreted."[4] Of the Apollonian plastic urge Nietzsche observes, "The image of Apollo must incorporate that thin line which the dream image may not cross, under penalty of becoming pathological, of imposing itself on us as crass reality" (21). The Apollonian is not the mundane opposite of inspiration; rather, at its healthiest, it is the materialization of the Dionysian. It is spirit made flesh, the ineffable bolted down to its concrete foundations.

Thus, the exclusivity often assumed to inhere in the seemingly oppositional Apollonian/Dionysian terminology is a mistaken assumption, and the apparent bivalent duality Nietzsche famously speaks of is, as even Nietzsche says, the result of his expressing himself through the imprecise, bivalently predicated languages of Kant and Schopenhauer rather than the result of some truly oppositional symmetry that the terms (and often the descriptions) imply. Perhaps with today's conceptions of fuzzy logic and a language derived from such logic, Nietzsche (like Aristotle before him) would have been better able to articulate his own Dionysian/Apollonian conceptions.

Here is where I feel many critics have failed Shaffer. Alan Strang's first tragedy is not that Apollonian civilization destroyed his Dionysian frenzy. Rather, it is the case that civilized prudery and guilt destroys the possibility of embracing the complex interaction of Apollonian/ Dionysian worship. Until his guilt-catalyzing encounter with Jill, Alan's worship often rose to being the incarnated blend of the Dionysian *and* Apollonian. He was ecstatic and dream artist participating in the life dance and articulating that participation through his verbalized rituals. Seeded in his psyche, however, were the socialized patterns of guilt that would infect his worship and destroy any hoped for edge-of-chaos balance. His own incipient guilt leads him to blind his Equus god. Dysart's role, ultimately, is to finish the process already begun by Strang's parents, finishing off Alan's religion in the process. Instead of an inaccurate depiction of Dionysian freedom struggling against Apollonian order, we see far more accurately the Dionysian/Apollonian fusion defeated by resistant social doctrine.

Dysart comes to realize his role in completing Strang's alienation from god/life/nature, realizing, too, his own metaphorically blinded alienation. Temporarily cut loose, Dysart is invited into the Dionysian/ Apollonian world, but he is already too filled with socialized guilt to indulge and concretize his dream state. In scene 14 Dysart recounts a dream he has following his first full encounter with Alan: "That night, I had this very explicit dream. I'm a chief priest in Homeric Greece. I'm wearing a gold mask, all noble and bearded. . . . I'm standing by a thick round stone and holding a sharp knife. . . . The sacrifice is a herd of children."[5] Being a child psychologist, Dysart realizes the parallels between his dream and reality, seeing also the self-doubt he has sensed for some time surfacing in the dream: "I know that if ever those two assistants so much as glimpse my distress—and the implied doubt that this repetitive and smelly work is doing any social good at all—I will be the next across the stone" (29–30). The Dionysian dream arises, and the scales are lifted from Dysart's eyes. But he fails to pursue an Apollonian response to the dream, namely, to act upon it. During waking hours Dysart also sees his tragic dilemma through Strang's case, aware of Apollonian/Dionysian interactive necessity but too cowardly to engage the processes.

This play makes it painfully clear that Dysart's life cannot and will not be saved by his revelation, and it is not merely a case of Dysart confessing his cowardice, that he would change if he only had the courage. Rather, the tragedy is that, even if he did have the courage, he lacks the ability, evident most fervently through the ossified thought process encapsulated in the play's structure, which is a reflection of his mind. The events within the play reveal nothing at the discursive level about *how* to gain what he lacks. They only reveal *what* he lacks. So, too, at least on the surface, does the play's dichotomous structure seem to misguide the audience, since it is apparently as currently ill equipped as Dysart.

Here is where *theater,* the dramatic experience onstage, influences in ways discursive language/thought fails. I would suggest that the tragedy in the play is almost purely structural, and it is best experienced performatively. Dysart's "flaw" in the scripted narrative is cowardice, hardly *a tragic* flaw. Dysart's narrative structuring and the epistemological traces it reveals is actually the site of the tragedy rather than the "tragic" tale itself. Experiencing Dysart's thought process by ourselves ambivalently experiencing the structure in operation reveals to us the true tragedy in its full though fleetingly complex symmetry. Our own consciousnesses, mistakenly seeing the correctness of bivalent thought, is where the tragedy of inadequacy is revealed.

Dysart's is a tragedy *we all* experience in the performance of *Equus,* at least those of us either attracted to the bivalent order of the text or drawn to the order but realizing its inadequacies. In either case we experience the acculturated entrapment of not being able clearly to articulate alternatives to Shaffer's sirenlike, bivalent-seeming package. Shaffer has even identified for us the failings of most art in its attempts to "capture" reality via the standard means and traditional logic typically utilized. Shaffer's play is the thing wherein human tragedy is embedded. Dysart—the Dysart whose mind is revealed through the play's structure—is us, and so, too, he is Shaffer, who reprises central characters who repeatedly demonstrate the complex and complicated inadequacies of a logic and consciousness we have grown dependent upon while to some degree sensing its inadequacies. In some sense this inability to find conformity between our serial mind and parallel brain (as well as the parallel natural world that brain reflects and absorbs) is the heart of all tragedy.

But within tragedy also exists a cathartic hint—again, usually beyond discursivity—of a means of salvation. Even as the inadequacies are made clear, Shaffer's plays do more than reveal those inadequacies. He allows the plays to operate in a pandemonium of ways, stepping beyond simple linear, oppositional treatises and offering something more than explication of the human dilemma. Here is where emergence emerges in the theater, moving to yet another level of theater experience.

A pseudo-Nietzschean act of will to return to some delusional Dionysian primitivism won't work. Changing our modes and goals of perceptive (that is, more strongly parallel and multivalent) awareness/ consciousness, however, may lead to a change as vital and essential as the reductive urge to primitivism it will need to replace. If Dysart could fully engage a multivalent logic, if he could *see* nature and his place in it more fully, completely, and roundedly, then perhaps his consciousness could engage a nature with postmodern sophistication, minus primitive mystery but with a contemporary material reenchantment replacing that mystery. The difference between saying this and actually offering a parallel experience of this parallel potentiality is what separates discursivity from the theater experience.

The hint is in Shaffer's description of the staged horses/gods in *Equus*. These horses should always be perceived as actors *playing* horses: "Any literalism which could suggest a cosy familiarity of a domestic animal—or, worse, a pantomime horse—should be avoided." Shaffer adds, "Great care must also be taken that the masks are put on before the audience with very precise timing—the actors watching each other, so that the masking has an exact and ceremonial effect" (17). That the actors are humans playing horses/gods—rather than that they are mimetically to pretend actually to be horses—is critical to the play's parallel experience. That Strang created his god, complete with Strang's own idiosyncratic qualities, is clearly important, given the play's narrative, though Strang's creation is a psychotic failure. What Strang's process suggests at the performance level, however—seeing mere actors/humans "deified" onstage without illusion, or magic—is that, as humanity perhaps comes better to know itself, so can it come closer to knowing god (again, from the bottom up) void of the mysteries traditionally attributed to the top-down pursuit. As the gods/horses of the stage are in essence human, so must humans know god through themselves (an observation echoing Kushner's thesis). The actors' Equus dance on stage is mystery made flesh, the immaterial made material through the human body (echoing Grotowski). It is a transformative process of material creation that audience members themselves must also imaginatively overlay upon the framework of these creatures, as Strang could only incompletely do (because of his own incompleteness) and as Dysart never really attempts. The process is not complete until consciousness folds into the materiality placed before it. Is this a popular attempt to achieve Brook's Holy Theatre?

What has just been suggested rings like a Sunday sermon, but the point is far less mystical. What this reading of *Equus* suggests is not that we return to mystical religious pursuits (Shaffer would likely argue against pursuit of traditional religious understanding) but that we adjust and adapt to receive nature multivalently and from the bottom up, on nature's terms, rather than on mystical top-down terms (disenfranchising nature in the process) or on any of our manipulative serialized terms that reduce nature to some reductive scientific specimen. To effect that end humanity must move away from bivalence, from tidy linearity. In essence we must move away from the thought patterns that produce the dramatic structures that Dysart, Salieri, and others produce. Shaffer presents on stage the thing to assault.

Ironically, the criticism that plagues Shaffer's theater is necessarily the first step, albeit a step that unfortunately has led to an assault on Shaffer as playwright rather than on his characters as failed minds. Can Dysart, who worships the God of Normal, learn to adjust his mental machinations, mature, escape normalcy, and develop his own "equus"? Can *Amadeus*'s Salieri adjust his merchant's mind and, instead of worshiping his mediocre, bivalent God of Bargains (a lumbering god limited to linear trade/exchange of base products), can he develop a new capacity to create and sight a multivalent God of Creativity that can emergently leap and bound, turning lead to gold and a profane Mozart to sacred musical instrument? The god we see is ultimately the humans we are. Although change never fully occurs in Shaffer's plays, change is forever on the verge, actually awaiting the change to occur beyond the footlights among the audience, cutting across its sight lines for at least the moment.

Sam Shepard's Assault upon Bivalent Consciousness

Sam Shepard's career first as foremost experimentalist and then as apparent compromiser with prevailing dramatic/theatrical orthodoxy has forced a re-viewing of Shepard by numerous critics and scholars. Perhaps most relevant to this discussion is Michael Vanden Heuvel's work *Performing Drama / Dramatizing Performance,*[6] which sees Shepard (and other contemporary practitioners) engaging in a rich interplay between performance and text. For Vanden Heuvel "text/drama is best understood as representative . . . of a larger cognitive activity of imposing structure or meaning on reality" (3); performance, on the other hand, "is activated by nonperiodic, nonlinear activities—improvisation, play, transformation, parataxis, game structures . . . break[ing] down the illusion of rational control and power over meaning . . . and substitut[ing] a dispersal of order into disorganization" (5). Regarding the matter of receptivity, Vanden Heuvel could be interpreted to suggest that text is equated with the linear, serial, rational processes we've generally associated with consciousness (that higher manifestation we now know to be only one end of a broad spectrum), while performance attempts to capture the nonlinear, parallel, and sensory processes operating along the preconscious neural network.

This suggestion seems loosely valid (though too bivalently articulated) regarding Shepard in particular, given that Vanden Heuvel reminds us that even Shepard acknowledges that the main theme of his works is "the idea of consciousness" (200). Vanden Heuvel remarks: "Even during the height of the nonverbal, nontextual experiments of the sixties and seventies, there were those unwilling to accept unexamined some of the extreme claims of performance and its promise of a theater that could operate as a reality of its own or as the first principle for transcending the burdens of consciousness" (193). Indeed, it seems nearly absurd—at very least naive—for anyone truly to have wanted to aspire to escape the "burdens of consciousness" in light of our inescapably verified reliance on consciousness (its linear processes certainly included) as the central tool for human adaptation and survival. What seems central, however, and what perhaps more sensible or sophisticated practitioners such as Shepard have settled upon, is the realization that linear levels of consciousness themselves are inescapable but could in subtle ways be reconceptualized and perhaps even actually reconfigured or rewired. Linearity has its inescapable virtues, but so too, do the information and processes occupying nonlinear recesses preceding linear transformation. This information and these processes could assist in rewiring the mechanism of consciousness itself.

At these intersections is where Shepard's theater engages the imagination. In his phenomenological approach to Shepard, Stanton B. Garner Jr. sees Shepard's stage clutter as central to understanding the playwright's agenda. Like Mamet's *American Buffalo* or Pinter's *The Caretaker* (which both engage a similar agenda), Shepard's stages are filled with junkyard clutter. But the sights, sounds, and smells of Shepard's stage engage more than a sociological and discursive level of comprehension and critique. They virtually clutter themselves beyond the stage and into the audience: consider the amplified sounds/noises in *A Fool for Love* and *States of Shock* and aromas of boiling artichokes in *The Curse of the Starving Class,* for example. Far more than being simple efforts at being "more real" on stage or at commenting on our culture's consumerist urges, such efforts, according to Garner, "reinstate the human within its field, an arena now stripped of its functional objectivity and available to more primitive, physiological modes of habitation."[7] The stage absorbs and contextualizes character into a materialist environment, and the actor's body becomes part of the world it inhabits. In Shepard, according to Garner, we see "a rootedness of the body in its physical field, a phenomenal mode of being present that these characters, for all their linguistic flights to other times and places, cannot escape" (99).

And neither can we, the audience, escape our preconscious sensory rootedness in the world Shepard's theater creates. We must also remind ourselves that with Shepard text itself often operates in a fuzzy fashion to undermine serial coherence even as performance frequently contributes in a fuzzy manner to that urge for coherence. Between text and performance exists a rich interplay, once again belying simple dichotomies. The conscious mind may try serially to order the play on stage (text as well as performance), but the senses experience and perceive the total performative environment in which they are placed through a parallel receptivity that precedes and overrules—or at least requests a reassessment of—the slower, more deliberate orderings of our higher conscious states. Shepard enters the stream of audience consciousness both linearly/serially and nonlinearly/parallelly, engaging consciousness all along its neural network, with the result being our serial conclusions are often undermined or even altered. The undermining process/result conforms to an agenda historically sighted in much of the theatrical work of the 1960s. For Shepard, however, the efforts at alteration seem more completely to acknowledge the inescapable necessity of relying on the higher (still an unpalatable term) serial levels of consciousness in order to exist while suggesting the possibility of breaking through the rigidified forms—bivalence included—imposed by an unchallenged, unassaulted, unquestioned, exclusively linearly fabricated consciousness.

Indeed, the healthy iconoclasms of the 1960s among the experimentalists and avant-gardists of the stage were a necessary first step, but they led to results/conclusions that undermined even the positive features and necessities of human evolution. The need to confront and adjust rather than merely to explode linear, bivalent consciousness seems to be precisely the reason Shepard turned to the more traditional linear-based mode of realism, altered significantly, however, to reconstitute perhaps subtle but nonetheless fundamental reroutings of our neural systems. Willie, in *The Unseen Hand,* observes, "Whenever I think beyond a certain circumference of a certain circle there's a hand that squeezes my brain."[8] Self-imposed or culturally inherited, the unseen hand of strict linear consciousness is the force Shepard tries to move beyond, though he realizes that he (and we) can never fully escape its clutches. Nor do we really want full freedom from its influences, only less tyrannical control.

One inescapable problem is that consciousness at its most rudimentary level, as Unamuno observes, reduces to consciousness of death:

> It is impossible for us, in effect, to conceive of ourselves as not existing, and no effort is capable of enabling consciousness to realize absolute unconsciousness, its own annihilation. Try, reader, to imagine to yourself, when you are wide awake, the condition of your soul when you are in a deep sleep; try to fill your consciousness with the representation of no-consciousness, and you will see the impossibility of it. The effort to comprehend it causes the most tormenting dizziness. We cannot conceive ourselves as not existing.[9]

Strictly speaking, Unamuno is accurate, reflecting again the likely primary cause of the "unhappy conscious" sighted by Hegel. But in Shepard, and in consciousness theories in general, there is an approach that mollifies the truth of Unamuno's observations. The first point involves escaping the tyranny of the excluded middle, the illusion that we are either conscious or unconscious or even that we are either alive or dead. Recall that in *A Lie of the Mind* Jake insists his wife, Beth, is dead even though she is "only" severely brain damaged. And, though Jake himself appears fully (and is physically) alive on this either/or scale of life-or-death, his mental surrender results in a sort of living death. Implicit is a modified notion of death equated with an inability fully to activate our consciousnesses. Although negatively cast in these descriptions, there is also a positive way to see Jake's and Beth's situations: succumbing as they have to less than fully serial consciousness has succeeded at attuning them to rhythms inhering beneath the processes of full linearizing consciousness. To be able to move beyond the either/or propositions Unamuno presumes, we must recognize that consciousness is process in flow—including extremes of death (no consciousness), life (total awareness), and the countless degrees in between—and that apparent discreteness derived through conscious awareness is not entirely distinct from the rest of physical creation, of which we remain an integral part, dead or alive. Unamuno operates from an incipient dualist prejudice that infects Western culture but which the new theories of consciousness are beginning to undermine.

None of what I've said, however, will ever fully eradicate the pervasive sense that consciousness infects us with an unhappy, discrete awareness of death that will never fully be circumvented. And herein lies the conflict that obsesses Shepard and all Western thought (indeed, all *human* thought). Recognizing our more central place in the physical world, however, may achieve some of the peace we all seek. Metaphysically speaking, moving away from top-down mysticism and toward bottom-up physical comprehension first of personal consciousness and then perhaps of a more universal, emergent consciousness may finally draw us closer than expected to the final answers of purpose, place, and even godhead. Shepard's path through the physical to the numerous subtle pulses he sees operating beneath the surfaces seems exactly the path consciousness theory advocates. The cautious hope Shepard holds out—if we can agree that there is hope—is of the sort and on the order that may best serve his culture.

Shepard's empiricist "mysticism," his flow of performance energy into textual orders, parallels the work of Dennett and other materialist advocates of consciousness. We see in Shepard the body reconnected to its environment and consciousness reconnected to its body. Furthermore, we see in Shepard consciousness altering itself to recognize not merely its discreteness as an individual, "soul-ful" entity but also its place in a yet higher stream of consciousness. Shepard essentially breaks through the block set up by Cartesian dualism and reunites the individual to a larger, more embracing context, creating, by extension, a more embracing consciousness. The fact that memic alteration allows the individual to sacrifice itself, if need be, represents a recognition that there is more to existence than merely discretely individuated biological continuation at any cost.

So, Hoss in *The Tooth of Crime* ironically sacrifices himself precisely in order to preserve his selfhood, inscribed as it is in a grander scheme. And Crow's triumph over Hoss ushers in an apparently even more vital and embracing sense of organic selfhood reflecting the natural flow of change itself. It may also be that Crow's triumph is a step backward in human development (as some critics would argue), but the key point is that the process is ongoing and evolving rather than static and linearly/bivalently definitive. Finding a place in existence entails the self-awareness of the individual finding its place in the grander scheme. As Hoss forced his predecessors consciously to recognize their place and as Crow forces Hoss to acquire an awareness of his place, so will the next generation force Crow to become more fully conscious/aware of his place among the dynamic flow of human self-awareness.

The seeming opposites we see in *Fool for Love, True West,* and *A Lie of the Mind,* for example, are not representative so much of schematized polarities. That would be an error in critical assessment similar to the error seen in assessing Shaffer's characters. Rather, they are the honed-down, bare-boned acknowledgments that context is crucial in the effort to come to terms with our linear self-awareness of discrete existence as well as parallel comprehension of a larger context. In the balance hangs the dilemma of being a "me" or a "we," or, better put, the dilemma of recognizing "I" am a "me" as well as a "we." We must recognize simultaneously that "I think; therefore, I am" as well as "I have context; therefore, I am."

The shifting ground that is Shepard's realism is a sort of heightened recognition of reality itself, blending the external natural world with the internal world of consciousness, revealing in the process the false dichotomy we've previously assumed to inhere in reality. The world is not either "out there" or "in here" but is, quantumlike, both out there and in here, inseparably and unisolatably.

Turning to family as Shepard does in his later works is a turn that I suggest fortunately modifies his earlier, more naive, experimental phase. Stephen J. Bottoms seems to agree:

> His [Shepard's] previous treatments of family themes—*The Rock Garden* and *The Holy Ghostly*—had both presented a son attempting (ambivalently) to shake off the influence of parents. Yet . . . Shepard now felt it was necessary to confront and embrace his origins, rather than avoid them: "I've been trying to escape myself ever since I left home," he wrote in a draft of a letter to his mother, "and I now realize that I have to face things, I can't run forever."[10]

Bottoms describes this search, however, as more than simply constructing a family tree because it evolves to be far more than merely Shepard's own physical search for place and identity as, say, an "American." While recountings of his father's death in a Mexican border town inhabit several of Shepard's plays, Shepard's work does more than exorcize personal demons. Through his stagecraft the recountings develop an almost mythical resonance. Thomas Nash observes of *Buried Child,* for example, "In the course of plot development, the influence of folklore and mythology becomes more forceful, so that the realism of the early scenes fades like twilight,"[11] and he calls the play's plot "a modern version of the central theme of Western mythology, the death and rebirth of the Corn King" (486). Although such intertextuality may not be quite as evident in Shepard's other works, the realism of his other "realist" works nevertheless also fades "like twilight" into a realm of mood that compromises the plays' realist initiations even as they build upon those initiations. The consciously aware serial realm of the real merges with the preconscious parallelly received realm identified by Nash as myth.

Myth, of course, concretizes patterns perceived universally to inhere in the field of human action. As accurate as Nash is regarding *Buried Child,* his observation relates equally well to the flux of Shepard's subsequent writings. They generally begin discretely, as any realist play does, but move into the broader field of vision—recall Gertrude Stein's use of the term *landscape*—designed to be absorbed in a nonlinear, parallel fashion that taps into universals found in nature and finally reflected, though incompletely, in linear consciousness. Consider the following from F. David Peat's *Synchronicity: The Bridge between Mind and Matter:*

> Nature . . . is somewhat like a ballet dancer, the meaning of whose gestures are contained in the whole movement. While it is possible to analyze the motion of a dancer's body by means of photographs, it is clear that each element has its origin in the entire gesture and any static element is therefore incomplete.[12]

Peat continues: "The parallelism between the objective and the subjective aspects of the universe do not so much arise through causal connections, or linear patterns in time, but out of underlying dynamics that are common to both" (115). Mind and matter, claims Peat—along with other proponents of materialist consciousness such as Penrose—are governed *together* by parallel patterns that themselves can only be perceived by parallel reception. The landscapes captured as myth are what Shepard reveals, proceeding from discrete linear—and incomplete—descriptions to parallel descriptions that become, simply, autonomous self-descriptions only incompletely capable of being linearly or discursively described. As they unfold, the plays are essentially the best descriptions of our inner and outer landscapes taken in as a whole in hopes of opening up our serial processes to, at very least, recognize their own incompleteness.

The success of this agenda seems at first glance a mixed blessing, for it reveals the fundamental dilemma of the human condition, namely, that we are simultaneously part of and distinct from the context in which we exist. It is important, however, to recognize that acknowledging this simultaneity is a necessary adjustment, given our centuries-old insistence on exclusively seeing ourselves as distinct from and beyond our context. On the other hand, longing for unadulterated "synchronicity" with our environment—swinging the pendulum to an opposite extreme in this false dichotomy—while obviously (and, by some accounts, tragically) being impossible, may not necessarily be the preferred option either. Recalling the pitfalls of the excluded middle, longing for one extreme over the other very likely should be adjusted to accepting the fact that possessing a mix of both extremes may be less humanity's curse—its problems notwithstanding—than it is humanity's ultimate blessing.

In this mix of equations we see the emergence of complexity theory wherein the whole is more than the sum of its parts. When this recognition is made, insistence on discrete reality diminishes, though the consequences may not always be fully positive. When the empty amoral positivist Duncan in Stoppard's *Jumpers,* for example, senses that altruism is a possibility—that an individual *can* be concerned with more than self-survival—his whole egocentric world system comes crashing down. On the other hand, we *can* refuse to succumb to despair at the sight of such a revelation, as Jerry in Albee's *The Zoo Story* does, literally sacrificing himself so that Peter can be saved from a middle-class, conformist, living death. And, when Hamlet gives in to the special providence found in the fall of sparrow, he becomes more than himself even as he sacrifices himself. The result is we see a system of contextualizing altruism breathing life into a world saved from its stultifying and isolated efforts to negotiate existence in an abstracted void. If an individual is willing selflessly to sacrifice himself for the good of something other than selfhood, then the concrete fabric of self-centered materialism must give way either to mysticism or some materialist replacement. In Shepard's case the materialist replacement is gaining the upper hand.

Theater, Peter Shaffer, and *The Gift of the Gorgon*

Given that Peter Shaffer's agenda aligns so appropriately, and popularly, with the theses of this study, I return to him one last time, looking at his

The Gift of the Gorgon (1993). The play retells the life of a deceased playwright whose work found inspiration in Greek mythology, the presumptive ancient cornerstone of Western civilization. The gathering narrative of this play—told in flashback by the widow of the deceased playwright to his long-lost son of an earlier affair—presents the passion of a man seeking truth in a mundane, civilized world that sets up barriers and refuses to confront primitive passions. This playwright's essential primitivism is confronted by his learned wife, who pleads for restraint while being herself swept into the ravaging current of her husband's earthy passions. At least this is what appears to occur in the play.

As with his earlier works, what Staffer gives us is far more than a tale of irresolvable conflict or hopeless dichotomies. And he also goes further than in his earlier works, for in this tale of a life in the theater informed by Greek sources, Shaffer actually suggests the critical need of the resurrection of theater within our culture, what could reasonably be described as literally approaching Brook's Holy Theatre, wherein the primitive and civilized commingle. In terms of consciousness we see again in this play the need for the parallel brain and serial mind to interact along the very continuum materialist scientists have identified. The linear activities of consciousness, when given full reign, result in static, deathlike existence under the illusion of life. And parallel activities of preconsciousness, when unchecked, lead to an unchecked pandemonium reduced to randomness and inevitable self-destruction. The theater when it is holy—and the mind when it is healthy—encourages a range of interplay between the two, a life on the edge of chaos all-too-infrequently encouraged by modern culture. Furthermore, this interaction can only remain viable and escape the empty solipsism of dualism by recognizing its essential materialist roots.

The scripted narrative of *The Gift of the Gorgon* informs the play, while the play sets the stage for theater performatively to exhibit theater's actual essential function in this play's ambitious undertaking: to materialize in a contemporary frame those universals that were materialized by other means in other times for those ancient predecessors to postmodernism. In essence Shaffer presents an example in which the theater performatively makes *flesh* for postmodernism what myth and religion made flesh for earlier cultures but whose incarnations fail today to speak directly and meaningfully to us.

A look at the philosophy of Shaffer's central character, playwright Edward Damson, reveals Damson's fundamental materialist urge to manifest the mysteries of existence physically. His urge, at least initially, appears in perfect conformity with the materialist urges of contemporary society. Intriguingly, Damson looks for inspiration in Greek mythology and the actual histories of not only the ancient world but also of Cromwellian and contemporary England. Important here is that Damson's (and Shaffer's and contemporary theater's) goal is not new but is virtually as primordial as human consciousness itself: the need to materialize the immaterial, to explain mystery as much as possible, preferably—though rarely in modern times—while preserving the enchantment whose source inspires our continued urge to confront and comprehend that mystery.

Damson speaks of the theater in terms of magic and mystery, but the magic is real, actually a material reality: "At its height, centuries ago in England just as much as Greece, the theater gave us faith and True Astonishment."[13] He continues:

> The audience assembled before it, and peered into it together, in communion. They saw themselves enlarged—made legendary as well as particular, in all their glory and ghastliness. It faced them with towering shapes of their most intense and terrible desires. Undeniable pictures, formed of blazing words. (20)

The "legendary" was made particular, "desire" was given shape, and "words" made pictures. From this materialization of the immaterial Damson concludes the effect:

> They [audiences] came away astounded. Scared. Exalted. Seeing themselves, perhaps for the first time, and their world—which they'd always thought ordinary—lit with the fire of *transformation*! . . . As they walked home, they'd suddenly really *see* the "dragon-wing of night o'erspread the earth"! And inside themselves the glint of their own true beings. Theatre was an *illuminant,* sacred and indispensable. (20–21)

This impassioned speech speaks to the role of theater as distilling reality by making it material on stage and then offering it to the audiences to see, thanks to the glinting illumination before them. *Glint* is a term Damson continually uses to describe those "people who catch the light" (14). Those who "glint" are those who escape the limitations of restrictive, linear sightings to take in the larger landscape of existence. Damson claims to see this glint in his mate, Helen.

In this description we see the illusion of dualism (the Cartesian theater) redirected and bridged by bottom-up material reality. Theater reminds us that the magic or enchantment of reality comes from the very fact that reality need not invoke some ethereally predicated magic to explain itself: its self-evident materialist complexity is itself magic. The dualism of idea versus manifestation, of spirit/soul versus materiality/reality is only illusion. And theater forces us to take the path that dispenses with any need for dualist considerations. Theater brings to the "eye" what the "I" itself desperately needs to undertake: a conscious acceptance of its concrete, integrated reality. The true theater (Holy Theatre?) reminds us that the process of materialization is already complete in the world out there; humans only need to develop an in-here consciousness that comprehends reality as such. The theater re-minds our consciousness, literally and in a material way, to that in us that can attune to the patterns inherent in that reality.

Damson's play within Shaffer's play, *Icons,* presents this theme of the Western world's turning its eyes away from striving to see the real. His play exacts that theme by dramatizing the struggles of Iconoclasm in eighth-century Byzantium. Damson explains: "The quarrel enshrines the most fundamental division in the human race: between abstract mind and concrete mind. Between those who believe God is always invisible—and those who need *illustration* to make them perceive it" (41). Seeing God as flesh, not in a metaphorical but in a literally real sense, and understanding that religious icons were designed to illuminate that truth and, in fact, incarnate that truth are what the eighth-century Iconoclasts assaulted. So, too, argues Damson, was Cromwell (the subject of Damson's second play) a dualistic, pro-idealistic iconoclast of his age (seventeenth-century England) who, like the Byzantine Iconoclasts, destroyed statues and images and insisted on maintaining a separation between the material/real and immaterial/ideal. Damson's argument additionally leaves little doubt why the theaters closed in England and undoubtedly in Constantinople (in fact, in the ancient world in general, once overtaken by Christianity) during these times of iconoclastic ascendancy. Dualism was forcibly imposed on civilization *twice,* as Western theater itself twice discovered its genesis prior to the iconoclastic religious assaults. (It could actually be argued that we're still trying to recover from the spirit that gave rise to Cromwell, who was, not coincidentally, a near contemporary of Descartes.)

Speaking in *Icons,* Emperor Constantine's mother—opposed to her iconoclast son—observes: "Twice He [Christ] has appeared on earth! Once in flesh, now again in *paint!* . . . This is the amazing and the appalling truth. God's Son said, 'I will be seen again by man!' and *my* son said, '*No! I forbid it!*" (45). What is described here is the historical root of a double conspiracy against materialist consciousness from opposite poles, one by iconoclastic spiritualists forbidding materialist contacts and the other by reductive empiricists discounting any spiritual emergence in material reality. Historically, when such enterprises as alchemy attempted to bridge the chasm, they were generally met with one form of hostility or another, either initiated by spiritualists/clergy or materialists/scientists, and usually by both.

So, too, we see the same assault on what Artaud would consider the alchemical nature of the theater. Theaters close or struggle for survival or become entertainment venues when dualism prevails in a culture. Secular as well as religious cultures in effect forbid seeing or even looking for material manifestations of the mysteries and enchantments of existence, opting for dualist ghettoizing by housing spirit in sanctuaries far from the material realities of existence, theater certainly included.

Damson seems accurate in arguing for the materiality of the rhythms and patterns of the world once described by our culture's mystical predecessors as the hand of God. Through understanding material reality, we come closer to understanding that which we formerly understood to be the mystery of the creator. To put Damson's thoughts in terms of consciousness theory, his is an argument favoring a vision of the world enchanted by complexity and chaos, quantum potential, and material consciousness. And within this materialism it is mystery, or at least enchantment toward our sightings of the world, that remains intact.

The problem for the doomed Damson ("damned son") is not his materialist urgings, and it is certainly not his belief that theater effects this materiality. Rather, it is once again (as seen in Shaffer's other works) the dichotomous radicality in which he sees this materiality at work. *Icons* is a smashing success in part because of the tempering influence of Helen, Damson's wife, who insists that he not fully indulge his pandemonious, uncontrolled blood lust on the stage by blinding the iconoclast Constantine onstage, as Damson originally proposed. Rather, she has him reluctantly offer an onstage speech justifying the blinding that will occur offstage.

Here we see an important distinction in Shaffer's play. The stage *can* materialize almost anything it chooses. It *can* present the most cruel of human/natural urges as precisely as life itself—theater's "double"—but perhaps it shouldn't. Here we see the potentially totally liberated parallel urge of the preconscious—complete with its primal and amoral fight-flight responses—checked by a morally predisposed linear consciousness that has before it the choice to accommodate an edge of chaos middle ground between unacceptably absolute randomness (spinning off to death) or similarly unacceptable total control (death by ossification). Clearly, an overweening dependence on conscious linear urges has reduced Helen's classics professor father to the crusty pedant he has become. But Helen's own classical sense that "measure is everything" is appropriately asserted (47). The interactive balance between the primitive, parallelly inspired mental functions and potentially overriding serial mental functions must be maintained.

Failure to maintain some sort of balance results in either sterile pedantry or devastating savagery. Damson, born into a sterile contemporary culture obsessed with serial control, is obsessed with choosing/endorsing the savage alternative. Unfortunately, he is engrossed in bivalence, imprecisely seeing this more savage element of bivalence as the height of Hellenistic civilization (the Apollonian/ Dionysian misapplication described earlier). He has failed to realize the true sophistication of the Greek theater and culture, that it manifested events of savagery *tempered;* its cruelty remained onstage—or, more precisely, offstage—providing a life in the theater for our primitive, even savage, urges but controlling them so that they will *not* spill into the streets of daily existence. The experience in the theater obviates the need for the experience to be experienced beyond the theater.

Damson's *Icons*—thanks to Helen's insistence—succeeded at this level, blending preconscious parallel urges with conscious serial controls. Damson's subsequent efforts do not blend. For *Prerogative,* his Cromwell play, Damson envisions an audience turned rabid by viewing his play and lusting to rip an effigy of the iconoclast Cromwell to shreds, an effigy that is "only canvas and paper—but by the miracle of art . . . will become transubstantiated." Although Helen insists, "All revenge is diseased," Damson responds, "No—only when it's kept unfulfilled" (56).

Damson's third play, *IRE,* depicts a woman's revenge on a terrorist who has killed her child in a bombing. In this work Damson goes utterly unchecked and depicts a ritual murder onstage followed by an invitation to the audience to partake in the ritual. The result is predictable: the audience is overwhelmed by the dramatized cruelty and merely laughs at the play's concluding invitation. Damson—a twisted but gifted psychotic, a grotesque misinterpretation of an Artaudian hero—approaches a solution to contemporary illness and self-delusion but fails to achieve his ends because he fails to comprehend the need for interactive balance rather than an extreme alternative. The failure is a result of not realizing the need to balance the preconscious urges with conscious reflection. Clearly in line with Artaud, Damson is aware of our culture's need to reengage the preconscious. But, ironically, his use of theater forgets the nature of Artaudian doubling: theater and life are each other's double, but they are not the same.

Shaffer, however, does not expose himself to the same fate with his own play. *The Gift of the Gorgon* rather sensationally concludes with a blood-letting in the form of a reenactment of Damson's own ritual sacrifice. And that event satisfies Helen's own primitive urges even as they horrifically work against her conscious controlling mechanisms. As she inadvertently enacts her revenge on Damson, she satisfies an urge that could only be satisfied inadvertently, by a sleight of hand. (Damson tricks her into destroying him.) Paradoxically, the revenge satisfies even as it horrifies. For Helen preconscious urges are satisfied even as the conscious mind/self remains essentially free of responsibility, revealing that in Helen primitivism is alive but controlled, the very thing that makes her alive.

This complex mix also succeeds in the theater among the audience to Shaffer's play but in a more healthy way. Throughout the performance we have witnessed preconscious transgressive urges manifest on the stage, purging us of the basic urges reminiscent of our fight-flight instincts buried beneath our higher linear consciousnesses. Our civilized, controlling linear consciousness has temporarily been circumvented by the materializing machinations of the stage, kindling an awareness of our preconscious survivalist instincts in ways that we would never (or should never) allow ourselves to indulge in our pre- or posttheatrical experiences. Shaffer neither requires audiences to partake of a blood communion, nor does he force audiences to accept the sacrifice in mythic/theological/magical terms. Rather, the play offers a concluding sacrifice of Damson that experientially recalls our primitive preconscious urges. And, simultaneously, while we are likely actually to be impelled to want to see Damson's death, the play also excites a counter-urge for forgiveness, given that the play ends with a reflective winding down, also experiential. We see both urges dramatized through Helen even as Shaffer has effected the experience among his audience members.

Shaffer has engaged his audience in the material experience. The complex feelings *experienced* by *witnessing* the play—as the ancients had themselves seen the world anew in their theaters—forces upon Shaffer's audiences the opportunity to judge their own responses to the intensely problematic conditions concluding the play. Shaffer's play offers a modern audience essentially what Damson claimed ancient theater did for its audiences: to see and test responses within the theater in such a way that, "as they walked home, they'd suddenly really *see* the 'dragon-wing of night o'erspread the earth'!" (21). The theater is quite literally a performing *thought experiment.*

The theater's material reality provides the experience of such taboo urges, thereby possibly alleviating the urge to commit such acts beyond the theater. In the process the performance experience loosens the grip of untested linear conclusions and allows a reconfiguration of assumptions and dispositions in the process. Here we can return to the play's title and to Nietzsche, who observed of Dionysian frenzy:

> It would appear that the Greeks were for a while quite immune from these feverish excesses which must have reached them by every known land or sea route. What kept Greece safe was the proud, imposing image of Apollo, who in holding up the head of the Gorgon to those brutal and grotesque Dionysiac forces subdued them.[14]

The alternating poisoning and sanctifying blood of the Gorgon, controlled by Apollo, led to "rites of universal redemption, of glorious transfiguration," as Nietzsche puts it (26). As a result, "It is as though in the Greek festivals a sentimental trait of nature were coming to the fore, as though nature were bemoaning the fact of her fragmentation, her decomposition into separate individuals" (27). Shaffer's play—a play, not a novel—invites something far less ferocious than Damson's "neo-ancient" theater, for Shaffer's very balance signals its health. We enter a field of experience that puts our neural networks to the test and allows for necessary adjustments.

The theater, Shaffer demonstrates, is a windowed mirror allowing us experientially to apprehend processes of conscious consideration either ignored or left unconsidered/unexamined through the course of daily life. Finally, theater promotes the experience of heightened consciousness. But it is not a ratification of linear processing over the non-linear, or vice versa; rather, it is a demonstration of the necessary interaction situated somewhere between the extremes of the exclusively parallel and the exclusively serial. In *The Gift of the Gorgon* Shaffer has created theater in which these processes of heightened consciousness operate, loosening rigid rationalism and opening mind more fully to a balance between parallel and serial operating mode, creating a nonlinear infusion overriding—though not totally defeating or invalidating—linear constructions.

Moving toward a Unified Cultural Consciousness:
David Edgar's *Pentecost*

In *Six Degrees of Separation* (1990) John Guare places the following lines in the mouth of Ouisa, his tried-and-failed liberal heroine:

> I read somewhere that everybody on this planet is separated by only six other people. Six degrees of separation. Between us and everybody else on this planet. . . . I find that A] tremendously comforting that we're so close and B] like Chinese water torture that we're so close. Because you have to find the right six people to make the connection. . . . I am bound to everyone on this planet by a trail of six people.[15]

This observation of human interconnectivity stems from an actual piece of scientific research that worked from the assumption that each individual is connected to a hundred friends and acquaintances, each of whom has one hundred friends and acquaintances, etc.[16] The math concludes that all humans are separated from one another by only six degrees. The point Guare picks up from this calculation is that we are a species linked closer to one another than either we previously knew or than we'd often like to think. We are all part of a vast but intricately connected human network.

This network of six degrees among members of the human community in many ways echoes the human neural network, though to a less expansive degree given that each human neuron actually has around a thousand contacts each. If we accept the assumptions of the materialist position that consciousness is a decentralized process rising from the bottom up, then it is possible to connect these human and neural-networked observations and envision the human cultural network as at least potentially reflecting the network that produces human consciousness. Given that consciousness is itself a process emerging from lower-order interactions rising to levels that are more than the sum of their parts, it is further possible to envision the networked human community achieving at least some degree of collective consciousness, if not finally achieving that higher-order level of self-awareness equivalent to that which we generally label full human consciousness/awareness. Patricia Churchland, in Roger Lewin's book *Complexity,* makes the following observation regarding the human neural system:

> The nervous system is a parallel-processing device, and this conveys several interesting properties. For a start, signals are processed in many different

networks simultaneously. Next, neurons are themselves very complex little analogue computers. Last, the interactions *between* neurons are nonlinear and modifiable. Real neuron networks are nonlinear dynamic systems,
and hence new properties can emerge at the network level.[17]

It is not at all far-fetched to see parallels between the neural network and
the human communal network, wherein the limited capacities of the
discrete individual can network and emergently produce collective
human capacities greater than the sum of their discrete parts.

Studies of the sociability of ants, for example, have uncovered parallels between ant colonies and the neural network. Edward O. Wilson
observes: "An individual social insect processes less information than an
individual solitary insect, but as part of an aggregate activity, the social
insect contributes to more complex computation. The colony works as
a single organism."[18] Given the bottom-up concept presumed in the
materialist enterprise, this idea of discrete entities combining to create a
"superorganism" through emergent, greater-than-the-parts processes
applies not only to ant communities but potentially to human ones as
well. At whatever level along this collective neural network we may
legitimately be able collectively to aspire, it seems we need more fully to
be aware of our collective potential and to aspire to go as far as possible.

David Edgar's *Pentecost* (1995) is a play that reveals the current
human failure to accept and utilize this communal consciousness paradigm, mired as we are in the modern world with the notion either of
hopeless and irreconcilable individuation or of some ultimate top-down
controlling agent akin to the illusion of a central operating unit. The two
misconceptions actually go hand in hand. Because of the putative triumph of the individual, if there is to be order to our Western social constructs it has generally been assumed that there is a need for at least some
form of a central controlling agent—a government—directing otherwise
randomly discrete human events. After all, our obsession with discrete
individuality has led to top-down assumptions that have affected social
structure from the level of individual human activity to levels of ethnic,
religious, and national groupings, first-, second-, and third-world status,
and East versus West dichotomies, seemingly verifying that there is no
bottom-up rising organizing principle in operation. Organization must
therefore be imposed directly from a top-down authority. Or so it
seems.

Humanity's failure, it appears, is a failure to recognize our interrelated status, which actually surfaces despite our selfish, individualistic

urges to deny it. Dynamic, emergent changes occur despite such resistance, in many cases precisely on the edge of chaos as science predicts. And, despite pervading suspicions, there is evidence that decentralizing our controls on human activity may result in new, productive, viable bottom-up social structures. In the case of *Pentecost* Edgar tests this thesis by placing us at an actual geopolitical edge of chaos—the Balkans—a contact zone of influence resisted by a dominant, European culture. In "Rewriting Europe: *Pentecost* and the Crossroads of Migration" Stanton B. Garner Jr. observes:

> As the categories of East and West become freed from the imposition of Cold War bipolarity, a Europe still constructed in terms of western identity has become, once again, a Border Theater, where efforts to create an internally border-free economic zone are matched by heightened anxiety concerning contamination from the outside and radical population shifts within.[19]

While the perceived contamination "pollutes" the purity of discrete Eurocentric identity, Edgar proposes that this ostensible pollution should, instead, be considered interactive pollenization or fertilization, something that, in fact, historically predates the currently dramatized interaction. Simply put, such pollution or pollenization—whichever term suits—is the very thing that created the Europe we now know and are working so hard to preserve from further pollenization/pollution.

Pentecost recounts a fictional case wherein an archaeological discovery in an unspecified Balkan country—the geographical edge between West and East, developed world and third-world—by art historians leads to a debate on the historical origins of thought leading to the European Renaissance, previously believed to have sprung almost mystically (idiopathically?) from European roots and first sprouted in Italy. The suggestion Edgar makes—a valid one—is that non-Western sources influenced this rebirth, that this rebirth, in fact, owes a debt to non-Western allies in thought that the triumphant West has refused to acknowledge.

The focus in the play involves the unveiling of the revolutionary concept of perspective in art thought to have originated in Italy by the artist Giotto, working in the 1300s at "the frontier between the medieval and modern world."[20] The traditional Western presumption, of course, is that this discovery of perspective was somehow spontaneous and, furthermore, that it originated in Europe, demonstrating the superiority of Western European thought over that of other cultures. What evolves in the plot of the play is a quite feasible suggestion that at this Balkan edge of chaos between East and West (though this actual geographic location may better be considered a metaphor for some intellectual "place" between East and West) a rich and dynamic pandemonium of circumstances led multivalently and multiculturally to this breakthrough in perception and the arts. As one of the play's art historians, Oliver, observes:

> We have this mindset, still, about the mediaeval period. That everybody knows their places, no-one travels, no-one moves. To each his walled garden. Whereas actually mediaeval Europe was a chaos of diaspora. Every frontier teeming, every crossroads thronged. So it is frankly more than possible that a painter could have set off in the early years of the thirteenth century. From what perils we cannot imagine. And coming to this place [in the Balkans], and being taken captive, and offering for his release to paint a picture, here, so akin to nature that its figures seem to live and breath. (98)

This chaos of diaspora, this pandemonium of existence, reconverges and rises emergently from the bottom up to produce this breakthrough of perspective:

> So he [the artist] has two eyes, and they tell him things have three dimensions, and [equipped with the geometry of the East] he paints the world that way. With all the innocence, that freshness and that rage [upon first hearing the Western myth of Christ's passion], we bring to things when we come upon them for the very first—first time. (99)

The idea of diaspora is earlier brought up by the play's Balkan minister Czaba, who reminds us, "Is it not Babel, where God invented all different language, to stop mankind build stairway to heaven?" (20). In the Judeo-Christian myth God creates the babel of tongues to minimize the emergent potential of a unified humanity in order to prevent our self-manufactured bottom up "stairway to heaven," as Czaba describes it. If in this myth God initiated this fragmentation of humanity, we now see that humanity itself is self-inflicted with the resignation to fragmentation. We actually need no longer insert a willful God into the story.

This notion of a self-willed fragmentation is the cornerstone of several significant subplots in the play, the overriding issue involving Asian, African, and non-Western European refugees pleading for asylum in the West only to be destroyed by a Western counterterrorist assault that destroys virtually everything in its sight—refugees as well as innocent bystanders—including the painting that likely verified that perspectivism was actually a multicultural triumph. As the culmination of a pervading self-interest presented throughout the play, the counterterrorist assault preserves ego-centered self-interest at the expense of an incipient, bottom-up recognition of a common, emergent humanity.

Beyond the narrative of the play, however, what evolves for the audience is a growing awareness of a common humanity whose essence transcends, or should transcend, such superficial distinctions as religious affiliation, economic status, geographical and national origin, race, gender. Edgar inserts a cacophony of national and ethnic variety—a literal Babel—providing onstage opportunities to develop sympathies for all factions, offering no single centralized truth except that centralized control of any sort hinders or defeats the natural processes that could be expected if only discrete self-interest would give way to decentralized emergence. Garner accurately observes of this multilingual onslaught—seeing the stage as "a place of verbal multiplicity" (8)—that it "subvert[s] the idea of unitary perspective and the fiction of an invisible universalizing subject" (9). Difference is celebrated even as common roots are acknowledged.

Tragically, as such revelations are crystallized, the play terminates with the militaristic incursion, supported presumably by the United States, and a return to a fragmented status quo dominated by centralized authority is guaranteed. The triumphant Czaba summarizes the doctrine of centralized control, here regarding antiterrorist tactics but representative of all top-down control of the natural process:

> First you limit access of world outside. Move everything from field of vision. Don't give phone number so they must always wait for you to call. Change over guy on phone so different languages [contribute to the confusion]. Then slowly build up routine. You order mealtime. Control all aspects of environment. Heat, light. And gradually they turn to child. (102)

The strict linear control of all input reduces the life and the options of those resisting top-down domination, in this or other situations. Add to this the practice of reducing the united group into a bunch of discrete units by granting some but not all the members a promise of asylum—having them move from solidarity to discrete self-interest—and the status quo will undoubtedly triumph over any possibility of fruitful integrating change.

Garner makes an interesting additional point regarding the play, seeing displacement and migration as being increasingly the modern human condition. He agrees with James Clifford's criticism of "twentieth-century ethnography for privileging relations of dwelling over relations of travelling and proposed a revised ethnographic practice that would approach cultures in terms of movements, interactions, border crossings, hybridity" (10). The play, of course, supports this proposed shift in perspective, and the perspective intriguingly supports that which we previously saw supported by David Bohm's linguistic "rheomode" proposal. Movement, flow, and becoming should be privileged over discrete concepts of place and being.

The various discrete postures and "identities" *Pentecost* positions against one another aptly summarizes contemporary cultures as fragmented and ego ridden by design, in which self-interest finds reward primarily at the expense of some demonized other. This is Darwinism interpreted and culturally adopted in its most competitively individualistic manifestation. Recently, however, the new sciences have begun to reinterpret the conclusions of Darwinism, not to discredit it but to realign it in ways that better fit the data provided by nature. This reinterpretation has accepted the notion of survival of the fittest as indeed central to evolutionary processes but suggests its meaning has less to do with individualistically competitive fitness than it has with a collectively cooperative fitness, an ability harmoniously to negotiate an appropriate and appropriately flexible place within the flow that is nature. The Western ideal of rugged individualism—more a cultural desire spawned by an "evolution" of the rights of man than a natural reality—is now being replaced by a sense of cooperative communalism: often, species survive better in groups than as individual units.

Within the sciences of complexity and consciousness the example of slime mold is often cited as a sort of paradigm.[21] Slime mold is a life form that alternately operates as a single cell and as a collective organism. When food is plentiful, the mold operates as single cells, even propagating by cell division. But when food resources are depleted, the single autonomous cells collectivize and actually construct themselves into a relatively complex "slug," complete with specialized parts such as heads and tails. This slug-conglomerate then relocates through coordinated locomotion, generates spores (a fairly sophisticated and specialized propagation process), splits open, and casts its spores to the wind. This strange adaptation of collectivized awareness based on mutual need and the ensuing complex cooperation among previously discrete organisms summarizes in its most efficient form the function and process of consciousness as typified in virtually every natural occurrence: consciousness is the product of some recognition of the need for mutual cooperation in order to increase chances of survival, from an individual neural level potentially to a collectivized human level.

To less spectacular degrees this process of collective consciousness explains not only organic units such as animals but also insect colonies (as previously noted), fish schools, bird flocks, mammal herds, packs, and pods. Science is beginning to recognize the "consciousness of collective groups" devised in all its array of complexity as a means of increasing species survivability. These groups seem to have/be more than a sum of individual consciousnesses within the group, exhibiting something of an emergent consciousness that is more than a sum of its discrete conscious parts. (On a less positive note, think also of the consciousness of human mobs.) This neo-Darwinian vision that cooperation is crucial to survival is yet one more dimension to the changing notions of consciousness as an emergent, natural phenomenon. What we have here is a sort of "ecto"-consciousness similar in every crucial regard to the more traditional "endo"-consciousness we accept as inhering within living organisms.

What Edgar asks in *Pentecost,* and what we increasingly find in numerous other works of art as well, is that collective human consciousness be allowed to grow and prosper from the bottom up and that it be activated for the greater good of the species. Virtually against our will, human history is dotted with bottom-up intercultural interactions that have resulted in "quantum leaps" of human advancement, improving in the process the likelihood of continued human survival and development. As Shaffer's *Gift of the Gorgon* warned against the dangers of indulging a too-dominant pandemonium of primitive impulses unchecked by our higher self-awareness, so Edgar's *Pentecost* (and Kushner's *Angels in America,* too) warns us of the danger of a too-self-aware urge toward discrete, individualistic self-control and static order controlled from the top down. It's a dangerous individualism sighted either literally at the individual level, or, more generally, at the level wherein pockets of individuated difference are valorized over our common human and integral emergent potential. In both cases we need to realize that the law of excluded middle needs to be challenged in favor of exploring the vast middle ground between the extremes of parallel non-self-aware input and serial self-aware control from above. We need to adjust our own understanding of consciousness away from the central homunculus idea and toward a decentralized sense of flow along a neural continuum.

Although slime mold is hardly an attractive image, it nonetheless captures the essential idea of Edgar's play. Furthermore, it articulates/projects the material and demystified nature of consciousness that theater itself strives to materialize before us via emergent patterns and rhythms, uniting its participants (onstage and in the audience) in a cohering cooperative movement in sympathy with the patterns and rhythms of nature, themselves already configured within our consciousness. In *Pentecost* Edgar dramatizes the literal Babel of human language (at least five languages are utilized with much frequency) separating individuals, despite the common roots they reveal by the frequent retelling of folk myths/stories on the stage. And many of the refugees disenfranchised by disrupting international politics are interestingly "naturally multilingual," coming from locations with multiple identities and ultimately no stable identities. The idea of discrete identity is dissolved here on the edge of Western certainty and non-Western uncertainty (uncomfortable dichotomies to be sure but at least an apt general mapping of the issue). Perhaps the Balkans, and all destabilized regions of our planet, is where our lessons on the future of humanity lies—literally, on the geographical frontiers of order/disorder as well as consciously on the same frontier between the pandemonium of parallel input and the seriality of self-consciousness.

Searching for and exclusively insisting upon difference, finally, undermines the emergent potential of our human cultural neural network. Edgar's painting, on center stage, is the image that pulls the point together onstage. But the audience experience is perhaps even more central. We experience, first of all, the humanity of these other refugees so often demonized by media and standard, Western-created histories. We follow a complex web of clues and dead ends in what becomes a hunger actually to verify the authenticity of the theory pertaining to the painting, namely, that it is the result of a creative interplay between East and West. And, clearly, rather than experiencing relief that the refugees' hostages are freed by the commando assault (most of them, anyway), we are dismayed by the brutality of the event, especially considering the media spin that would likely be placed on such a "terrorist" event if it were real (and likely has been placed on such events in our actual history). The recognition that we have failed to recognize our six degrees of separation in the past is almost overwhelming.

To coin a phrase, Edgar espouses an ecto-ecological consciousness in his theater, cooperatively interactive (ecto) and aware of its crucial interrelation with nature (ecology). If competitiveness and isolated/fragmented consciousnesses were somehow necessary in our most recent stages of human development (an arguable point), it has now become increasingly evident that we are entering a time when an ecto-ecological consciousness may become absolutely vital to human survival. The theater both informs us of the need and (re)awakens within us the mechanisms needed to surface in order to exact the change.

The patterns of existence reverberating within materiality are the "things" theater fleetingly captures as its life hangs onstage in the balance between existence and memory, a place of no-place revealing a thing that is no-thing. Consciousness, too, is in effect a no-thing and no-place, but, like theater, its emergent qualities can literally effect reality/materiality. Awareness of new paradigms borne of dire necessity can exact material change through the potential of memic alteration. Edgar asks for such changes in consciousness and for material changes naturally to follow as well.

That Edgar ends *Pentecost* so devastatingly and bleakly speaks to Edgar's personal pessimism (or perhaps only to his sense of the melodramatic), but it is evident that resignation to and acceptance of the status quo will lead to no good—to put it mildly.

Looking Forward

Materializations of heightened and altered consciousness abound in the theater in almost precisely the ways that materialist theories of consciousness found in the sciences would predict, aiding in approaching a fuller understanding of the magic of theater. Shakespeare, again, reminds us of the material reality of the "ineffable." In *A Midsummer Night's Dream* Theseus observes:

> as imagination bodes forth
> The forms of things unknown, the poet's pen
> Turns them to shapes, and gives to airy nothing
> A local habitation and a name.
> (5.1.14–17)

This transformation of airy nothings to material reality may at first sight be the work of a poetical alchemist. But we now realize that, in fact, the transformation is really "merely" a re-formation, a return of idea to its material roots.

Getting precisely at the heart of this formative, materializing magic may never be fully achieved, as getting at the heart of consciousness itself may ultimately never fully be achieved. But we surely can squeeze the domain that we attribute to magic, or mystery, as we come closer and closer to understanding various elements and events formerly hidden under that enfolding (though receding) mystical veil. In the process we may do well to reconsider how we use such terms. Colin McGinn, for example, observes: "When I say consciousness is a mystery, I'm making a naturalistic point about human cognitive abilities, not about any mystical quality of consciousness itself. Consciousness may be a rather simple biological characteristic, like digestion."[1] Subscribing to a materialist bottom-up agenda rather than presuming a vitalist top-down insertion, our pursuit of the mysteries of consciousness, theater, life itself, need not

result in our giving over the search to inscrutability; rather, we can progressively close in on the mysterious, at very least until we hit some wall
through which we are cognitively unable to pass. Finding god need not
be any more of a separate epistemological enterprise than the scientific
pursuit of, say, life or consciousness, or the heart of Holy Theatre.

At this point I find several theater events worth mentioning, productions that have embedded themselves in my consciousness for reasons I had not comprehended until I began this project. One was experienced nearly two decades ago, the other quite recently. That first one
was Théâtre du Soleil's production of Shakespeare's *Richard II,* performed in French (in Paris) on a minimalist black stage intermittently
assaulted by waves of backdrop color (in the form of parachute lengths
of vivid supple cloth of gold and red). Invading the darkness, percus-
sionists punctuated an aggressive Kabuki-style acting mode. In part
because the subtleties of Shakespeare's characterization were minimized
by the formalized acting style and because Shakespeare's poetry fell vic-
tim to the aggressive vocalizations of the speeches, what surfaced as clear
as anything I've ever seen on the stage was the unadulterated necessity of
literally and materially placing on the stage not characters but *rhythm* and
pattern. Here I saw it highlighted, and that experience has drawn me to
conclude that patterns and rhythms are essential to every successful (perhaps, here I mean "Holy") stage product. At that point I felt I understood Artaud, but, until I read and digested the materialist theories of
consciousness put forward by the new sciences of complexity and chaos,
I didn't quite grasp what Artaud had to do with the world, other than,
say, in a metaphorical and poetically abstract sense.

My second moving theater experience occurred in Galway, Ireland,
at a performance of the Druid Theatre's production of Vincent Woods's
At the Black Pig's Dyke. The production integrated a traditional
O'Casey-esque drama of betrayal and suffering with a mummer's play
serving seamlessly, though peripherally, as nondiscursive commentary.
The mummers quickly outdistanced the play's realist narrative in effect
and interest. But the rhythms and underpinnings of the mummers would
very likely have been lost in impressionistic abstraction without the narrative it reflected and commented upon. One interdependently required
the other.

It seems that these rhythms and patterns, cited by chaos and complexity theories and now studied under light of consciousness theory,
have revealed the reasons for their resonance. They beg that we consider
a new form of epistemological structuralism but one that is biologically

rather than linguistically predicated. After all, the hard wiring of human brains is a structural human constant, and the rhythms and patterns the brain is designed to intercept are the rhythms and patterns that order nature and that, through neural evolution, helped to build the brain and, ultimately, mind. Quite simply, the rhythms and patterns sighted by chaos/complexity theory to inhere in nature have contributed to the evolutionary development of the brain, resulting in an effective, even miraculous, circularity.

It is becoming increasingly apparent that the universe and the brain/mind are naturally sympathetically synchronized: when a natural rhythm occurs, the brain is there naturally to receive and respond. Ultimately, we need the vibrations of preconscious experience at least as much as we need accesses to linearly conscious mind in, say, the form of language and discursivity.

Clearly, these theory models of the brain/mind inform more than just theater. They inform us of theater's function and mysteries, and they then work with theater to tell us much about existence. For example, what we have seen of the hard-wire structure of the brain supports the notion of Jungian archetypes, tied in as they must be to fundamental universal cognition. And it explains why Artaud could be so attracted to exotic Balinese dance, why Yeats was drawn to Noh drama. It's because we all have much in common, thanks to universal mental hard wiring, despite culturally manufactured soft-wire differences. Through this retooled lens of science (and theater) we also now see more clearly how our soft-wire potentialities explain those cultural difference, the result of various independent culturally manufactured memic (r)evolutions of our soft wiring networks. A point further should be made that, though these differences are factually real, they are truly materially superficial. Ultimately, we have more *in common* with one another than the current apparent evidence suggests. Together, that blend typically described as preconscious and conscious is what should give humanity reason for hope, rather than a sense of inescapable or unavoidable entropic despair.

So, when Tony Kushner's *Angels in America* blends significant realism with the very nearly supernatural in ways that insist on sighting the higher levels of an almost mystically patterned consciousness, it is the grounding in the linearly concrete events exhibited in plot that feed back into a hope for materially emergent transformation. The grounding is the key in thinking about and producing the play. Ignoring this crucial point jeopardizes the success of any production of the work.

Then, too, there's Tom Stoppard's *Arcadia,* simultaneously talking its way through chaotics and structurally performing the processes discursively presented. The nonlinear performance mode infects the brain's neural system even as the text speaks to the linear processing units of mind. And the painful, poignant final dance of bivalence into overlapping multivalent realities and potentialities sticks with the audience even if the discursive wit sometimes escapes our focused, linearizing mental gaze.

The ways in which the rhythms of such works ground themselves in and rely upon the materiality of what went on onstage are the things that make them magical, to use that precritical, prematerial term. But, of course, that sort of vague assessment leaves a taste in one's mouth that something more must be said, that something more than inexplicable magic has occurred. Perhaps still unacceptably short of full explanation by many critical standards, consciousness theory does, nonetheless, come closer to understanding what made these works magical, equipped as we now are with the tools borrowed from science to understand the interaction between material reality and consciousness as it is now described.

The point is that sightings of instances of resistance to reductionism, linearity, bivalence, and dualism exist at many turns in the theater. Looking for them with the clarity offered by the rigors of the new sciences should open our eyes to new ways of viewing works of theater. Furthermore, perhaps by being equipped with these new scientifically endorsed and formalized understandings, theater practitioners may be better able to move forward in their efforts to assist in exacting the sorts of paradigm shifts they and their scientific colleagues have striven to promote. While Hamlet was correct in his day to warn his friend, "There are more things in heaven and earth, Horatio, / Than are dreamt of in your philosophy," Hamlet was not aware that "philosophy" (that is, "natural philosophy," or science) would someday evolve to the point it has today. The result has been a sort of groping forward—two steps forward and one step back—in that march toward clarity that has very likely benefited from the musings of the artist, current impressions of the value of art notwithstanding.

Indeed, I would suggest that the interaction between the two camps is mutually beneficial, for scientists can only benefit from the imaginative rigors of the theater by moving out of laboratories and into auditoriums to see exactly the things they are searching for but in another light and from a different perspective.

United—or reunited—the sciences and arts could effect the changes envisioned by cutting-edge artists and scientists alike. Perhaps evolving to be foes no longer, artists and scientists are beginning directly to influence one another in numerous fruitful ways. Tom Stoppard, for example, has been directly influenced by quantum mechanics and chaos theory in his plays *Hapgood* and *Arcadia*. Michael Frayn, too, has seen the value of blending science into art in his work *Copenhagen*. And, as noted earlier, even unabashed scientific reductionists such as Francis Crick have evoked a need to discover some as-yet undiscovered Shakespeare to convert scientific equations to a language fit for public staging. F. David Peat, another from that cutting-edge "new" scientific camp, is even reported to have entered the world of theater, among other arts, writing for both stage and radio.

The list of those actively bridging the two worlds of arts and sciences is still quite finite. Less obvious are the occasions when a sort of emergent osmosis occurs. Attending plays today often leaves me with a sense that playwrights and directors must surely know the work of these new scientists. And the reverse is true when I read the writings of these scientists: surely, they must know Wilson, Shepard, Shaffer, Edgar. Usually, of course, I simply *wish* they knew each other's work, knowing full well that it is not often yet the case.

In one case in which the nexus has been directly made, the results have been very satisfying. The science specialist Roger Highfield (coauthor of *Frontiers of Complexity* [1995], among others) attended and actually reviewed Tom Stoppard's *Arcadia* in the *London Daily Telegraph* (15 April 1993), observing of the performance, "I felt moved to shout for an encore on its opening night." Indeed, I think shouts of "encore" could resound within the scientific community as well as in the theater world if only each camp would at least occasionally visit the camp of the other.

This book has attempted to outline avenues through which these visitations could be most productively engaged. In the process it has additionally attempted to put at ease yet another camp. Those who adhere to traditional religious beliefs should not be disheartened by either the new sciences or the theater. It seems to me that church/synagogue, stage, and lab are all in search of the same things and that no one venue will ever fully displace another. If, as I've suggested, science and stage have succeeded at putting us closer in touch with materializations of "soul," they have nonetheless *not* disproved the possibility of some moral creationist/god existing beyond the physical world. If one chooses to terminate a forever-receding sense of essence by positing a first cause, then god is an excellent choice. If the patterns we are now working more fully to come into contact with must also be commingled with a moral originator, then so be it. The god of traditional religions perhaps has its place.

On the other hand, if the amoral rhythms and patterns cited/sighted here to be the essence of existence are sufficient, then so be it as well. In the spirit of Occam's razor and Pascal's wager, a natural morality predicated on a notion of ecological good is the result. But note that we are approaching an integrationist view here of the material and spiritual. One perspective does not deny/disconfirm the other; it merely redirects focus. True religion—either gathered from hallowed texts or gleaned from nature—honors the world of which we are part. True religion advocates natural morality, arguing that what is "good" is good universally. It argues against *ego*system and for *eco*system.

This, I believe, is what the new sciences call for, a call that rejects the reductionist abuses and logical manipulations of the past in favor of an integrationist, increasingly fully conscious and fluid reengagement with a nature we have until only recently worked so hard to deny as part of our own beings, choosing, instead, to manipulate it as some "other" set out there for our own egotistical gains.

Theater and science are increasingly rejoining to present an awareness of selfhood, but it is a selfhood that is developing an inescapable, heightened awareness of our place within the whole. We've heard this refrain in the past; we now have a culture looking to the future and positioned on the verge of rediscovering its essential, critical truth.

Notes

Notes to Chapter 1

1. Joseph Wood Krutch, *The Measure of Man: On Freedom, Human Values, Survival, and the Modern Temper* (1953; rpt., New York: Grosset and Dunlap, 1968), 177.

2. Laurie Garret, *The Coming Plague: Newly Emerging Diseases in a World Out of Balance* (New York: Farrar, Straus and Giroux, 1995).

3. William W. Demastes, *Theater of Chaos: Beyond Absurdism, into Orderly Disorder* (New York: Cambridge University Press, 1998).

4. Quoted in Lawrence Leshan, *The Medium, the Mystic and the Physicist* (New York: Viking Press, 1966), 85.

5. Elinor Fuchs, *The Death of Character* (Bloomington: Indiana University Press, 1995).

6. Robert P. Crease, *The Play of Nature: Experimentation as Performance* (Bloomington: Indiana University Press, 1993), 109.

7. Gordon Armstrong, "Theatre as a Complex Adaptive System," *New Theatre Quarterly* 13:51 (August 1997): 278.

8. See Peter Brook, *The Empty Space* (New York: Atheneum, 1968).

9. Peter Brook, "Any Event Stems from Combustion: Actors, Audiences, and Theatrical Energy," *New Theatre Quarterly* 8:30 (May 1992): 107.

10. Bert O. States, *Great Reckonings in Small Rooms: On the Phenomenology of Theater* (Berkeley: University of California Press, 1985).

11. Quoted in States, *Great Reckonings in Small Rooms*, 61, from Émile Zola, "A Naturalism on the Stage," *The Experimental Novel and Other Essays*, trans. Belle M. Sherman (New York: Haskell House, 1964), 151.

12. David H. Hesla, *The Shape of Chaos: An Interpretation of the Art of Samuel Beckett* (Minneapolis: University of Minnesota Press, 1971), 193.

13. See Robert Brustein, *The Theatre of Revolt* (Boston: Little, Brown, 1964).

14. In *Art and Physics* (New York: William Morrow, 1991) Leonard Shlain brilliantly explains how modern and contemporary art both reflect and encourage recent scientific visions of the world. A similar case can be made of much modern and contemporary experimental theater. What is missing in these arguments, however, is the point that, such art-science connections notwithstanding, neither the art nor science community has succeeded in capturing the popular imagination. This study will, in fact, observe experimental breakthroughs. But I will extend the point by noting limitations in popular reception and digestion, suggesting the need to highlight such advances not just to an elite few but to larger sections of our population as well, through the larger venues of the popular theater experience.

Notes to Chapter 2

1. Stuart Kauffman, *At Home in the Universe: The Search for Laws of Self-Organization and Complexity* (New York: Oxford University Press, 1995), 92.

2. Gordon Armstrong, "Theatre as a Complex Adaptive System," *New Theatre Quarterly* 51 (August 1997): 278.

3. Antonio R. Damasio, *Descartes' Error: Emotion, Reason, and the Human Brain* (New York: G. P. Putnam's Sons, 1994), 248.

4. Erich Harth, *The Creative Loop: How the Brain Makes a Mind* (Reading, Mass.: Addison-Wesley, 1993), xvii.

5. Daniel C. Dennett, *Consciousness Explained* (Boston: Little, Brown, 1991), 29.

6. Gilbert Ryle, *The Concept of Mind* (London: Hutchinson, 1949), 15–16.

7. A notable example is Arthur Koestler, *The Ghost in the Machine* (Chicago: Henry Regnery Co., 1967).

8. Owen Flanagan, *The Science of Mind,* 2d ed.(Cambridge: MIT Press, 1991), 310.

9. David J. Chalmers, *The Conscious Mind* (New York: Oxford University Press, 1996).

10. Bert O. States, *Great Reckonings in Little Rooms: On the Phenomenology of Theater* (Berkeley: University of California Press, 1985), 80.

11. See Stanton B. Garner Jr., *Bodied Spaces: Phenomenology and Performance in Contemporary Drama* (Ithaca: Cornell University Press, 1994).

12. Maurice Merleau-Ponty, *Phenomenology of Perception,* trans. Colin Smith (London: Routledge, 1962), 57.

13. Elinor Fuchs, *The Death of Character: Perspectives on Theater after Modernism* (Bloomington: Indiana University Press, 1996), 5.

14. Francis Crick, *The Astonishing Hypothesis: The Scientific Search for the Soul* (New York: Touchstone, 1994).

15. William R. Uttal, *The Psychobiology of Mind* (Hillsdale, N.J.: Lawrence Erlbaum, 1978), 208.

16. John C. Eccles, *Evolution of the Brain: Creation of the Self* (London: Routledge, 1989), 237.

Notes to Chapter 3

1. J. L. Styan, *Modern Drama in Theory and Practice,* 3 vols. (New York: Cambridge University Press, 1981).

2. Bert O. States, *Great Reckonings in Little Rooms: On the Phenomenology of Theater* (Berkeley: University of California Press, 1985), 80.

3. Marc Robinson, *The Other American Drama* (New York: Cambridge University Press, 1994), 2.

4. Gordon Armstrong, "Theatre as a Complex Adaptive System," *New Theatre Quarterly* 51 (August 1997): 280.

5. Arthur Miller, *Death of a Salesman* (New York: Viking Press, 1949), 11.

6. Eric Bentley, Review of *Cat on a Hot Tin Roof*, *New Republic* (4 April 1955): 22.

7. Owen Flanagan, *The Science of the Mind*, 2d ed. (Cambridge: MIT Press, 1991), 316.

8. Laurene V. Faussett, *Fundamentals of Neural Networks: Architectures, Algorithms, and Applications* (Englewood Cliffs, N.J.: Prentice-Hall, 1994), 3.

9. Oscar Wilde, *The Importance of Being Earnest* (New York: Avon, 1965), 28.

10. Leo Jacubinsky, qtd. in Boris Eichenbaum, "The Theory of the Formal Method," in *Russian Formalist Criticism: Four Essays,* ed. Lee T. Lemon and Marion J. Reis (Lincoln: University of Nebraska Press, 1965), 108.

11. Roland Barthes, *Image-Music-Text* (New York: Hill and Wang, 1977), 52.

12. Michel Foucault and Ludwig Binswanger, *Dream and Existence* (Seattle: Review of Existential Psychology and Psychiatry, 1986), 43.

13. Herbert Blau, *Blooded Thought: Occasions of Theater* (New York: Performing Arts Journals Publication, 1982), 39.

14. Michael Vanden Heuvel, *Performing Drama / Dramatizing Performance: Alternative Theater and the Dramatic Text* (Ann Arbor: University of Michigan Press, 1991), 13.

15. Gertrude Stein, *The Autobiography of Alice B. Toklas* (New York: Harcourt, Brace and Co., 1933), 259.

16. Gertrude Stein, *Lectures in America* (Boston: Beacon Press, 1985), 119.

17. Bonnie Marranca, *Ecologies of Theater* (Baltimore: Johns Hopkins University Press, 1996), 6.

18. Elinor Fuchs, *The Death of Character: Perspectives on Theater after Modernism* (Bloomington: Indiana University Press, 1996), 96–97.

19. Bernard J. Baars, *In the Theater of Consciousness* (New York: Oxford University Press, 1997), 80.

20. Philip Moeller, foreword to Elmer Rice, in *The Adding Machine* (New York: Doubleday, 1923), ix.

21. Harold Clurman, *Ibsen* (New York: Macmillan, 1977), 178.

22. Kenneth Burke, *On Symbols and Society* (Chicago: University of Chicago Press, 1989), 77.

23. Jean Cocteau, preface to *The Eiffel Tower Wedding Party,* trans. Dudley Fitts, in *The Infernal Machine and Other Plays by Jean Cocteau* (New York: New Directions, 1963), 154.

24. Leonard Shlain, *Art and Physics: Parallel Visions in Space, Time, and Light* (New York: William Morrow, 1991).

25. Tom Stoppard, *Arcadia* (London: Faber and Faber, 1993), 45.

26. Luigi Pirandello, preface to *Six Characters in Search of an Author,* trans. Eric Bentley, in *Naked Masks,* ed. Eric Bentley (New York: E. P. Dutton, 1952), 367.

27. Samuel Beckett, *Endgame and Act without Words* (New York: Grove Press, 1958), 1.

28. Samuel Beckett, *Happy Days* (New York: Grove Press, 1961), 27.

29. David H. Hesla, *The Shape of Chaos: An Interpretation of the Art of Samuel Beckett* (Minneapolis: University of Minnesota Press, 1971), 195.

30. Jean-Paul Sartre, *Being and Nothingness: An Essay on Phenomenological Ontology,* trans. Hazel E. Barnes (New York: Philosophical Library, 1956), liii.

31. Samuel Beckett, *Not I,* in *Ends and Odds, Nine Dramatic Pieces by Samuel Beckett* (New York: Grove Press, 1974), 17.

32. Samuel Beckett, *Waiting for Godot* (New York: Grove Press, 1954), 41b.

33. Stanton B. Garner Jr., *Bodied Spaces: Phenomenology and Performance in Contemporary Drama* (Ithaca: Cornell University Press, 1994), 79–80.

Notes to Chapter 4

1. Jan Christian Smuts, *Holism and Evolution,* 2d ed. (1926; rpt., London: Macmillan, 1927), 16.

2. Bart Kosko, *Fuzzy Thinking: The New Science of Fuzzy Thinking* (New York: Hyperion, 1993).

3. George Ledyard Stebbins, *Darwin to DNA, Molecules to Humanity* (New York: W. H. Freeman, 1982), 222.

4. Roger Penrose, *Shadows of the Mind: A Search for the Missing Science of Consciousness* (Oxford: Oxford University Press, 1994).

5. Douglas Hofstadter, *Gödel, Escher, Bach: An Eternal Golden Braid* (1979; rpt., New York: Vintage, 1989), 17.

6. In my own discussions in *The Theatre of Chaos* I accepted the prevailing view that quantum physics did not actually affect the visible world, that at best it could be used metaphorically to explain the visible world. From Penrose's view I failed to give quantum physics its due macrocosmic attention, a view I now tend to agree with but which does not undermine other related points I have previously made.

7. Michael Frayn, *Copenhagen* (London: Methuen, 1998), 94.

8. Qtd. in M. Mitchell Waldrop, *Complexity: The Emerging Science at the Edge of Order and Chaos* (New York: Simon and Schuster, 1992), 118.

9. F. David Peat, *Synchronicity: The Bridge between Matter and Mind* (New York: Bantam, 1988); David Bohm, *Wholeness and the Implicate Order* (New York: Routledge, 1980).

10. Qtd. in Waldrop, *Complexity,* 108.

11. Stuart Kauffman, *At Home in the Universe: The Search for Laws of Self-Organization and Complexity* (New York: Oxford University Press, 1995), 145.

12. See Richard Dawkins, *The Selfish Gene* (Oxford: Oxford University Press, 1976).

13. Qtd. in Waldrop, *Complexity,* 108.

14. Francis Crick, *The Astonishing Hypothesis: The Scientific Search for the Soul* (New York: Simon and Schuster, 1995), 260.

15. Roger Lewin, *Complexity: Life on the Edge of Chaos* (London: J. M. Dent, 1993), 156.

16. Jacques Derrida, "The Theater of Cruelty and the Closure of Representation," *Writing and Difference,* trans. Alan Bass (Chicago: University of Chicago Press, 1978), 236.

17. Elinor Fuchs, *The Death of Character: Perspectives on Theater after Modernism* (Bloomington: Indiana University Press, 1996), 107.

Notes to Chapter 5

1. David Bohm, *Wholeness and the Implicate Order* (New York: Routledge, 1980), 173.

2. Bart Kosko, *Fuzzy Thinking: The New Science of Fuzzy Logic* (New York: 1993).

3. Richard Schechner, *Between Theatre and Anthropology* (Philadelphia: University of Pennsylvania Press, 1985), 118.

4. Peter Brook, "Any Event Stems from Combustion: Actors, Audiences, and Theatrical Energy," *New Theatre Quarterly* 8:30 (May 1992): 108.

5. Brian Swimme, "The Cosmic Creation Story," in *The Reenchantment of Science: Postmodern Proposals,* ed. David Ray Griffin (Albany: State University of New York Press, 1988), 48.

6. Jan Christian Smuts, *Holism and Evolution,* 2d ed. (1926; rpt., London: Macmillan, 1927), 1–2.

7. Kenneth Burke, *On Symbols and Society* (Chicago: University of Chicago Press, 1989), 84.

8. Antonin Artaud, *The Theater and Its Double,* trans. Mary Caroline Richards (New York: Grove Press, 1958), 47.

9. Eugenio Barba and Nicola Savarese, *The Secret Art of the Performer: A Dictionary of Theatre Anthropology* (London: Routledge, 1991), 55.

10. Cited in Eric Sellin, *The Dramatic Concepts of Antonin Artaud* (Chicago: University of Chicago Press, 1968), 93.

11. Timothy J. Wiles, *The Theater Event: Modern Theories of Performance* (Chicago: University of Chicago Press, 1980), 123.

12. Elaine Scarry, *The Body in Pain: The Making and Unmaking of the World* (New York: Oxford University Press, 1985), 34.

13. Bettina Knapp, *Antonin Artaud: Man of Vision* (New York: David Lewis, 1969), 38.

14. Susan Sontag, "Approaching Artaud," in *Selected Writings,* trans. Helen Weaver (New York: Farrar, Straus and Giroux, 1976), lvii.

15. Jane Goodall, *Artaud and the Gnostic Drama* (Oxford: Clarendon, 1995), 2.

16. Jerzy Grotowski, "He Wasn't Entirely Himself," *Towards a Poor Theater* (New York: Simon and Schuster, 1968), 118–19.

17. Jerzy Grotowski, "Towards a Poor Theater," *Towards a Poor Theater* (New York: Simon and Schuster, 1968), 17.

18. Jennifer Kumiega, *The Theater Of Grotowski* (London: Methuen, 1987), 96.

Notes to Chapter 6

1. Bill Viola, *Reasons for Knocking at an Empty House: Writings, 1973–1994* (Cambridge: MIT Press, 1995), 255.

2. See Bonnie Marranca, ed., *The Theater of Images* (New York: Drama Book Specialists, 1977).

3. Bonnie Marranca, *Ecologies of Theater* (Baltimore: Johns Hopkins University Press, 1996), 39.

4. Arthur Holmberg, *The Theatre of Robert Wilson* (New York: Cambridge University Press, 1996), 121.

5. Interview, in *Brooklyn Academy of Music Presents* Einstein on the Beach: *The Changing Image of Opera* (video documentary), 1986.

6. Stefan Brecht, qtd. in Laurence Shyer, *Robert Wilson and His Collaborators* (New York: Theatre Communications Group Press, 1989), 217.

7. Qtd. in Shyer, *Robert Wilson,* 218.

8. Qtd. in *Brooklyn Academy of Music Presents* Einstein on the Beach: *The Changing Image of Opera* (video documentary), 1986.

9. Michael Vanden Heuvel, *Performing Drama / Dramatizing Performance: Alternative Theater and the Dramatic Text* (Ann Arbor: University of Michigan Press, 1991), 160.

10. Qtd. in Vanden Heuvel, *Performing Drama,* 160–61. Original in C. W. E. Bigsby, *A Critical Introduction to Twentieth-Century American Drama,* vol. 3: *Beyond Broadway* (Cambridge: Cambridge University Press, 1985), 165.

11. Richard Schechner, *The End of Humanism* (New York: Performing Arts Journal Press, 1982), 18.

12. Hebert Blau, *The Eye of Prey: Subversions of the Postmodern* (Bloomington: Indiana University Press, 1987), xxv.

13. Herbert Blau, *Blooded Thought: Occasions of Theatre* (New York: Performing Arts Journal Press, 1982), 41.

14. C. W. E. Bigsby, *A Critical Introduction to Twentieth Century America Drama,* vol. 3: *Beyond Broadway* (Cambridge: Cambridge University Press, 1985), 34.

15. Elinor Fuchs, *The Death of Character: Perspectives on Theater after Modernism* (Bloomington: Indiana University Press, 1996), 84

16. Kate Davy, ed., *Richard Foreman: Plays and Manifestos* (New York: New York University Press, 1976), ix.

17. Susan Sontag, "On Art and Consciousness," *Performing Arts Journal* 2:2 (Fall 1977): 28.

18. For an extended discussion of Gray's relationship with Schechner and the Wooster Group, see David Savran, *Breaking the Rules: The Wooster Group* (New York: Theatre Communications Group Press, 1988).

19. Spalding Gray, "About Three Places in Rhode Island," *The Drama Review* 23:1 (1979): 36.

20. Una Chaudhuri, *Staging Place: The Geography of Modern Drama* (Ann Arbor: University of Michigan Press, 1995), 83.

21. Gay Brewer, "Talking His Way Back to Life: Spalding Gray and the Embodied Voice," *Contemporary Literature* 37:2 (1996): 237–38.

22. Eleanor Wachtel, "Spalding Gray," interview, *Writers and Company* (Toronto: Knopf Canada, 1993), 39.

23. Wachtel, "Spalding Gray," 34.

24. Spalding Gray, "Perpetual Sundays," *Performing Arts Journal* 6:1 (1981): 48.

25. Vincent Canby, "Soloists on the Big Screen," *New York Times,* 22 March 1987, 2:19. Curiously enough, Spalding Gray not only stands up in his recent piece,

Morning, Noon, and Night, he actually dances toward the end of his monologue, a true coup de theater!

26. Spalding Gray, *Swimming to Cambodia* (New York: Theatre Communications Group Press, 1985), 59.

27. Spalding Gray, *Gray's Anatomy* (New York: Vintage, 1993), 9, 8.

28. Tony Kushner, *Angels in America,* pt. 1: *Millennium Approaches* (New York: Theatre Communications Group, 1992); *Angels in America,* pt. 2: *Perestroika* (New York: Theatre Communications Group, 1992).

Chapter 7

1. Tom Stoppard, *Hapgood* (London: Faber and Faber, 1988), 72.

2. Gene A. Plunka, "'Know Thyself': Integrity and Self-Awareness in the Early Plays of Peter Shaffer," in *Peter Shaffer: A Casebook,* ed. C. J. Gianakaris (New York: Garland Press, 1991), 57.

3. Though *Amadeus* was a great cinematic success, I would argue it was not a successful filming of the play because the film medium undermines—by its objectifying nature—the very subjectivity that gives the play its epistemological focus, theme, and complexity. On the screen we see a "history" related rather than a mind dramatically and materially unfolding, as in the play. The same is true in the less successful filmed version of *Equus,* which erroneously opted to use real horses rather than the imaginative, consciously formulated facsimiles used in the play.

4. Friedrich Nietzsche, *The Birth of Tragedy,* in *The Birth of Tragedy* and *The Genealogy of Morals,* trans. Francis Golfing (New York: Anchor, 1956), 20.

5. Peter Shaffer, *Equus* (New York: Avon, 1974), 29.

6. Michael Vanden Heuvel, *Performing Drama / Dramatizing Performance: Alternative Theater and the Dramatic Text* (Ann Arbor: University of Michigan Press, 1991).

7. Stanton B. Garner Jr., *Bodied Spaces: Phenomenology and Performance in Contemporary Drama* (Ithaca: Cornell University Press, 1994), 98.

8. Sam Shepard, *The Unseen Hand and Other Plays* (New York: Bantam, 1986), 7.

9. Miguel de Unamuno, *The Tragic Sense of Life,* trans. J. E. Crawford Flitch (New York: Dover, 1954), 38.

10. Stephen J. Bottoms, *The Theatre of Sam Shepard: States of Crisis* (Cambridge: Cambridge University Press, 1998), 154.

11. Thomas Nash, "Sam Shepard's *Buried Child:* The Ironic Use of Folklore," *Modern Drama* 26:4 (December 1983): 486.

12. F. David Peat, *Synchronicity: The Bridge between Mind and Matter* (New York: Bantam, 1987), 54.

13. Peter Shaffer, *The Gift of the Gorgon* (Harmondsworth, Eng.: Viking, 1993), 20.

14. Friedrich Nietzsche, *The Birth of Tragedy and The Genealogy of Morals,* trans. Francis Golffing (New York: Anchor, 1956), 26.

15. John Guare, *Six Degrees of Separation* (New York: Random House, 1990), 81.

16. See James J. Collins and Carson S. Chow, "It's a Small Word," *Nature* 393 (4 June 1998): 409–10.

17. Patricia Churchland, qtd. in Roger Lewin, *Complexity: Life on the Edge of Chaos* (London: J. M. Dent, 1993), 164.

18. Qtd. in Lewin, 175.

19. Stanton B. Garner Jr., "Rewriting Europe: *Pentecost* and the Crossroads of Migration," *Essays in Theatre* 16:1 (November 1997): 5.

20. David Edgar, *Pentecost* (London: Nick Hern Books, 1995), 25.

21. See Peter Coveney and Roger Highfield, *Frontiers of Complexity: The Search for Order in a Chaotic World* (New York: Fawcett Columbine, 1995), 214–15, for a fuller explanation.

Conclusion

1. Colin McGinn, qtd. in Roger Lewin, *Complexity: Life on the Edge of Chaos* (London: J. M. Dent, 1993), 169.

Bibliography

Armstrong, Gordon. "Theatre as a Complex Adaptive System." *New Theatre Quarterly* 13:51 (August 1997): 277–88.

Artaud, Antonin. *The Theater and Its Double*. Trans. Mary Caroline Richards. New York: Grove Press, 1958.

Baars, Bernard J. *In the Theater of Consciousness*. New York: Oxford University Press, 1997.

Barba, Eugenio, and Nicola Savarese. *The Secret Art of the Performer: A Dictionary of Theatre Anthropology*. London: Routledge, 1991.

Barthes, Roland. *Image-Music-Text*. New York: Hill and Wang, 1977.

Beckett, Samuel. *Endgame, a Play in One Act, Followed by Act without Words, a Mime for One Player*. Trans. from the French by the author. New York: Grove Press, 1958.

———. *Happy Days*. New York: Grove Press, 1961.

———. *Not I*. In *Ends and Odds: Nine Dramatic Pieces by Samuel Beckett*, 13–23. New York: Grove Press, 1974.

———. *Waiting for Godot*. New York: Grove, 1954.

Bentley, Eric. Review of *Cat on a Hot Tin Roof*. *New Republic*, 4 April 1955, 20.

Bigsby, C.W.E. *A Critical Introduction to Twentieth Century American Drama*. Vol. 3: *Beyond Broadway*. London: Cambridge University Press, 1985.

Blau, Herbert. *Blooded Thought: Occasions of Theatre*. New York: Performing Arts Journal Press, 1982.

———. *The Eye of Prey: Subversions of the Postmodern*. Bloomington: Indiana University Press, 1987.

Bohm, David. *Wholeness and the Implicate Order*. New York: Routledge, 1980.

Bottoms, Stephen J. *The Theatre of Sam Shepard: States of Crisis*. Cambridge: Cambridge University Press, 1998.

Brewer, Gay. "Talking His Way Back to Life: Spalding Gray and the Embodied Voice." *Contemporary Literature* 37.2 (1996): 237–57.

Briggs, John, and F. David Peat. *Turbulent Mirror*. New York: Harper and Row, 1988.

Brook, Peter. "Any Event Stems from Combustion: Actors, Audiences and, Theatrical Energy." *New Theatre Quarterly* 8:30 (May 1992): 107–12.

———. *The Empty Space*. New York: Atheneum, 1968.

Brooklyn Academy of Music Presents Einstein on the Beach: *The Changing Image of Opera*. Video documentary, 1986.

Brustein, Robert. *The Theatre of Revolt*. Boston: Little, Brown, 1964.

Burke, Kenneth. *On Symbols and Society*. Chicago: University of Chicago Press, 1989.

Canby, Vincent. "Soloists on the Big Screen." *New York Times,* 22 March 1987, 2:19.

Chalmers, David J. *The Conscious Mind: In Search of a Fundamental Theory.* New York: Oxford University Press, 1996.

Chaudhuri, Una. *Staging Place: The Geography of Modern Drama.* Ann Arbor: University of Michigan Press, 1995.

Clurman, Harold. *Ibsen.* New York: Macmillan, 1977.

Cocteau, Jean. Preface to *The Eiffel Tower Wedding Party.* Trans. Dudley Fitts. In *The Infernal Machine and Other Plays,* 151–60. New York: New Directions, 1963.

Cobb, John B., Jr. "The Postmodern Heresy: Consciousness as Causal." In *The Reenchantment of Science: Postmodern Proposals.* Ed. David Ray Griffin, 99–114. Albany: State University of New York Press, 1988.

Collins, James J., and Carson C. Chow. "It's a Small World." *Nature* 393, 4 June 1998, 409–10.

Coveney, Peter, and Roger Highfield. *Frontiers of Complexity: The Search for Order in a Chaotic World.* New York: Fawcett Columbine, 1995.

Crease, Robert P. *The Play of Nature: Experimentation as Performance.* Bloomington: Indiana University Press, 1993.

Crick, Francis. *The Astonishing Hypothesis: The Scientific Search for Soul.* New York: Scribner's, 1994.

Damasio, Antonio R. *Descartes' Error: Emotion, Reason, and the Human Brain.* New York: G. P. Putnam's Sons, 1994.

Davy, Kate, ed. *Richard Foreman: Plays and Manifestos.* New York: New York University Press, 1976.

Dawkins, Richard. *The Selfish Gene.* Oxford: Oxford University Press, 1976.

Demastes, William W. *Theatre of Chaos: Beyond Absurdism, into Orderly Disorder.* New York: Cambridge University Press, 1998.

Dennett, Daniel C. *Consciousness Explained.* Boston: Little, Brown, 1991.

Derrida, Jacques. *Writing and Difference.* Trans. Alan Bass. Chicago: University of Chicago Press, 1978.

Descartes, René. *The Philosophical Works of Descartes.* 2 vols. Trans. Elizabeth S. Haldane and G. R. T. Ross. London: Cambridge University Press, 1975.

Eccles, John C. *Evolution of the Brain: Creation of the Self.* London: Routledge, 1989.

Edgar, David. *Pentecost.* London: Nick Hern Books, 1995.

Eichenbaum, Boris. "The Theory of Formal Method." In *Russian Formalist Criticism: Four Essays.* Ed. Lee N. T. Lemon and Marion J. Reis, 56–62. Lincoln: University of Nebraska Press, 1965.

Foucault, Michel, and Ludwig Biswanger. *Dream and Existence.* Seattle: Review of Existential Psychology and Psychiatry, 1986.

Faussett, Laurene. *Fundamentals of Neural Networks: Architectures, Algorithms, and Applications.* Englewood Cliffs, N.J.: Prentice Hall, 1994.

Flanagan, Owen. *The Science of Mind,* 2d ed. Cambridge: MIT Press, 1991.

Frayn, Michael. *Copenhagen.* London: Methuen, 1998.

Fuchs, Elinor. *The Death of Character: Perspectives on Theater after Modernism.* Bloomington: Indiana University Press, 1996.

Garner, Stanton B., Jr. *Bodied Spaces: Phenomenology and Performance in Contemporary Drama.* Ithaca: Cornell University Press, 1994.

————. "Rewriting Europe: *Pentecost* and the Crossroads of Migration. *Essays in Theatre*" 16.1 (November 1997): 3–14.

Garrett, Laurie. *The Coming Plague: Newly Emerging Diseases in a World Out of Balance*. New York: Farrar, Straus, and Giroux, 1995.

Gianakaris, C. J., ed. *Peter Shaffer: A Casebook*. New York: Garland, 1991.

Gleick, James. *Chaos: Making a New Science*. New York: Viking Penguin, 1987.

Goodall, Jane. *Artaud and the Gnostic Drama*. Oxford: Clarendon, 1995.

Gray, Spalding. "About Three Places in Rhode Island." *The Drama Review (TDR)* 23:1 (1979): 31–42.

————. *Gray's Anatomy*. New York: Vintage, 1993.

————. "Perpetual Sundays." *Performing Arts Journal* 6:1 (1981): 46–49.

————. *Swimming to Cambodia*. New York: Theatre Communications Group, 1985.

Griffin, David Ray, ed. *The Reenchantment of Science: Postmodern Proposals*. Albany: State University of New York Press, 1981.

Grotowski, Jerzy. *Towards a Poor Theatre*. New York Simon and Schuster, 1968.

Guare, John. *Six Degrees of Separation*. New York: Ransom House, 1990.

Harth, Erich. *The Creative Loop: How the Brain Makes a Mind*. Reading, Mass.: Addison-Wesley, 1993.

Heisenberg, Werner. *The Physicist's Conception of Nature*. New York: Harcourt, Brace, 1958.

Hesla, David H. *The Shape of Chaos: An Interpretation of the Art of Samuel Beckett*. Minneapolis: University of Minnesota Press, 1971.

Hofstadter, Douglas. *Gödel, Escher, Bach: An Eternal Golden Braid*. 1979. Reprint. New York: Vintage, 1989.

Holmberg, Arthur. *The Theatre of Robert Wilson*. New York: Cambridge University Press, 1996.

Husserl, Edmund. *Meditations: An Introduction to Pure Phenomenology*. Trans. Dorion Cairns. The Hague: Martinus Nijhof, 1960.

————. "Philosophy as Rigorous Science." In *Phenomenology and the Crisis of Philosophy*. Trans. Quentin Lauer. New York: Harper and Row, 1965.

Kauffman, Stuart. *At Home in the Universe: The Search for Laws of Self-Organization and Complexity*. New York: Oxford University Press, 1995.

Knapp, Bettina. *Antonin Artaud, Man of Vision*. New York: David Lewis, 1969.

Koestler, Arthur. *The Ghost in the Machine*. Chicago: Henry Regnery Co., 1967.

Kosko, Bart. *Fuzzy Thinking: The New Science of Fuzzy Logic*. New York: Hyperion, 1993.

Krutch, Joseph Wood, *The Measure of Man: On Freedom, Human Values, Survival, and the Modern Temper*. 1953. Reprint. New York: Grosset and Dunlap, 1968.

Kumiega, Jennifer. *The Theatre Of Grotowski*. London: Methuen, 1987.

Kushner, Tony. *Angels in America*. Pt. 1: *Millennium Approaches*. New York: Theatre Communications Group, 1992.

————. *Angels in America*. Pt. 2: *Perestroika*. New York: Theatre Communications Group, 1992.

Leshan, Lawrence. *The Medium, the Mystic and the Physicist*. New York: Viking Press, 1966.

Lewin, Roger. *Complexity: Life on the Edge of Chaos*. London: J. M. Dent, 1993.

Marranca, Bonnie. *Ecologies of Theater*. Baltimore: Johns Hopkins University Press, 1996.

———, ed. *The Theater of Images*. New York: Drama Book Specialists, 1977.

Merleau-Ponty, Maurice. *Phenomenology of Perception*. Trans. Colin Smith. London: Routledge, 1962.

———. "The Primacy of Perception and Its Philosophical Consequence." Trans. James N. Edie. In *The Primacy of Perception and Other Essays on Phenomenological Psychology, the Philosophy of Art, History and Politics*. Ed. James M. Edie, 12–42. Evanston: Northwestern University Press, 1964.

Miller, Arthur. *Death of a Salesman*. New York: Viking Press, 1949.

Moeller, Philip. Foreword to *The Adding Machine* by Elmer Rice, vii–x. New York: Doubleday, 1923.

Nash, Thomas. "Sam Shepard's *Buried Child*: The Ironic Use of Folklore." *Modern Drama* 26.4 (December 1983): 486–91.

Nietzsche, Friedrich. *The Birth of Tragedy; and, The Genealogy of Morals*. Trans. Francis Golffing. New York: Anchor, 1990.

Peat, F. David. *Synchronicity: The Bridge between Matter and Mind*. New York: Bantam, 1988.

Penrose, Roger. *The Emperor's New Mind*. Oxford: Oxford University Press, 1989.

———. *Shadows of the Mind: A Search for the Missing Science of Consciousness*. Oxford: Oxford University Press, 1994.

Pirandello, Luigi. Preface to *Six Characters in Search of an Author*. Trans. Eric Bentley. In *Naked Masks*. Ed. Eric Bentley, 363–75. New York: E. P. Dutton, 1952.

Plunka, Gene A. "Know Thyself': Integrity and Self-Awareness in the Early Plays of Peter Shaffer." In *Peter Shaffer: A Casebook*. Ed. C. J. Gianakaris, 57–74. New York: Garland, 1991.

Robinson, Marc. *The Other American Drama*. New York: Cambridge University Press, 1994.

Ryle, Gilbert. *The Concept of Mind*. London: Hutchinson, 1949.

Sartre, Jean-Paul. *Being and Nothingness: An Essay on Phenomenological Ontology*. Trans. Hazel E. Barnes. New York: Philosophical Library, 1956.

Savran, David. *Breaking the Rules: The Wooster Group*. New York: Theatre Communications Group Press, 1988.

Scarry, Elaine. *The Body in Pain: The Making and Unmaking of the World*. New York: Oxford University Press, 1985.

Schechner, Richard. *Between Theatre and Anthropology*. Philadelphia: University of Pennsylvania Press, 1985.

———. *The End of Humanism*. New York: Performing Arts Journal Press, 1982.

Searle, John R. *The Rediscovery of the Mind*. Cambridge: MIT Press, 1992.

Sellin, Eric. *The Dramatic Concepts of Antonin Artaud*. Chicago: University of Chicago Press, 1968.

Shaffer, Peter. *Equus*. New York: Avon, 1974.

———. *The Gift of the Gorgon*. Harmondsworth, Eng.: Viking, 1993.

Shepard, Sam. *The Unseen Hand and Other Plays*. New York: Bantam, 1986.

Shlain, Leonard. *Art and Physics: Parallel Visions in Space, Time, and Light*. New York: William Morrow, 1991.

Shyer, Lawrence. *Robert Wilson and His Collaborators*. New York: Theatre Communications Group Press, 1989.

Smuts, Jan Christian. *Holism and Evolution*. 1926. Reprint. London: Macmillan, 1927.

Sontag, Susan. "Approaching Artaud." In *Selected Writings*. Trans. Helen Weaver. New York: Farrar, Straus and Giroux, 1976.

―――. "On Art and Consciousness." *Performing Arts Journal* 2:2 (Fall 1977): 25–32.

States, Bert O. *Great Reckonings in Small Rooms: On the Phenomenology of Theater*. Berkeley: University of California Press, 1985.

Stebbins, George Ledyard. *Darwin to DNA, Molecules to Humanity*. San Francisco: W. H. Freeman, 1982.

Stein, Gertrude. *The Autobiography of Alice B. Toklas*. New York: Harcourt, Brace, and Co., 1933.

―――. *Lectures in America*. Boston: Beacon Press, 1985.

Stoppard, Tom. *Arcadia*. London: Faber and Faber, 1993.

―――. *Hapgood*. London: Faber and Faber, 1988.

Styan, J. L. *Modern Drama in Theory and Practice,* 3 vols. New York: Cambridge University Press, 1981.

Swimme, Brian. "The Cosmic Creation Story." In *The Reenchantment of Science: Postmodern Proposals*. Ed. David Ray Griffin, 47–56. Albany: State University of New York Press, 1988.

Unamuno, Miguel de. *The Tragic Sense of Life*. Trans. J. E. Crawford Flitch. New York: Dover, 1954.

Uttal, William R. *The Psychobiology of Mind*. Hillsdale, N.J.: Lawrence Erlbaum, 1978.

Vanden Heuvel, Michael. *Performing Drama / Dramatizing Performance: Alternative Theater and the Dramatic Text*. Ann Arbor: University of Michigan Press, 1991.

Viola, Bill. *Reasons for Knocking at an Empty House: Writings, 1973–1994*. Cambridge: MIT Press, 1995.

Wachtel, Eleanor. "Spalding Gray." Interview. *Writers and Company,* 33–48. Toronto: Knopf Canada, 1993.

Waldrop, M. Mitchell. *Complexity. The Emerging Science at the Edge of Order and Chaos*. New York: Simon and Schuster, 1992.

Wilde, Oscar. *The Importance of Being Earnest*. New York: Avon, 1965.

Wiles, Timothy J. *The Theater Event: Modern Theories of Performance*. Chicago: University of Chicago Press, 1980.

Williams, Raymond. *The Drama from Ibsen to Brecht*. New York: Oxford University Press, 1969.

Zola, Émile. *The Experimental Novel and Other Essays*. Trans. Belle M. Sherman. New York: Haskell House, 1964.

Index